Harry Escombe
A Tale of Adventure in Peru

by

Harry Collingwood

Harry Escombe
A Tale of Adventure in Peru
by Harry Collingwood

Copyright © 2024

All Rights reserved.

ISBN: 978-93-62206-36-7

Published by

DOUBLE 9 BOOKS

2/13-B, Ansari Road
Daryaganj, New Delhi – 110002
info@double9books.com
www.double9books.com
Tel. 011-40042856

ABOUT THE AUTHOR

Harry Collingwood was the pseudonym of William Joseph Cosens Lancaster (23 May 1843 - 10 June 1922), a British civil engineer and novelist who wrote over 40 boys' adventure tales, the majority of which were set on the sea. Collingwood was the eldest son of master mariner Captain William Lancaster (1813 - (1861 - 1871)) and Anne, née Cosens. According to his birth certificate, he was born on May 23, 1843 at 9:30 a.m. at Concord Place in Weymouth, Dorset. According to the Oxford Dictionary of National Biography, the majority of references, with the exception of his birth certificate, identify his birth date as 1851. According to his application for Associate Membership in the Institution of Civil Engineers, he was born on May 23, 1846. Collingwood was the first of the couple's three children. He was eight years old when his sister Ada Louise was born, and twelve when his sister Sarah Anne (1 June 1853 - 27 December 1941) was born. Both ladies were listed as draper helpers on the 1871 census. Collingwood's father had died by that time, and his mother lived with her daughters until her death. Ada never married and lived with her sister after leaving her family home. Sarah Anne married Mathew Smellie in St Michaels, Toxteth, Liverpool, Lancashire, on June 30, 1880. Harold Ernest Smellie, born on April 11, 1881, died on April 30, 1961. Harold, Collingwood's nephew, registered his death in 1922.

CONTENTS

Chapter One
How the Adventure Originated

The hour was noon, the month chill October; and the occupants—a round dozen in number—of Sir Philip Swinburne's drawing office were more or less busily pursuing their vocation of preparing drawings and tracings, taking out quantities, preparing estimates, and, in short, executing the several duties of a civil engineers' draughtsman as well as they could in a temperature of 35° Fahrenheit, and in an atmosphere surcharged with smoke from a flue that refused to draw—when the door communicating with the chief draughtsman's room opened and the head of Mr Richards, the occupant of that apartment, protruded through the aperture. At the sound of the opening door the draughtsmen, who were acquainted with Mr Richards's ways, glanced up with one accord from their work, and the eye of one of them was promptly caught by Mr Richards, who, raising a beckoning finger, remarked:

"Escombe, I want you," and immediately retired.

Thereupon Escombe, the individual addressed, carefully wiped his drawing pen upon a duster, methodically laid the instrument in its proper place in the instrument case, closed the latter, and, descending from his high stool, made his way into the chief draughtsman's room, closing the door behind him. He did this with some little trepidation; for these private interviews with his chief were more often than not of a distinctly unpleasant character, having reference to some stupid blunder in a calculation, some oversight in the preparation of a drawing, or something of a similar nature calling for sharp rebuke; and as the lad—he was but seventeen—accomplished the short journey from one room to the other he rapidly reviewed his most recent work, and endeavoured to decide in which job he was most likely to have made a mistake. But before he could arrive at a decision on this point he was in the presence of Mr Richards, and a single glance at the chief draughtsman's face—now that it could be seen clearly and unveiled by a pall of smoke—sufficed to assure Harry Escombe that in this case at least he had nothing in the nature of censure to fear. For Mr Richards's face was beaming with satisfaction, and a large atlas lay open upon the desk at which he stood.

"Sit down, Escombe," remarked the dreaded potentate as he pointed to a chair.

Escombe seated himself; and then ensued a silence of a full minute's duration. The potentate seemed to be meditating how to begin. At length—

"How long have you been with us, Escombe?" he enquired, hoisting himself onto a stool as he put the question.

"A little over two years," answered Escombe. "I signed my articles with Sir Philip on the first of September the year before last, and came on duty the next day."

"Two years!" ejaculated Mr Richards. "I did not think it had been so long as that. But time flies when one is busy, and we have done a lot of work during the last two years. Then you have only another year of pupilage to serve, eh, Escombe?"

"Only one year more, Mr Richards," answered the lad.

"Ah!" commented Mr Richards, and paused again, characteristically. "Look here, Escombe," he resumed; "you have done very well since you came here; Sir Philip is very pleased with you, and so am I. I have had my eye on you, and have seen that you have been studying hard and doing your best to perfect yourself in all the details of your profession. So far as theory goes you are pretty well advanced. What you need now is practical, out-of-door work, and," laying his hand upon the open atlas, "I have got a job here that I think will just suit you. It is in Peru. Do you happen to know anything of Peru?"

Escombe confessed that his knowledge of Peru was strictly confined to what he had learned about that interesting country at school.

"It is the same with me," admitted Mr Richards. "All I know about Peru is that it is a very mountainous country, which is the reason, I suppose, why there is considerably less than a thousand miles of railway throughout the length and breadth of it. And what there is is made up principally of short bits scattered about here and there. But there is some talk of altering all that now, and matters have gone so far that Sir Philip has been commissioned to prepare a scheme for constructing a railway from a place called Palpa— which is already connected with Lima and Callao—to Salinas, which is connected with Huacho, and from Huacho to Cochamarca and thence to a place called Cerro de Pasco, which in its turn is connected with Nanucaca; and from Nanucaca along the shore of Lake Chinchaycocha to Ayacucho, Cuzco, and Santa Rosa, which last is connected by rail with Mollendo, on the coast. There is also another scheme afoot which will involve the taking of a complete set of soundings over the length and breadth of Lake Titicaca.

Now, all this means a lot of very important and careful survey work which I reckon will take the best part of two years to accomplish. Sir Philip has decided to entrust the work to Mr Butler, who has already done a great deal of survey work for him, as of course you know; but Mr Butler will need an assistant, and Sir Philip, after consultation with me, has decided to offer that post to you. It will be a splendid opportunity for you to acquire experience in a branch of your profession that you know very little of, as yet; and if the scheme should be carried out, you, in consequence of the familiarity with the country which you will have acquired, will stand an excellent chance of obtaining a good post on the job. Now, what do you say, Escombe; are you willing to go? Your pay during the survey will be a guinea a day—seven days a week—beginning on the day you sail from England and ending on the day of your return; first-class passage out and home; all expenses paid; twenty-five pounds allowed for a special outfit; and everything in the shape of surveying instruments and other necessaries, found. After your return you will of course be retained in the office to work out the scheme, at a salary to be agreed upon, which will to a great extent depend upon the way in which you work upon the survey; while, in the event of the scheme being carried out, you will, as I say, doubtless get a good post on the engineering staff, at a salary that will certainly not be less than your pay during the survey, and may possibly be a good deal more."

Young Escombe's heart leapt within him, for here was indeed a rosy prospect suddenly opening out before him, a prospect which promised to put an abrupt and permanent end to certain sordid embarrassments that of late had been causing his poor widowed mother a vast amount of anxiety and trouble, and sowing her beloved head with many premature white hairs. For Harry's father had died about four months before this story opens, leaving his affairs in a condition of such hopeless disorder that the family lawyer had only just succeeded in disentangling them, with the result that the widow had found herself left almost penniless, with no apparent resource but to allow her daughter Lucy to go out into a cold, unsympathetic world to earn her own living and face the many perils that lurk in the path of a young, lovely, innocent, and unprotected girl. But here was a way out of all their difficulties; for, as Harry rapidly bethought himself, if all his expenses were to be paid while engaged upon the survey, he could arrange for at least three hundred pounds of his yearly salary to be paid to his mother at home, which, with economy and what little she had already, would suffice to enable her and Lucy to live in their present modest home, free from actual want.

There was but one fly in his ointment, one disturbing item in the alluring programme which Mr Richards had sketched out, and that was

Mr Butler, the man who was to be Escombe's superior during the execution of the survey. This man was well known to the occupants of Sir Philip Swinburne's drawing office as a most tyrannical, overbearing man, with an arrogance of speech and offensiveness of manner and a faculty for finding fault that rendered it absolutely impossible to work amicably with him, and at the same time retain one's self respect. Moreover, it was asserted that if there were two equally efficient methods of accomplishing a certain task, he would invariably insist upon the adoption of that method which involved the greatest amount of difficulty, discomfort, and danger, and then calmly sit down in safety and comfort to see it done. Mr Richards had said that Escombe would, upon his return to England, be retained in the office to work out the scheme, at a salary the amount of which would "to a great extent depend upon the way in which he worked on the survey"; and it seemed to Harry that Sir Philip's estimate of the way in which he worked on the survey would be almost entirely based upon Mr Butler's report. Now it was known that, in addition to possessing the unenviable attributes already mentioned, Butler was a most vindictive man, cherishing an undying enmity against all who had ever presumed to thwart or offend him, and he seemed to be one of those unfortunately constituted individuals whom it was impossible to avoid offending. It is therefore not to be wondered at if Escombe hesitated a moment before accepting Mr Richards's offer.

"Well, Escombe, what do you say?" enquired the chief draughtsman, after a somewhat lengthy pause. "You do not seem to be very keen upon availing yourself of the opportunity that I am offering you. Is it the climate that you are afraid of? I am told that Peru is a perfectly healthy country."

"No, Mr Richards," answered Escombe. "I am not thinking of the climate; it is Mr Butler that is troubling me. You must be fully aware of the reputation which he holds in the office as a man with whom it is absolutely impossible to work amicably. There is Munro, who helped him in that Scottish survey, declares that nothing would induce him to again put himself in Mr Butler's power; and you will remember what a shocking report Mr Butler gave of Munro's behaviour during the survey. Yet the rest of us have found Munro to be invariably most good natured and obliging in every way. Then there was Fielding—and Pierson—and Marshall—"

"Yes, I know," interrupted Mr Richards rather impatiently. "I have never been able to rightly understand those affairs, or to make up my mind which was in the wrong. It may be that there were faults on both sides. But, be that as it may, Mr Butler is a first-rate surveyor; we have always found his work to be absolutely accurate and reliable; and Sir Philip has given him this survey to do; so it is too late for us to draw back now, even if Sir Philip would, which I do not think in the least likely. So, if you do not feel inclined to take on the job—"

"No; please do not mistake my hesitation," interrupted Escombe. "I will take the post, most gratefully, and do my best in it; only, if Mr Butler should give in an unfavourable report of me when all is over, I should like you to remember that he has done the same with everybody else who has gone out under him; and please do not take it for granted, without enquiry, that his report is perfectly just and unbiased."

This was a rather bold thing for a youngster of Escombe's years to say in relation to a man old enough to be his father; but Mr Richards passed it over—possibly he knew rather more about those past episodes than he cared to admit—merely saying:

"Very well, then; I dare say that will be all right. Now you had better go to Mitford and draw the money for your special outfit; also get from him a list of what you will require; and to-morrow you can take the necessary time to give your orders before coming to the office. But you must be careful to make sure that everything is supplied in good time, for you sail for Callao this day three weeks."

The enthusiasm which caused Escombe's eyes to shine and his cheek to glow as he strode up the short garden path to the door of the trim little villa in West Hill, Sydenham, that night, was rather damped by the reception accorded by his mother and sister to the glorious news which he began to communicate before even he had stepped off the doormat. Where the lad saw only an immediate increase of pay that would suffice to solve the problem of the family's domestic embarrassments, two years of assured employment, with a brilliant prospect beyond, a long spell of outdoor life in a perfect climate and in a most interesting and romantic country, during which he would be perfecting himself in a very important branch of his profession, and, lastly, the possibility of much exciting adventure, Mrs Escombe and Lucy discerned a long sea voyage, with its countless possibilities of disaster, two years of separation from the being who was dearer to them than all else, the threat of strange and terrible attacks of sickness, and perils innumerable from wild beasts, venomous reptiles and insects, trackless forests, precipitous mountain paths, fathomless abysses, swift-rushing torrents, fierce tropical storms, earthquakes, and, worse than all else, ferocious and bloodthirsty savages! What was money and the freedom from care and anxiety which its possession ensured, compared with all the awful dangers which their darling must brave in order to win it? These two gently nurtured women felt that they would infinitely rather beg their bread in the streets than suffer their beloved Harry to go forth, carrying his life in his hands, in order that they might be comfortably housed and clothed and sufficiently fed! And indeed the picture which they drew was sufficiently alarming to have daunted a lad of nervous and timid temperament, and perhaps have turned him from his purpose. But Harry Escombe was a youth of very different mould, and was built of much sterner stuff. There was nothing of the milksop about him, and the dangers of which his mother and sister spoke so eloquently had no terrors for him, but, on the contrary, constituted a positive and very powerful attraction; besides, as he pointed out to his companions, he would not always be clinging to the face of a precipice, or endeavouring to cross an impassable mountain torrent. Storms did not rage incessantly in Peru, any more than they did elsewhere; Mr Richards had assured him that the climate was healthy; ferocious animals and deadly reptiles did not usually attack a man unless they were interfered with; and reference to an Encyclopaedia disclosed the fact that Peru, so far from swarming with untamed savages, was a country enjoying a very fair measure of civilisation. Talking thus, making light of such dangers as he would actually have to face, and dwelling very strongly upon the splendid opening which the offer afforded him, the lad gradually brought his mother and sister into a more reasonable frame of mind, until at length, by the time that the bedroom candles made their appearance, the two women, knowing how completely Harry had set his heart upon going, and recognising also the strength of his contention as to the advantageous character of the opening afforded him by Mr Richards's proposal, had become so far reconciled to the prospect of the separation that they were able to speak of it calmly and to conceal the heartache from which both were suffering. So on the following morning Mrs Escombe and Lucy were enabled to sally forth with cheerful countenance and more or less sprightly conversation as they accompanied the lad to town to assist him in the purchase of his special outfit, the larger portion of which was delivered at The Limes that same evening, and at once unpacked for the purpose of being legibly marked and having all buttons securely sewn on by two pairs of loving hands.

The following three weeks sped like a dream, so far as the individual chiefly interested was concerned; during the day he was kept continually busy by Mr Butler in the preparation of lists of the several instruments, articles, and things—from theodolites, levels, measuring chains, steel tapes, ranging rods, wire lines, sounding chains, drawing and tracing paper, cases of instruments, colour boxes, T-squares, steel straight-edges, and drawing pins, to tents, camp furniture, and saddlery—and procuring the same. The evenings were spent in packing and re-packing his kit as the several articles comprising it came to hand, diversified by little farewell parties given in his honour by the large circle of friends with whom the Escombes had become acquainted since their arrival and settlement in Sydenham. At length the preparations were all complete; the official impedimenta—so to speak—had all been collected at Sir Philip Swinburne's offices in Victoria Street, carefully packed in zinc-lined cases, and dispatched for shipment in the steamer which was to take the surveyors to South America. Escombe had sent on all his baggage to the ship in advance, and the morning came when he must say good-bye to the two who were dearest to him in all the world. They would fain have accompanied him to the docks and remained on board with him until the moment arrived for the steamer to haul out into the river and proceed upon her voyage; but young Escombe had once witnessed the departure of a liner from Southampton and had then beheld the long-drawn-out agony of the protracted leave taking, the twitching features, the sudden turnings aside to hide and wipe away the unbidden tear, the heroic but futile attempts at cheerful, light-hearted conversation, the false alarms when timid people rushed ashore, under the unfounded apprehension that they were about to be carried off across the seas, and the return to the ship to say goodbye yet once again when they found that their fears were groundless. He had seen all this, and was quite determined that his dear ones should not undergo such torture of waiting, he therefore so contrived that his good-bye was almost as brief and matter of fact as though he had been merely going up to Westminster for the day, instead of to Peru for two years. Taking the train for London Bridge, he made his way thence to Fenchurch Street and so to Blackwall, arriving on board the s.s. *Rimac* with a good hour to spare.

But, early as he was, he found that not only had Mr Butler arrived on board before him, but also that that impatient individual had already worked himself into a perfect frenzy of irritation lest he—Harry—should allow the steamer to leave without him.

"Look here, Escombe," he fumed, "this sort of thing won't do at all, you know. I most distinctly ordered you to be on board in good time this morning. I have been searching for you all over the ship; and now, at a quarter to eleven o'clock, you come sauntering on board with as much deliberation as though you had days to spare. What do you mean by being so late, eh?"

"Really, Mr Butler," answered Harry, "I am awfully sorry if I have put you out at all, but I thought that so long as I was on board in time to start with the ship it would be sufficient. As it is I am more than an hour to the good; for, as you are aware, the ship does not haul out of dock until midday. Have you been wanting me for anything in particular?"

"No, I have not," snapped Butler. "But I was naturally anxious when I arrived on board and found that you were not here. If you had happened to miss the ship I should have been in a pretty pickle; for this Peruvian survey is far too big a job for me to tackle singlehanded."

"Of course," agreed Escombe. "But you might have been quite certain that I would not have been so very foolish as to allow the ship to leave without me. I am far too anxious to avail myself of the opportunity which this survey will afford me, to risk the loss of it by being late. Is there anything that you want me to do, Mr Butler? Because, if not, I will go below and arrange matters in my cabin."

"Very well," assented Butler ungraciously. "But, now that you are on board, don't you dare to leave the ship and go on shore again—upon any pretence whatever. Do you hear?"

"You really need not feel the slightest apprehension, Mr Butler," replied Harry. "I have no intention or desire to go on shore again." And therewith he made his way to the saloon companion, and thence below to his sleeping cabin, his cheeks tingling with shame and anger at having been so hectored in public; for several passengers had been within earshot and had turned to look curiously at the pair upon hearing the sounds of Butler's high-pitched voice raised in anger.

"My word," thought the lad, "our friend Butler is beginning early! If he is going to talk to me in that strain on the day of our departure, what will he be like when we are ready to return home? However, I am not going to allow him to exasperate me into forgetting myself, and so answering him as to give him an excuse for reporting me to Sir Philip for insolence or insubordination; there is too much depending upon this expedition for me to risk anything by losing my temper with him. I will be perfectly civil to him, and will do my duty to the very best of my ability, then nothing very serious can possibly happen."

Upon entering his cabin Escombe was greatly gratified to learn from the steward that he was to be its sole occupant. He at once annexed the top berth, and proceeded to unpack the trunk containing the clothing and other matters that he would need during the voyage, arranged his books in the rack above the bunk, and then returned to the deck just in time to witness the operation of hauling out of dock.

He found Butler pacing the deck in a state of extreme agitation.

"Where have you been all this while?" demanded the man, halting abruptly, square in Escombe's path. "What do you mean by keeping out of my sight so long? Are you aware, sir, that I have spent nearly an hour at the gangway watching to see that you did not slink off ashore?"

"Have you, really?" retorted Harry. "There was not the slightest need for you to do so, you know, Mr Butler, for I distinctly told you that I did not intend to go ashore again. Didn't I?"

"Yes, you did," answered Butler. "But how was I to know that you would keep your word?"

"I always keep my word, sir; as you will learn when we become better acquainted," answered the lad.

"I hope so, for your sake," returned Butler. "But my experience of youngsters like yourself is that they are not to be trusted." Then, glancing round him and perceiving that several passengers in his immediate neighbourhood were regarding him with unconcealed amusement, he hastily retreated below. As he did so, a man who had been lounging over the rail close at hand, smoking a cigar as he watched the traffic upon the river, turned, and regarding Escombe with a good-natured smile, remarked:

"Your friend seems to be a rather cantankerous chap, isn't he? He will have to take care of himself, and keep his temper under rather better control, or he will go crazy when we get into the hot weather. Is he often taken like that?"

"I really don't know," answered Harry. "The fact is that I only made his acquaintance about three weeks ago; but I fear that he suffers a great deal from nervous irritability. It must be a very great affliction."

"It is, both to himself and to others," remarked the stranger dryly. "I have met his sort before, and I find that the only way to deal with such people is to leave them very severely alone. He seems to be a bit of a bully, so far as I can make out, but he will have to mind his p's and q's while he is on board this ship, or he will be getting himself into hot water and finding things generally made very unpleasant for him. You are in his service, I suppose?"

"Yes, in a way I am," answered Escombe with circumspection; "that is to say, we are both in the same service, but he is my superior."

"I see," answered the stranger. "How far are you going in the ship?"

"We are going to Callao," answered Harry.

"To Peru, eh?" returned the stranger. "So am I. I know the country pretty well. I have lived in Lima for the last nine years, and I can tell you that when your friend gets among the Peruvians he will have to pull in his horns a good bit. They are rather a peppery lot, are the Peruvians, and if he attempts to talk to them as he has talked to you to-day, he will stand a very good chance of waking up some fine morning with a long knife between his ribs."

"Oh, I hope it will not come to that!" exclaimed Escombe. "But—to leave the subject of my friend and his temper for the present—since you have lived in Peru so long, perhaps you can tell me something about the country, what it is like, what is the character of its climate, and so on. It is possible that I may have to spend a year or so in it. I should therefore be glad to learn something about it, and to get such tips as to the manner of living, and so on, as you can give me before we land."

"Certainly," answered the stranger; "I shall be very pleased indeed to give you all the information that I possibly can, and I fancy there are very few people on board this ship who know more about Peru than I do."

And therewith Escombe's new acquaintance proceeded to hold forth upon the good and the bad points of the country to which they were both bound, describing in very graphic language the extraordinary varieties of climate to be met with on a journey inland from the coast, the grandeur of its mountain scenery, the astonishing variety of its products, its interesting historical remains; the character of the aboriginal Indians, the beliefs they cherish, and the legends which have been preserved and handed down by them from father to son through many generations; the character and abundance of its mineral wealth, and a variety of other interesting information; so that by the time that Harry went down below to luncheon, he had already become possessed of the feeling that to him Peru was no longer a strange and unknown land.

Chapter Two
The Chief Officer's Yarn

Upon entering the saloon and searching for his place, Harry found that, much to his satisfaction, he had been stationed at the second table, presided over by the chief officer of the ship—a very genial individual named O'Toole, hailing from the Emerald Isle—and between that important personage and his recently-made Peruvian acquaintance, whose name he now discovered to be John Firmin; while Mr Butler, it appeared, had contrived to get himself placed at the captain's table, which was understood to be occupied by the élite of the passengers. With the serving of the soup Escombe was given a small printed form, which he examined rather curiously, not quite understanding for the moment what it meant.

Mr Firmin volunteered enlightenment. "That," he explained, "is an order form, upon which you write the particular kind of liquid refreshment—apart from pure water—with which you wish to be served. You fill it in and hand it to your own particular table steward, who brings you what you have ordered, and at the end of each week he presents you with the orders which you have issued, and you are expected to settle up in spot cash. Very simple, isn't it?"

"Perfectly," agreed Harry. "But supposing that one does not wish to order anything, what then?"

"You leave the order blank, that is all," answered Firmin. Then noticing that the lad pushed the form away, he asked: "Are you a teetotaler?"

"By no means," answered Harry; "I sometimes take a glass of wine or beer, and very occasionally, when I happen to get wet through or am very cold, I take a little spirits; but plain or aerated water usually suffices for me."

"I see," remarked Firmin. He remained silent for a few seconds, then turning again to Harry, he said: "I wonder if you would consider me very impertinent if, upon the strength of our extremely brief acquaintance, I were to offer you a piece of advice?"

"Certainly not," answered Harry. "You are much older and more experienced than I, Mr Firmin, and have seen a great deal more of the world than I have; any advice, therefore, that you may be pleased to give me I shall be most grateful for, and will endeavour to profit by."

"Very well, then," said Firmin, "I will risk it, for I have taken rather a fancy to you, and would willingly do you a good turn. The advice that I wish to give you is this. Make a point of eschewing everything in the nature of alcohol. Have absolutely nothing to do with it. You are young, strong, and evidently in the best of health; your system has therefore no need of anything having the character of a stimulant. Nay, I will go farther than that, and say that you will be very much better, morally and physically, without it; and even upon the occasions which you mention of getting wet or cold, a cup of scalding hot coffee, swallowed as hot as you can take it, will do you far more good than spirits. I am moved to say this to you, my young friend, because I have seen so many lads like you insensibly led into the habit of taking alcohol, and when once that habit is contracted it is more difficult than you would believe to break it off. I have known many promising young fellows who have made shipwreck of their lives simply because they have not possessed the courage and strength of mind to say 'no' when they have been invited to take wine or spirits."

"By the powers, Misther Firmin, ye niver spoke a thruer word in your life than that same," cut in the chief officer, who had been listening to what was said. "Whin I was a youngster of about Misther Escombe's age I nearly lost my life through the dhrink. I was an apprentice at the time aboard a fine, full-rigged iron clipper ship called the *Joan of Arc*. We were outward bound, from London to Sydney, full up with general cargo, and carried twenty-six passengers in the cuddy, and nearly forty emigrants in the 'tween decks. We had just picked up the north-east trades, blowing fresh, and the 'old man', who was a rare hand at carrying on, and was eager to break the record, was driving her along to the south'ard under every rag that we could show to it, including such fancy fakements as skysails, ringtails, water-sails, and all the rest of it. It was a fine, clear, starlit night, with just the trade-clouds driving along overhead, but there was no moon, and consequently, when an exceptionally big patch of cloud came sweeping up, it fell a bit dark. Still, there was no danger—or ought to have been none—for we were well out of the regular track of the homeward-bounders, and in any case, with a proper look-out, it would have been possible to see another craft plenty early enough to give her a good wide berth. But after Jack has got as far south as we then were he is apt to get a bit careless in the matter of keeping a look-out—trusts rather too much to the officer of the watch aft, you know, and is not above snatching a cat-nap in the most comfortable corner he can find, instead of posting himself on the heel of the bowsprit, with his eyes skinned and searching the sea ahead of him.

"Now, it happened—although none of us knew it until it was too late—that our chief mate had rather too strong a liking for rum; not that he was exactly what you might call a drunkard, you know, but he kept a bottle in his cabin, and was in the habit of taking a nip just whenever he felt like it, especially at night time; and on this particular night that I'm talking about he must have taken a nip too many, for when he came on deck at midnight to keep the middle watch he hadn't been up above an hour before he coiled himself down in one of the passenger's deck-chairs and—went to sleep. Of course, under such circumstances as those of which I am speaking—the weather being fine and the wind steady, with no necessity to touch tack or sheet—the watch on deck don't make any pretence of keeping awake; they're on deck and at hand all ready for a call if they're needed, and that's as much as is expected of 'em at night time, since there's no work to be done; and the consequence was that all hands of us were sound asleep long before the mate; and there is no doubt that the look-out—who lost his life, poor chap! through his carelessness—fell asleep too. As to the man at the wheel, well he is not expected to steer the ship and keep a look-out at the same time, and, if he was, he couldn't do it, for his eyes soon grow so dazzled by the light of the binnacle lamps that he can see little or nothing except the illuminated compass card.

"That, gentlemen, was the state of affairs aboard the *Joan of Arc* on the night about which I'm telling ye; the skipper, the passengers, the second mate, and the watch below all in their bunks; and the rest of us, those who were on deck and ought to have been broad awake, almost if not quite as sound asleep as those who were below. I was down on the main deck, sitting on the planks, with my back propping up the front of the poop, my arms crossed, and my chin on my chest, dhreaming that I was back at school in dear old Dublin, when I was startled broad awake by a shock that sent me sprawling as far for'ard as the coaming of the after-hatch, to the accompaniment of the most awful crunching, ripping, and crashing sounds, as the *Joan* sawed her way steadily into the vitals of the craft that we had struck. Then, amid the yelling of the awakened watch, accompanied by muffled shrieks and shouts from below, there arose a loud twang-twanging as the backstays and shrouds parted under the terrific strain suddenly thrown upon them, then an ear-splitting crash as the three masts went over the bows, and I found myself struggling and fighting to free myself from the raffle of the wrecked mizenmast. I felt very dazed and queer, and a bit sick, for I was dimly conscious of the fact that I had been struck on the head by something when the masts fell, and upon putting up my hand I found that my hair was wet with something warm that was soaking it and trickling down into my eyes and ears. Then I heard the voice of the 'old man' yelling for the mate and the carpenter; and as I fought myself clear of the raffle I became aware of many voices frantically demanding to know what had happened, husbands calling for their wives, mothers screaming for their children, the sound of axes being desperately used to clear away the wreck, a sudden awful wail from somewhere ahead, and a rushing and hissing of water as the craft that we had struck foundered under our forefoot, and the skipper's voice again, cracked and hoarse, ordering the boats to be cleared away."

O'Toole paused for a moment and gasped as if for breath; his soup lay neglected before him, his elbows were on the table, and his two hands locked together in a grip so tense that the knuckles shone white in the light that came streaming in through the scuttles in the ship's side, his eyes were glassy and staring into vacancy with an intensity of gaze which plainly showed that the whole dreadful scene was again unfolding itself before his mental vision, and the perspiration was streaming down his forehead and cheeks. Then the table steward came up, and, removing his soup, asked him whether he would take cold beef, ham-and-tongue, or roast chicken. The sound of the man's voice seemed to bring the dazed chief officer to himself again; he sighed heavily, and as though relieved to find himself where he was, considered for a moment, and, deciding in favour of cold beef, resumed his narrative.

"The next thing that I can remember, gentlemen," he continued, "was that I was on the poop with the skipper, second and third mates, the carpenter, and a few others, lighting for our lives as we strove to keep back the frantic passengers and prevent them from interfering with the hands who were cutting the gripes and working furiously to sling the boats outboard. We carried four boats at the davits, two on each quarter, and those were all that were available, for the others were buried under the raffle and wreckage of the fallen masts, and it would have taken hours to clear them, with the probability that, when got at, they would have been found smashed to smithereens, while a blind man could have told by the feel of the ship that she was settling fast, and might sink under us at any moment. At last one of the boats was cleared and ready for lowering, and as many of the women and children as she would carry were bundled into her, the third mate, two able seamen, and myself being sent along with them by the skipper to take care of them. I would willingly have stayed behind, for there were other women and children—to say nothing of men passengers—to be saved, but I knew that a certain number of us Jacks must of necessity go in each boat to handle and navigate her, and there was no time to waste in arguing the matter; so in I tumbled, just as I was, and the next moment we were rising and falling in the water alongside, the tackle blocks were cleverly unhooked, and we out oars and shoved off, pulling to a safe distance and then lying on our oars to wait for the rest.

"I shall never, to my dying day, forget the look of that ship as we pulled away from her. The *Joan* had been as handsome a craft as ever left the stocks when we hauled out of dock at London some three weeks earlier; but now — her bows were crumpled in until she was as flat for'ard as the end of a sea-chest; her decks were lumbered high with the wreckage of her masts and spars; the standing and running rigging was hanging down over her sides in bights; and she had settled so low in the water that her channels were already buried; while her poop was crowded with madly struggling figures, from which arose a confused babel of sound—shouting, screaming, and cursing—than which I have never heard anything more awful in all my life.

"When we had pulled off about fifty fathoms the third mate, who was in charge of the boat, ordered us to lie upon our oars; and presently we saw that the second quarter-boat was being lowered. She reached the water all right, and then we heard the voice of the second mate yelling to the hands on deck to let run the after tackle. The next moment, as the sinking ship rolled heavily to starboard, we saw the stern of the lowered boat lifted high out of the water, the bow dipped under, and in a second, as it seemed, she had swamped, and the whole load of people, some twenty in number, were struggling and drowning alongside as they strove ineffectually to scramble back into the swamped boat, which had now by some chance become released from the tackle that had held her.

"For a moment we, in the boat that had got safely away, sat staring, dumb and paralysed with horror at the dreadful scene that was enacting before our eyes. But the next moment those of us who were at the oars started madly backing and pulling to swing the boat round and pull in to the help of the poor wretches who were perishing only a few fathoms away from us. We had hardly got the boat round, however, when Mr Gibson, the third mate, gave the order for us to hold water.

"'We mustn't do it,' he said. 'The boat is already loaded as deep as she will swim, and the weight of even one more person would suffice to swamp her! As it is, it will take us all our time, and tax our seamanship to the utmost, to keep her afloat; you can see for yourselves that it would be impossible for us to squeeze more than one additional person in among us, and, even if we had the room, we could not get that one in over the gunnel without swamping the craft. To attempt such a thing would therefore only be to throw away uselessly the lives of all of us; we must therefore stay where we are, and endure the awful sight as best we can—ah, there you have a hint of what will happen if we are not careful!'—as the boat, lying broadside-on to the sea, rolled heavily and shipped three or four bucketfuls of water—'pull, starboard, and get her round stem-on to the sea; and you, O'Toole, get hold of the baler and dish that water out of her.'

"It was true, every word of it, as a child might have had sense to see. We could do absolutely nothing to help the poor wretches who were drowning there before our very eyes; and in a few minutes all was over, so far as they were concerned. Two or three men, I believe, managed to get back aboard the sinking ship by climbing up the davit tackles; but the rest quickly drowned—as likely as not because they clung to each other and pulled each other down.

"But the plight of those aboard the *Joan* was rapidly becoming desperate; and we could see that they knew it by observing the frantic efforts which they were making to get the other two boats into the water. We could distinctly hear the voice of the skipper rising from time to time above the clamour, urging the people to greater efforts, encouraging one, cautioning another, entreating the maddened passengers to keep back and give the crew room to work. Then, in the very midst of it all there came a dull boom as the decks blew up. We heard the loud hissing of the compressed air as it rushed out between the gaping deck planks; there arose just one awful wail—the sound of which will haunt me to my dying day—and with a long, sliding plunge the *Joan* lurched forward and dived, bows first, to the bottom.

"As for us, we could do nothing but just keep our boat head-on to the sea and let her drift, humouring and coaxing her as best we could when an extra heavy sea appeared bearing down upon us, and baling for dear life continuously to keep her free of the water that, in spite of us, persisted in slapping into her over the bows. The Canaries were the nearest bits of dry land to us, but Mr Jellicoe, the third mate, reckoned that they were a good hundred and fifty miles away, and dead to wind'ard; so it was useless for us to think of reaching them in a boat with her gunnels awash, and not a scrap of food or a drop of fresh water in her. The only thing that we could do was to exert our utmost endeavours to keep the craft afloat, and trust that Providence would send something along soon to pick us up. But— would you believe it?—although we were right in the track of the outward-bound ships, and although we sighted nine sailing craft and three steamers, nothing came near enough to see us, lying low in the water as we were, until the ninth day, when we were picked up by a barque bound for Cape Town. But by that time, gentlemen, Mr Jellicoe, one seaman, and I were all that remained alive of the boatload that shoved off from the stricken *Joan of*

Arc on that fatal night. Don't ask me by what means we contrived to keep the life in us for so long a time, for I won't tell you. Thus you see that, of the complete complement of ninety-two persons who left London in the *Joan of Arc*, eighty-nine were drowned—to say nothing of those aboard the craft that we had run down—because the mate couldn't—or wouldn't—control his love of drink. Since that day, gentlemen, coffee is the strongest beverage that has ever passed my lips."

"I am delighted to hear it," remarked Firmin, "for observation has led me to the conviction that at least half the tragedies of human life have originated in the craving for intoxicants; and therefore,"—turning to Escombe—"I say again, my young friend, have absolutely nothing to do with them. I have no doubt that, ere you have been long in Peru, you will have made the discovery that it is a thirsty country; but, apart of course from pure water, there is nothing better for quenching one's thirst than fresh, sound, perfectly ripe fruit, failing which, tea, hot or cold—the latter for preference—without milk, and with but a small quantity of sugar, will be found hard to beat. Now, if you are anxious for hints, there is one of absolutely priceless value for you; but I present it you free, gratis, and for nothing."

"Thanks very much!" returned Harry. "I will bear it in mind and act upon it. No more intoxicants for me, thank you. Mr O'Toole, accept my thanks for telling us that terrible story of your shipwreck. It has brought home to me, as nothing else has ever done, the awful danger of tampering with so insidious an enemy as alcohol, which I now solemnly abjure for ever."

Meanwhile, at the captain's table, Mr Butler was expressing his opinion upon various subjects in loud, strident tones, and with a disputatiousness of manner that caused most of those about him mentally to dub him a blatant cad, and to resolve that they would have as little as possible to do with him.

One afternoon, when the *Rimac* had reached the other side of the Atlantic, Butler called Harry into the cabin of the former and said: "I understand that we shall be at Montevideo the day after to-morrow. Now I want you to understand that I shall expect you not to go on shore either at Montevideo or either of the other places that the *Rimac* will be stopping at. She will only remain at anchor at any of these places for a few hours; and if you were to go on shore it would be the easiest thing in the world for you to get lost and to miss your passage; therefore in order to obviate any such possibility I have decided not to allow you to leave the ship. Do you understand?"

"Yes," answered Escombe, "I understand perfectly, Mr Butler, what you mean. But I certainly do not understand by what authority you attempt to interfere with my personal liberty to the extent of forbidding me to go on shore for a few hours when the opportunity presents itself. I agreed with Sir Philip Swinburne to accompany you to Peru as your assistant upon the survey which he has engaged you to make; and from the moment when that survey commences I will render you all the obedience and deference due to you as my superior, and will serve you to the best of my ability. But it was no part of my contract that I should surrender my liberty to you during the outward and homeward voyage; and when it comes to your forbidding me to leave the ship until our arrival at Callao, you must permit me to say that I feel under no obligation to defer to your wishes. And, quite apart from that, I may as well tell you that I have already accepted an invitation to accompany Mr and Mrs Westwood and a party ashore at Montevideo, and I see no reason why I should withdraw my acceptance."

"W-h-a-t!" screamed Butler; "do I understand that you are daring to disobey and defy me?"

"Certainly not, sir," answered Harry, "because, as I understand it, disobedience and defiance are impossible where no authority exists; and I beg to remind you that your authority over me begins only upon our arrival at Callao. Yet, purely as a matter of courtesy, I am of course not only prepared but perfectly willing to show all due deference to such reasonable wishes as you may choose to express. But I reserve to myself the right of determining where the line shall be drawn."

"Very well, sir," stuttered Butler, "I am glad to learn thus early what sort of behaviour I may expect from you. I shall write home at once to Sir Philip, reporting to him what has passed between us, and requesting him to send me out someone to take your place—someone who can be depended upon to render me implicit obedience at all times." And therewith he whirled about and marched off to his own cabin, where, with the heat of his anger still upon him, he sat down and penned to Sir Philip Swinburne a very strong letter of complaint of what he was pleased to term young Escombe's "insolently insubordinate language and behaviour". As for Harry, Butler's threat to report him to Sir Philip furnished him with a very valuable hint as to the wisest thing to do under the circumstances, and he too lost no time in addressing an epistle to Sir Philip, giving his own version of the affair. Thenceforward Butler pointedly ignored young Escombe's existence for the remainder of the voyage; but by doing so he only made matters still more unpleasant for himself, for his altercation with Harry had been overheard by certain of the passengers, and by them repeated to the rest, with the final result that Butler was promptly consigned to Coventry, and left there by the whole of the saloon passengers.

Harry duly went ashore with his friends at Montevideo and—having first posted his letter to Sir Philip and another to his mother and sister— went out with them by train to Bellavista, where they all enjoyed vastly the little change from the monotony of life at sea, returning in the nick of time to witness a violent altercation between Butler and the boatman who brought him off from the shore. Also Harry went ashore for an hour or two at Punta Arenas, in the Straits of Magellan; and again at Valparaiso and Arica; finally arriving at Callao something over a month from the day upon which he sailed from London.

Chapter Three
Butler the Tyrant

At this point Escombe acknowledged himself to be legitimately under Butler's rule and dominion, to obey unquestioningly all the latter's orders, to go where bidden and to do whatever he might be told, even as did the soldiers of the Roman centurion; and Butler soon made him understand and feel that there was a heavy score to be wiped off—a big wound in the elder man's self esteem to be healed. There were a thousand ways now in which Butler was able to make his power and authority over Harry felt; he was careful not to miss a single opportunity, and he spared the lad in nothing. He would not even permit Harry to land until the latter had personally supervised the disembarkation of every item of their somewhat extensive baggage; and when this was at length done he insisted that Escombe should in like manner oversee the loading of them into a railway wagon for Lima, make the journey thither in the same truck with them—ostensibly to ensure that nothing was stolen on the way—and finally, upon their arrival in Lima, he compelled Harry to remain by the truck and mount guard over it until it was coupled to the train for Palpa, and then to proceed to that town in the same truck without seeing anything more of the capital city than could be seen from the station yard. Then, again, at Palpa he insisted that Harry should remain by the truck and supervise the unloading of the baggage and its transference to a lock-up store, giving the lad to understand that he would be held responsible for any loss or damage that might occur during the operation; so that by the time that all this was done poor Escombe was more dead than alive, so utterly exhausted was he from long exposure to the enervating heat, and lack of proper food.

But Harry breathed no word of expostulation or complaint. He regarded everything that he now did as in the way of duty and merely as somewhat unpleasant incidents in the execution of the great task that lay before him, and he was content, if not quite as happy and comfortable as he might have been under a more congenial and considerate leader. Besides, he was learning something every minute of the day, learning how to do things and also how not to do them, for he very quickly recognised that although Butler might possibly be an excellent surveyor, he was but a very poor hand at organisation. Then, too, Butler had characteristically neglected the acquisition of any foreign language, consequently they had no sooner arrived at Palpa than he found himself absolutely dependent upon Harry's knowledge of Spanish; and this advantage on Escombe's part served in a great measure to place the two upon a somewhat more equal footing, and gradually to suppress those acts of petty tyranny which Butler had at first evinced a disposition to indulge in.

Palpa was the place at which their labours were to begin, and here it became necessary for them to engage a complete staff of assistants, comprising tent bearers, grooms, bush cutters, porters, cooks, and all the other attendants needed for their comfort and convenience during a long spell of camp life in a tropical climate, and in a country where civilisation is still elementary except in the more important centres. Luckily for them, the first section of their work comprised only a stretch of a little more than thirty miles of tolerably flat country, where no serious natural difficulties presented themselves, and that part of their work was soon accomplished. Yet Escombe found even this trifling bit of the great task before him sufficiently arduous; for Butler not only demanded that he should be up and at work in the open at daybreak, and that he should continue at work so long as daylight lasted, but that, when survey work was no longer possible because of the darkness, the lad should "plot" his day's work on paper before retiring to rest. Thus it was generally close upon midnight before Escombe was at liberty to retire to his camp bed and seek his hard-earned and much-needed rest.

But it was when they got upon the second section of their work— between Huacho, Cochamarca, and Cerro de Pasco—that their real troubles and difficulties began, for here they had to find a practicable route up the face of the Western Cordillera in the first instance, and, having found it, to measure with the nicest accuracy not only the horizontal distances but the height of every rise and the depth of every declivity in the face of a country made up to a great extent of lofty precipices and fathomless ravines, the whole overgrown with dense vegetation through which survey lines had to be cut at enormous expense of time and labour. And here it was that Butler's almost fiendish malice and ingenuity in the art of making things unpleasant for other people shone forth conspicuously. It was his habit to ride forth every morning accompanied by a strong band of attendants armed with axes and machetes, and well provided with ropes to assist in the scaling of precipitous slopes, for the purpose of selecting and marking out the day's route, a task which could usually be accomplished in a couple of hours; and then to return and supervise the work of his subordinate, which he made as difficult and arduous as possible by insisting upon the securing of a vast amount of superfluous and wholly unnecessary information, in the obtaining of which Harry was obliged to risk his life at least a dozen times a day. Yet the lad never complained; indeed he could not have done so even had he been so disposed, for it was for Butler to determine what amount of information and of what nature was necessary for the proper execution of the survey; but Escombe began to understand now the means by which his superior had acquired the reputation of an accomplished surveyor. It is easy for a man in authority to stand or sit in safety and command another to perform a difficult task at the peril of his life!

And if Butler was tyrannically exacting in his treatment of Harry, he was still more so toward the unfortunate peons in his service, and especially those whom he detailed to accompany him daily to assist in the task of selecting and marking out the route of the survey line. These people knew no language but their own, and since Harry was always engaged elsewhere with theodolite, level, and chain, and was, therefore, not available to play the part of interpreter, it became necessary for Butler to secure the services of a man who understood enough English to translate his orders into the vernacular; and because this unfortunate fellow was necessarily always at Butler's elbow, he became the scapegoat upon whose unhappy head the sins and shortcomings of the others were visited in the form of perpetual virulent abuse, until the man's life positively became a burden to him, to such an extent, indeed, that he would undoubtedly have deserted but for the fact that Butler, suspecting his inclination perhaps, positively refused to pay him a farthing of wages until the conclusion of his engagement. It can easily be understood, therefore, that, under the circumstances described, an element of tragedy was steadily developing in the survey camp.

But although the overbearing and exacting behaviour of the chief of the expedition was thus making matters particularly unpleasant for everybody concerned, nothing of a really serious character occurred until the second section of the survey had been in progress for a little over two months, by which time the party had penetrated well into the mountain fastnesses, and were beginning to encounter some of the more formidable difficulties of their task. Butler was still limiting his share of the work to the mere marking out of the route, leaving Harry to perform the whole of the actual labour of the survey under his watchful eye, and stirring neither hand nor foot to assist the young fellow, although the occasions were frequent when, had he chosen to give a few minutes' assistance at the theodolite or level, such help would have saved young Escombe some hours of arduous labour, and thus expedited the survey.

Now, it happened that a certain day's work terminated at the edge of a *quebrada*, and Butler informed Harry that the first task of the latter, upon the following morning, would be to take a complete set of accurate measurements of this *quebrada*, before pushing on with the survey of the route. A *quebrada*, it may be explained, is a sort of rent or chasm in the mountain, usually with vertical, or at least precipitous sides, and very frequently of terrific depth, the impression suggested by its appearance being that at some period of the earth's history the solid rock of the mountain had been riven asunder by some titanic force. Sometimes a *quebrada* is several hundreds of feet in width, and of a depth so appalling as to unnerve the most hardy mountaineer. The *quebrada* in question, however, was of comparatively insignificant dimensions, being only about forty feet wide at the point where the survey line crossed it, and some four hundred feet deep.

Now, although Harry was only an articled pupil, he knew quite enough about railway engineering to be perfectly well aware that the elaborate measurements which Butler had instructed him to take were absolutely unnecessary, the accurate determination of the width at the top—where a bridge would eventually have to be thrown across—being all that was really required. Yet he made no demur, for he had already seen that it would be possible to take as many measurements as might be required, with absolute accuracy and ease, by the execution of about a quarter of an hour's preliminary surveying. But when, on the following morning, he commenced this bit of preliminary work, Butler rushed out of his tent and interrupted him.

"What are you doing?" he harshly demanded. "Have you forgotten that I ordered you to measure very carefully the *quebrada* this morning, before doing anything else?"

"No, sir," answered Harry, "I have not forgotten. I am doing it now, or, rather, doing the necessary preliminary work."

"Doing the necessary preliminary work?" echoed Butler. "What do you mean? I don't understand you."

"Then permit me to explain," said Harry suavely. "I have ascertained that, by placing the theodolite over that peg yonder,"—pointing to a newly driven peg some four hundred feet away to the left—"I shall be able to get an uninterrupted view of the *quebrada* from top to bottom, and, by taking a series of vertical and horizontal angles from the top edge, can measure the contour of the two sides, at the point crossed by the survey line, with the nicest accuracy."

"How do you mean?" demanded Butler.

Harry proceeded to elaborate his explanation, patiently describing each step of the intended operation, and making it perfectly clear that the elaborate series of unnecessary measurements demanded could be secured with the most beautiful precision.

"But," objected Butler, "when you have taken all those angles you will have done only part of the work; you will still have to calculate the length of the vertical and horizontal lines subtended by them—"

"A matter of about half an hour's work!" interjected Harry.

"Possibly," agreed Butler. "But," he continued, "I do not like your plan at all; I do not approve of it; it is amateurish and theoretical, and I won't have it. A much simpler and more practical way will be for you to go down the *quebrada* at the end of a rope, measuring as you go."

"That is one way certainly," assented Harry; "but, with all submission, Mr Butler, I venture to think that it will not be nearly so accurate as mine. Besides, consider the danger. If the rope should happen to be cut in its passage over the sharp edge of that rock—"

"Look here," interrupted Butler, "if you are afraid, you had better say so, and I will do the work myself. But I should like you to understand that timid people are of no use to me."

The taunt was unjust, for Harry was not afraid; but he was convinced that his own plan was far and away the more expeditious and the more accurate, also it involved absolutely no danger at all; while it was patent to even the dullest comprehension that there was a distinct element of danger attaching to the other, inasmuch as that if anything should happen to the rope, the person suspended by it must inevitably be precipitated to the bottom, where a mountain stream roared as it leaped and boiled and foamed over a bed of enormous boulders.

Had Escombe been ten years older than he actually was he would probably not have hesitated—while disclaiming anything in the nature of cowardice—to express very strongly the opinion that where there were two methods of executing a certain task, one of them perfectly safe, and the other seriously imperilling a human life, it was the imperative duty of the person with whom the decision rested to select the safer method of the two, particularly when that method offered equally satisfactory results with the other. But, being merely a lad, and as yet scarcely certain of himself, remembering also that his future prospects were absolutely at Butler's mercy, to make or mar as he pleased, Harry contented himself with a disclaimer of any such feeling as fear, and expressed his readiness to perform the task in any manner which Butler might choose to approve.

At the same time he confessed his inability to understand precisely how the required measurements were to be taken, and requested instructions.

"Why," explained Butler impatiently, "the thing is surely simple enough for a baby to understand. You will be lowered over the cliff edge and let down the cliff face exactly five feet at a time. As it happens to be absolutely calm, the rope by which you are to be lowered will hang accurately plumb; all that you will have to do, therefore, will be to measure the distance from your rope to the face of the rock, at every five feet of drop, and you will then have the particulars necessary to plot a contour of the cliff face, from top to bottom. You will do this on both sides of the *quebrada*, and then measure the width across at the top, which will enable us to produce a perfectly correct section of the gorge."

"But how am I to measure the distance from the rope to the cliff face?" demanded Harry. "For, as you will have observed, sir, the rock overhangs at the top, and the gorge widens considerably as it descends."

"You can do your measuring with a ranging-rod," answered Butler tersely; "and if one is not long enough, tie two together."

"Even so," persisted Harry, "I fear I shall not be able to manage—"

"Will you, or will you not, do as you are told?" snapped Butler. "If you cannot manage with two rods, I will devise some other plan."

"Very well, sir," said Harry. "If you are quite determined to send me over the cliff, I am ready to go. What rope is it your pleasure that I shall use?"

"Take the tent ropes," ordered Butler. "You will have an ample quantity if you join them all together. Make a seat for yourself in the end, and then mark off the rest of the rope into five-foot lengths, so that we may know exactly how much to pay out between the measurements. Then lash two ranging-rods together, and you will find that you will manage splendidly."

Harry had his doubts, for to his own mind the tent ropes seemed none too strong for such a purpose. Moreover, the clips upon them would render the paying out over the cliff edge exceedingly awkward; still, since it seemed that the choice lay between risking his life and ruining his professional prospects, he chose the former, and set about making his preparations for what he could not help regarding as a distinctly hazardous experiment. These did not occupy him very long, and in about twenty minutes he was standing at the cliff edge, with a padded bight of the rope about his body, and the two joined ranging-rods in his hand, quite ready to be lowered down the face. Then two peons whom he had specially selected for the task, drew in the slack of the rope, passed a complete turn of it round an iron bar driven deep into a rock crevice, and waited for the command of a third who now laid himself prone on the ground, with his head projecting over the edge of the cliff, to watch and regulate the descent. Then Harry, fully realising, perhaps for the first time, the perilous nature of the enterprise, laid himself down and carefully lowered himself over the rocky edge.

"Lower gently, brothers!" ordered the man who was supervising the operation, and the rope was carefully eased away until the first five-foot mark reached the cliff edge, while Butler, who now also began at last to recognise and appreciate the ghastly peril to which his obstinacy had consigned a fellow creature, moved off to a point about a hundred yards distant, from which he could watch the entire descent. And he no sooner reached it than he perceived that Harry's objections to the plan were well grounded, and that, even with the two joined rods, it would be impossible for the lad to take the required measurements over more than the first quarter of the depth. This being the case, it was obviously his duty at once to put a stop to so dangerous an attempt, especially as he knew perfectly well that it was as unnecessary as it was dangerous; but to do this would have been tantamount to confessing that he had made a mistake, and this his nature was too mean and petty to permit, so he simply sat down and watched in an ever-growing fever of anxiety lest anything untoward should happen for which he could be blamed.

Meanwhile, at the very first stoppage, Harry began to experience some of the difficulties that beset him in the task which he had undertaken. Despite the utmost care in lowering, the rope would persist in oscillating, very gently, it is true, but still sufficient to render it necessary to pause until the oscillation had ceased before attempting to take the measurement; also the torsion of the rope set up a slow revolving movement, so that, even when at length the oscillation ceased, it was only with difficulty that the correct measurement was taken and recorded in the book. This difficulty recurred as every additional five-foot length of rope was paid out, so that each measurement cost fully five minutes of precious time. Moreover, despite the padding of the rope, Harry soon began to find it cutting into his flesh so unpleasantly that he had grave doubts whether he would be able to endure it and hold out until the bottom, far below, should be reached.

At length, when about forty feet of rope had been very cautiously paid out, and some eight measurements taken, the peon who was superintending the operation of lowering was suddenly seen to stiffen his body, as though something out of the common had attracted his attention; he raised one hand as a sign to the other two to cease lowering, and gazed intently downward for several seconds. Then he signed for the lowering to be continued, and, to the astonishment of the others, wriggled himself back from the edge of the cliff until he had room to stand upright, when, scrambling hastily to his feet, he sprang to the two men who were lowering, and hissed between his set teeth:

"Lower! lower away as quickly and as steadily as you can, my brothers; the life of the young *Señor* depends upon your speed and steadiness. The rope has stranded—cut by the edge of the rock, most probably—and unless you can lower the *muchacho* to the bottom ere it parts altogether, he will be dashed to pieces!"

Meanwhile Harry, hanging there swinging and revolving in the bight of the rope, was not a little astonished when he found himself being lowered without pause, save such momentary jerks as were occasioned by the passage of the clips round the bar and over the cliff edge, and he instinctively glanced upward to see if he could discover what was wrong - for that something had gone amiss he felt tolerably certain. For a few seconds his eye sought vainly for an explanation, then his gaze was arrested by the sight of two severed ends of one strand of the rope standing out at a distance of about thirty feet above his head, and he knew!—knew that the strength of the slender rope had been decreased by one third, and that his life now depended upon the holding together of the two remaining strands!

Harry could see that those two remaining strands were stretched by his hanging weight to the utmost limit of their resistance, and he watched them with dull anxiety, as one in a dream, every moment expecting to see the yarns of which they were composed part one by one under the strain. And the worst of it was that that strain was not a steady one, otherwise there might be some hope that the strands would withstand it long enough to permit him to reach the bottom of the *quebrada*; but at frequent intervals there occurred a couple of jerks—one as a clip passed round the bar, and another as it slid over the cliff edge—and, of course, at every recurrence of the jerk the strain was momentarily increased to an enormous extent. And presently that which he feared happened, a more than usually severe jerk occurred, and one of the yarns in the remaining strands parted. Escombe dully wondered how far he still was from the bottom—a fearful distance, he believed—for he seemed to be cruelly close to the overhanging edge of the cliff, although he had been hanging suspended for a length of time that seemed to him more like hours than minutes. He did not dare to look down, for he had the feeling that if he removed his gaze from those straining and quivering strands for a single instant they would snap, and he would go plunging downward to destruction. Then, as he watched, another yarn parted, and another. A catastrophe was now inevitable, and the lad began to speculate curiously, and from a singularly impersonal point of view, what the sensation would be like when the last yarn had snapped. He had read somewhere that the sensation of falling from a great height was distinctly pleasurable; but what about the other, upon reaching the bottom? A quaint story came into his mind about an Irishman who was said to have fallen off the roof of a house, and who, upon being picked up, was asked whether he had been hurt by his fall, to which the man replied: "No, the fall didn't hurt me a bit, it was stoppin' so quick that did all the mischief!" The humour of the story was not very brilliant, yet somehow it seemed to Escombe at that moment to be ineffably amusing, and he laughed aloud at the quaintness of the conceit. And, as he did so, the remaining yarns of the second strand parted with a little jerk that thrilled him through and through, and he hung there suspended by a single strand, but still being lowered rapidly from above. His eyes were now fixed intently upon the unbroken strand, and he distinctly saw it stretching and straightening out under his weight, but, as it seemed to him, with inconceivable slowness. Then—to such a preternatural state of acuteness had his senses been wrought by the imminence and certainty of ghastly disaster—he saw the last strand slowly parting, not yarn by yarn but fibre by fibre, until, after what seemed to be a veritable eternity of suspense, the last fibre snapped, he heard a loud twang, and found himself floating—as it seemed to him—very gently downward, so gently, indeed, that, as he was swung round, facing the rocky wall, he was able to note clearly and distinctly every inequality, every projection, every crack, every indentation in the face of the rock; nay, he even felt that, were it worth while to do so, he would have had time enough to make sketches of every one of them as they drifted slowly upward. The next thing of which he was conscious was a loud swishing sound which rose even above the deafening brawl of water among rocks, that he now remembered with surprise had been thundering in his ears for—how many months—or years, was it? Then he became aware that he was somehow among leaves and branches; and again memory reproduced the scene upon which he had looked when, standing upon the cliff edge at a point from which he could command a view of the whole depth of the gorge, he had idly noted that, at the very bottom of it, a few inconsiderable shrubs or small trees, nourished by eternal showers of spray, grew here and there from interstices of the rock, and he realised that he had fallen into the heart of one of them. He contrived to grasp a fairly stout branch with each hand, and was much astonished when they bent and snapped like twigs as his body ploughed through the thick growth; but he knew that the force of his fall had been broken, and, for the first time since he had made the discovery of the severed strand, the hope came that, after all, he might emerge from this adventure with his life. Then he alighted—on his feet—on a great, moss-grown boulder, felt his legs double up and collapse under him, sank into a huddled heap upon the wet, slippery moss, shot off into the leaping, foaming water, and knew no more.

Chapter Four
Mama Cachama

When young Escombe regained his senses it was night, or so he supposed, for all was darkness about him, save for such imperfect illumination as came from a small wood fire which flickered and crackled cheerfully in one corner of the apartment in which he found himself. The apartment! Nay, it was far too large, much too spacious in every dimension, to be a room in an ordinary house, and those walls—or as much as could be seen of them in the faint, ruddy glow of the firelight—were altogether too rough and rugged to have been fashioned by human hands, while the roof was so high that the flickering light of the flames was not strong enough to reach it. It was a cavern, without doubt, and Harry began to wonder vaguely by what means he had come there. For, upon awakening, his mind had been in a state of the most utter confusion, and it was not until he had lain patiently waiting for his ideas to arrange themselves, and had thereby come to the consciousness that he was aching in every bone and fibre of his body, while the latter was almost entirely swathed in bandages, that the recollection of his adventure returned to him. Even then the memory of it was but a dreamy one, and indeed he did not feel at all certain that the entire incident was not a dream from beginning to end, and that he should not presently awake to find himself on the cot in his tent, with the cold, clear dawn peering in past the unfolded flap, and another day's arduous work before him. But he finally concluded that the fire upon which his eyes rested was too real, and, more especially, that his pain was too acute and insistent for him to be dreaming. Then he fell to wondering afresh how in the name of fortune he had found his unconscious way into that cave and upon the pallet which supported him.

The fire was the only thing in the cavern that was distinctly visible; certain objects there were here and there, a vague suggestion of which came and went with the rise and fall of the flame, but what they were Harry could not determine. There was, among other matters, an object on the far side of the fire, that looked not unlike a bundle of rags; but when Escombe, in attempting to turn himself over into a more comfortable position, uttered an involuntary groan as a sharp twinge of pain shot through his anatomy, the bundle stirred, and instantly resolved itself into the quaintest figure of a little, old, bowed Indian woman that it is possible to picture. But, notwithstanding her extreme age and apparent decrepitude, the extraordinary old creature displayed marvellous activity. In an instant she was on her feet and beside the pallet, peering eagerly and anxiously into Harry's wide-open eyes. The result of her inspection appeared to be satisfactory, for presently she turned away and, muttering to herself in a tongue which was quite incomprehensible to her patient, disappeared in the all-enveloping darkness, only to reappear a moment later with a small cup in her hand containing a draught of very dark brown, almost black, liquid of an exceedingly pungent but rather agreeable bitter taste, which she placed to his lips, and which the lad at once swallowed without demur. The effect of the draught was instantaneous, as it was marvellously stimulating and exhilarating; and it must also have possessed very remarkable tonic properties, for scarcely had Escombe swallowed it when a sensation of absolutely ravenous hunger assailed him.

HARRY FINDS HIMSELF IN STRANGE QUARTERS

Harry Escombe | 37

"Ah!" he sighed, "that was good; I feel ever so much better now. Mother," he continued in Spanish, "I feel hungry: can you find me something to eat?"

"Aha! you feel hungry, do you?" responded the old woman in the same language. "Good! I am prepared for that. Wait but a moment, *caro mio*, until I can heat the broth, and your hunger shall soon be satisfied." And with the birdlike briskness which characterised all her actions she moved away into the shadows, presently returning with three iron rods in her hand, which she dexterously arranged in the form of a tripod over the fire, and from which she suspended a small iron pot. Then, taking a few dry sticks from a bundle heaped up near the fire, she broke them into short lengths, which she carefully introduced, one by one, here and there, into the flame, coaxing it into a brisk blaze which soon caused a most savoury and appetising steam to rise from the pot. Next, from some hidden receptacle she produced a bowl and spoon, emptied the smoking contents of the pot into the former, and then, carefully propping her patient into a sitting position, proceeded to feed him. The stew was delicious, to such an extent, indeed, that Harry felt constrained to compliment his hostess upon its composition and to ask of what it was made. He was much astonished—and also, it must be confessed, a little disgusted—when the old lady simply answered, *Lagarto* (lizard). There was no doubt, however, that he had greatly enjoyed his meal, and felt distinctly the better for it; he therefore put his squeamishness on one side, and asked his companion to enlighten him as to the manner in which he came to be where he was.

"It is very simple," answered the old woman. "While my son Yupanqui was fishing in the river, two days ago, he caught sight of something unusual lying at the edge of a sandbank, and upon paddling his *balsa* to the spot, he found your insensible body lying stranded there, bruised and bleeding; so, like a sensible boy, he took you up and brought you hither as quickly as possible, in order that I might exercise my skill in the attempt to restore you to life. We managed to do so at last, between us; but you were *caduco* (crazy), and could tell us nothing of yourself, for you spoke persistently in a language that we did not understand; so, as soon as it was seen that you would live, I busied myself in dressing your wounds and bruises, after which I prepared for you a certain medicine which, as I expected, threw you into a deep sleep, from which you have at length awakened in your right mind. And now you have but to lie still and allow your wounds to heal. Which reminds me that now is a very favourable time to dress them afresh."

"Two days ago—stranded on a sandbank!" repeated Escombe in bewilderment. "I do not understand you, Mother. Surely I have not been lying insensible for two whole days! And how could I possibly have become stranded on a sandbank? I fell into the river in the *quebrada*, and I am prepared to avouch that there were no sandbanks there!"

"In the *quebrada*! Is it possible?" echoed the old woman. "Why, the end of the *quebrada* is more than a mile away from where Yupanqui found you! But I think I begin to understand a little. You are not a Spaniard—I can tell that by your accent—therefore you must be an Inglés, one of the *ingenieros* who are making the new railway among the mountains. Is it not so?"

"You have guessed it, Mother," answered Escombe. "Yes, I was taking some measurements in the *quebrada* when the rope by which I was hanging broke, and I fell into a tree, and thence on to the rocks beneath, after which I lost consciousness."

"Ah!" exclaimed the old woman, as she proceeded to remove deftly the bandages and re-dress Harry's hurts; "yes, it is wonderful—very wonderful; for if you had not chanced to fall into the tree before striking the rocks, you must certainly have been killed. That I can quite understand. But I cannot understand how, after having fallen into the river, you escaped being dashed to pieces upon the many rocks among which it flows, nor how, having escaped that death, you afterwards escaped drowning in the deep water, for you must have been swept along quite a mile after issuing from the *quebrada*. It is true that when Yupanqui found you, you were lying upon your back; so that, I suppose, is the reason why the river did not suffocate you. Your hurts are doing famously, *Señor Inglés*, thanks to my knowledge of simples. There is only one—this in your head—which is likely to give trouble; but we will soon mend that, if you can prevail upon yourself to lie still and not disturb the bandage."

"Oh!" answered Harry; "I will do that all right, now that my senses have come back to me, don't you fear; for I must get well quickly, and return to my work as soon as possible. Meanwhile, Mother, where is your son? I should like to send him with a message to the engineer's camp, if he will go, to let them know that I am alive."

"Assuredly, assuredly," assented the queer old creature, as she assiduously bathed the wound in Harry's head with a hot fomentation which she had specially prepared. "He is out hunting, now, but the evening is drawing in and I expect him back ere long. When he returns we will hear what he has to say about it. Doubtless he will willingly go; but if your camp is near the spot where I think you must have fallen, it will take him quite half a day to reach it."

"Half a day!" echoed Harry, aghast. "How is that? I should have thought that half an hour would have been nearer the mark."

"Nay, my son," answered the old woman, "he will have to travel fast to do it in half a day. You do not know how difficult it is to travel from place to place among these mountains, even when one knows the way. He will have to go a long way round to reach the spot of which I am thinking, for there are many impassable precipices in his course, to say nothing of bogs in which, if one be not very careful, one can disappear, leaving no trace behind."

Harry could understand this, now that it had been explained to him, for he had already had experience of the impassable precipices and bottomless morasses spoken of by his companion. But it was disconcerting, to say the least of it, that it would occupy so long to send a message to camp; for, taking into consideration the fact that he had already been two days absent, and that it would require another half-day to send a message, the chances were that, when Yupanqui reached the spot, he would find the survey party gone, and would be obliged to follow them up until he should overtake them. Also he began to wonder how long it would be before his injuries would be sufficiently healed to allow him to travel over a road of so difficult a character as that hinted at in his companion's remarks. He had only to attempt to move on his pallet, and to feel the intolerable aching in every limb that resulted from the effort, to understand that some days—probably at least a week—must elapse ere he would be fit to attempt the journey; and meanwhile where would the survey party be, and how would they be faring without him? What would Butler do? Would he take Harry's death for granted, and proceed singlehanded with the survey; or would he send out a search party to seek for traces of his lost assistant? He must of necessity do one or the other, and the comforting reflection came to Harry that, even if the first course were adopted, the party could not get very far away without being overtaken.

"How long do you think it will be, Mother, before I shall be able to rise and move about again?" he enquired.

"Nay, my son, who can tell save the good God who holds our lives in His hands?" answered the old woman. "It may be two weeks, or it may be two months, according to whether or not the fever returns. Much must depend upon yourself. If you keep quite quiet, and do not become impatient, you may be able to rise and go into the open for a short time in two weeks, possibly even in less. But you must do in all things exactly as I say, if you wish to get well quickly; and you may trust in me, for I have seen many years and have always been skilled in the art of healing."

"I will trust you, of course," answered Harry, reaching out at the cost of some pain and squeezing the old creature's clawlike hand. "Get me well as quickly as you can, Mother, and you will not find me ungrateful. I have the means of rewarding you liberally for all your trouble as soon as I can return to camp."

"Reward!" ejaculated the old woman, angrily snatching away her hand; "who spoke of reward? I require no reward, if by that you mean money payment. I have no need of money. This cave has provided me with dry and comfortable housing for many years, while the garden outside and my son's hunting and fishing furnish us with ample food. What need have we of money?"

"Pardon, Mother," exclaimed Harry penitently, "I did not mean to offend you. But if you do not need money, there are perhaps other things that you or your son may be glad to have, and you must let me show my gratitude to you in some way, for I cannot forget that to you and your son I owe my life."

"Ay, ay; ay, ay; that's as may be," muttered the old creature, as though speaking to herself. "There," she added, as, having completed the dressing of Escombe's injuries, she secured the last bandage, "that is done. Now, more medicine, and then more sleep." And therewith she bustled away into the shadows, returning, a few minutes later, with a generous draught that foamed and sparkled in the goblet like champagne, but left a taste of sickly sweetness upon the palate. As the invalid swallowed the dose a sensation of great ease and comfort permeated his entire system, and the next moment he was asleep.

When Harry next awoke, feeling very much better, he saw that his hostess, and a fine, stalwart, copper-coloured young Indian whom he took to be her son, were seated at a roughly framed table, at some little distance from his cot, taking a meal by the light of an earthenware lamp, and conversing together in low tones in a language with which he was unfamiliar. From the manner in which the pair glanced in his direction from time to time he rather suspected that he was the subject of their conversation, which was being conducted with much earnestness, especially by the old woman. That she was maintaining a very keen watch upon her patient was perfectly evident, for at Harry's first movement she sprang to her feet and, snatching up the lamp, rapidly approached his bedside, peering down into his eyes with the same intense eagerness that she had before exhibited, muttering and mumbling to herself excitedly the while.

"Ah, ah!" she exclaimed, in tones of much satisfaction, "so you are awake again at last! You have slept well and long, my friend—slept all through the night without a movement. And your skin is cool, too," she continued, laying her skinny hand on Harry's forehead; "cool and moist; no fever. But what of the pain? Is it still severe as ever?"

"The pain!" exclaimed Hal, moving himself slightly. "Why, no, it seems almost gone. What magic is this?"

"No magic at all," chuckled the quaint old creature, "but merely a poor old Indian woman's skill in simples. You are doing excellently well, *Señor Inglés*—better, even, than I dared hope. And now you are hungry, is it not so? Good! your breakfast is ready and shall be brought to you instantly; and when you have finished, there is my son Yupanqui, who is ready to take any message that you may desire to send to your camp."

An excellently roasted bird—which the patient subsequently learned was a parrot,—bread made of Indian corn flour, and a cup of delicious chocolate were speedily dispatched. Then Harry having asked for his notebook, which had been found in his pocket and carefully dried, he pencilled a note to Butler, briefly informing that individual of his escape, and of his hope that he would be sufficiently recovered from his injuries to rejoin the camp in about a fortnight's time, and dispatched Yupanqui with it, describing to the Indian the probable situation of the camp, as nearly as he could, and instructing the man to give it only into the hands of the Englishman, and to ask for a reply, which he was to bring back with him.

The next few days passed uneventfully, save that the invalid's progress toward recovery was so rapid and satisfactory that about midday of the third day Harry—who began to find bed becoming very wearisome—was allowed by his nurse to rise and, clad in trousers and the remains of his shirt, go as far as the entrance of the cave and sit there for an hour or two, enjoying the magnificent prospect which greeted his astonished eyes.

He found that the cave which had afforded him such perfect shelter during his helplessness formed a chamber, or rather a series of chambers, in an enormous mass of rock that rose sheer out of a little circular, basin-like valley through which flowed the stream from the *quebrada*, the water here spreading out in the form of a lake measuring about a mile across and evidently rather shallow, for here and there he could see small sandbanks showing clear of the water. It was upon one of these that he had been found stranded by Yupanqui. The *quebrada* died out in the valley about a mile from the mouth of the cave, as could be seen when the spot was indicated by the old Indian woman, and Escombe wondered more than ever by what chance his senseless body had been carried so far by the rushing water without destroying such life as remained in it. The ground sloped rather steeply from the cave down to the water's edge, and some eight or ten acres of it had been dug up at intervals and planted with maize, vegetables of various kinds, and fruit trees, among which Harry recognised the peach, the orange, the mulberry, and the cacao. It was no wonder, he told himself, that his queer but kind-hearted old hostess indignantly disclaimed any need of money. For, with the produce of the garden, and what Yupanqui could bring in from the forest and the river, it seemed to him that their every want, except perhaps in the matter of clothes, must be abundantly supplied. And, so far as clothes were concerned, doubtless the cultivated ground yielded a superabundance ample enough to afford them the means of bartering it for such simple clothing as they needed. The valley was of basin-like form, the sides of it growing ever steeper as they receded from the middle, until they eventually merged into the mountain slopes which hemmed in the valley on every side and went rolling away, ridge beyond ridge, in interminable perspective, until, in the extreme distance, they terminated in the snow-clad peaks of the Andes.

Harry's hostess—who now mentioned that she bore the name of Cachama—appeared to be in a singularly communicative mood that day, for she beguiled the time by not only pointing out and naming the principal peaks in sight, but she also related several very interesting legends connected with certain of them and with the country generally, going back to the time before the conquest, and painting in dazzling colours the glories of the Inca dynasty, and the incredible wealth of the ancient rulers of Peru. She appeared to be pretty intimately acquainted with the history of the conquest of the country by Pizarro, and had many bitter things to say of the strange pusillanimity of the Inca, Atahuallpa, on that fatal 16th of November, 1532, when he went, open-eyed, into the trap prepared for him at Caxamalca, and suffered himself to be seized, in the presence of his entire army, by a mere handful of Spaniards. She gave a most emphatic denial to the suggestion that the country had benefited by the civilised conditions that had followed the conquest.

"No, no," said she, "we are infinitely worse off in every way, to-day, than we were under the rule of the Incas. Poverty, misery, oppression, and suffering of every kind are to be met with on all hands and wherever one goes, while four hundred years ago we had a far higher state of civilisation than now exists, in which poverty and oppression, with their countless attendant evils, were unknown. But it will not last for ever, I tell you; brighter and happier days are in store for us of the ancient race, and perhaps even I, old as I am, may live to see it. Yes, I, poor though I am, and compelled to lodge my worn-out body in a cave, have royal blood in my veins, as had my husband, Yupanqui; we are both descended from Huayna Capac, and, but for Atahuallpa's incredible folly, I might have been enjoying comfort and affluence to-day; ay, and possibly my husband might also have been living."

Escombe had read Prescott's *Conquest of Peru* during his schooldays, and the romantic story had implanted within his mind a keen interest in everything pertaining to the history of the country, which had never waned, and which had received a fresh stimulus when he learned that he was not only to visit and spend some time in Peru but also to explore certain parts of it. And now, to find himself actually conversing with someone who claimed descent from those proud Incas, who appeared to have lived in a regal splendour only to be equalled by that of the potentates of the *Arabian Nights*, seemed to him to be a rare slice of good luck; he was therefore careful to say nothing calculated to divert the conversation from the channel in which it was so satisfactorily flowing, but, on the contrary, did everything he could to keep it there. He was, however, very much surprised to find his hostess looking forward so confidently to brighter and happier times for the despised Indian race; for if any one thing seemed absolutely certain, it was that the time was not very far distant when the few scattered survivors must perish, and the race vanish from the face of the earth. It was therefore in somewhat incredulous tones that he turned to Cachama and said:

"What grounds have you for the hope—or should I call it the certainty—that better days are in store for your race? To me it seems that there are very few of you left."

"Ay," she answered, "it may so seem to you, for you have as yet seen but little of the country save the *terra caliente*, and very few of us are now to be found near the coast. But when you get farther up among the mountains, and especially when you get into the neighbourhood of Lake Titicaca, you will find that we have not all perished. Furthermore, it is said—with what truth I know not—that when Atahuallpa fell into the hands of the *Conquistadors*, and was strangled by torchlight in the great *plaza* of Caxamalca, many of the nobles who had been with him fled with their families into the heart of the mountains, and, establishing themselves in a certain secret place, set to work, at the bidding of one Titucocha, a priest of the Sun, to build a new City of the Sun—beside the glories of which those of Cuzco were to be as nothing—against the time when our Lord the Sun should again send Manco Capac, the founder of the Inca dynasty, back to earth to restore the dynasty in all its ancient splendour."

"And do you really believe that such a restoration is possible?" asked Escombe with a smile at the old woman's credulity.

"Ay," answered Cachama with conviction, "I more than believe, I know! For I have the gift of foreknowledge, to a certain extent, and from my earliest childhood I have felt convinced that the prophecy is true—I cannot explain how, or why; I only know that it is so. And with the passage of the years I have ever felt that the time for its fulfilment was drawing nearer, until now I know that it is so close at hand that even I, old though I am, may live to see it. I would that I could feel as sure of the continuance of the dynasty as I am of its restoration; but I cannot; I can only see—dimly—up to a certain point, beyond which everything is misty and uncertain, with a vague suggestion of disaster which fills, me with foreboding."

Chapter Five
What has become of Butler?

On the second day after the dispatch of Yupanqui to the surveyors' camp, he had duly returned with a curt officially worded note from Butler acknowledging the receipt of Escombe's "report" of his accident and its result, and requesting the latter to rejoin the survey party with the least possible delay, "as his absence was the cause of much inconvenience and delay in the progress of the survey". Not a word of regret at the occurrence of the accident, much less anything that could be construed into an admission that the writer's own unreasonable demands and orders were the cause of the mishap; and not even a word of congratulation at Escombe's narrow escape from a terrible death; simply a formal request that he would rejoin, "with the least possible delay", for a certain good and sufficient reason. Poor Harry shrugged his shoulders with something very like contempt for the hidebound creature who was, to a great extent, the master of his fate, and who seemed to be absolutely destitute of the very smallest shred of good feeling. He felt that it would be quite hopeless to look for any praise or appreciation from such a man; he foresaw that the fellow would appropriate to himself whatever credit might result from the expedition, and lay upon his (Harry's) shoulders the onus of any shortcomings of complete success. And he came to the conclusion that since such a chief was not worth putting oneself out for, he would remain where he was until it was quite certain that he could travel with perfect safety, and resume duty immediately upon his return to camp. But he was young, and possessed a thoroughly sound constitution; moreover, he had miraculously escaped with unbroken bones, his recovery therefore was rapid, and on the nineteenth day after the accident he rejoined the camp and formally reported himself as prepared to resume duty.

It had been Butler's custom, from the commencement of the survey, to flag out a certain length of route daily, and to insist—without very much regard to the difficulties of the task—that that amount of work should be done by nightfall. This length of route usually amounted to from two to three miles, and Escombe had once or twice protested—when the natural difficulties of the work were excessive—that he could not undertake to guarantee the accuracy of his work if so much were demanded of him; to which Butler had retorted that, in his opinion, the amount of work demanded was exceedingly moderate, that he should expect it to be done, and that he should hold Escombe responsible for all inaccuracies. Yet, upon Escombe's return to camp he found that, during the nineteen days of his absence, Butler had advanced the survey by a distance of less than four miles! the explanation which the elder man condescended to make being that, during the four days immediately following the accident, no survey work at all had been done, the whole body of peons having been scattered in various directions, seeking some clue to Harry's fate.

For a week or two after Escombe's return to camp matters went very much more smoothly. Whether it was that Harry's accident had given Butler a wholesome fright, or that the conviction had been forced upon the latter that he had been outrageously exacting, there was nothing to show, but certain it was that, for a while, Escombe was allowed to take his own time over his work and do it his own way, with the result that while this state of affairs lasted the lad actually took pleasure in, nay, thoroughly enjoyed, his work. But on the third week after his return Harry began to detect signs that these agreeable conditions were drawing to an end. Thenceforth Butler allowed himself to gradually drift back into his former exacting and autocratic ways, until at length life in the camp again became a veritable purgatory for everybody concerned, Butler himself included, the natural result of his tyrannical conduct being that everybody—Harry excepted—did everything in his power to thwart him, while even the lad himself ceased to attempt the apparently impossible task of pleasing his chief.

In this unpleasant and unsatisfactory manner the railway survey proceeded for the two months following Escombe's return to duty; by which time Butler's behaviour had become so unendurable that nearly three-fourths of the peons originally engaged had deserted, notwithstanding the fact that their desertion involved them in the loss of a sum in wages that, to these humble toilers, represented quite a little fortune, and their places had been filled by others of a much less desirable type in every way. And this was all the more to be regretted since the surveyors were now in the very heart of the mountains, where the natural difficulties to be contended with were at their worst, while the newcomers, being of course utterly strange to such work, had to be taught their duties, down to the simplest detail, under the most adverse conditions possible. It can be readily understood that the attempt to instruct a set of ignorant, stupid, sullen, and lawless half-castes under such conditions was a task of surpassing difficulty, resulting in constant acute friction, and demanding the nicest judgment and the utmost diplomacy upon the part of the teachers. Harry met this difficulty by bringing to his assistance an almost sublime patience, that in the course of time—and not a very long time either—completely wore down the opposition of his unwilling pupils and brought a change in their mental attitude which was as surprising as it was satisfactory. Butler, however, knew not the meaning of the word "patience", nor did his character contain the smallest particle of that valuable quality; his method was what he termed "the rough-and-ready", and consisted in emphasising every order, and item of construction, with a kick! It was not surprising, therefore, that the relations between him and the peons daily grew more strained.

It was when the tension between Butler on the one hand and the peons on the other had developed to such an extent that the labourers had been goaded into a state of almost open mutiny, that the former set out as usual, on horseback, one morning, accompanied by a half-dozen of the new hands, to seek for and stake out a few miles farther of practicable route. Such a duty as this he usually contrived to complete in time to return to the camp for lunch, after which he was wont to saunter out along the line until he encountered Harry, when he would spend the remainder of the day in making the poor lad's life a burden to him by finding fault with everything he did, frequently insisting upon having some particularly awkward and difficult piece of work done over again. Consequently the progress of the survey was abnormally and exasperatingly slow; and when, upon the day in question, Butler failed to put in an appearance on the scene of operations, young Escombe's first feeling was one of gratification, for he was just then engaged upon an exceptionally difficult task which he was most anxious to complete without being interfered with. So absorbed was the lad in his work that he had not much thought to spare for speculation as to the reason for so unusual a piece of good luck, although it is true that, as the afternoon wore on, he did once or twice permit himself to wonder whether "perchance" he had to thank a slight touch of indisposition, or possibly a sprained ankle, for this unexpected and most welcome freedom from interruption. But when at length, upon his arrival in camp at the conclusion of his day's survey work, he learned, to his astonishment, that neither Butler nor his party of peons had returned, the impression forced itself upon him that something serious had happened, and mustering afresh his own gang of tired and hungry assistants, and providing them with lanterns, ropes, and other aids to a search, he led them forth along the survey line in quest of the absent ones.

For a distance of nearly two miles from the camp the route of the missing party was easily followed, being marked by stakes at frequent intervals, indicating the line chosen by Butler as that to be surveyed by Escombe. It ended at the foot of a precipitous slope of bare rock towering aloft some seven or eight hundred feet, with further heights beyond it. Here the searchers were brought to an abrupt halt, for Harry was fully aware that no sane engineer would for a single moment dream of carrying an ordinary railway up that rocky acclivity, while it was well understood that the rack system of construction was to be avoided, if possible, upon the score of expense. The probability was that Butler, upon reaching this point, and finding himself confronted by the necessity to make a wide détour, or, alternatively, to consider the question of a tunnel, had struck off, either to the right or to the left, on a tour of investigation; and there was the chance that, becoming involved in the maze-like intricacies of his surroundings, he had decided to camp out for the night rather than risk an accident by attempting to return in darkness over difficult ground. But this was a question which Harry felt ought to be settled forthwith, and he accordingly issued instructions to his peons to search for the spoor of the party and follow it up. To find the spoor was a very easy matter, for the last stake had been driven in comparatively soft ground, and despite the fact that it was by this time almost pitch dark, a short search, aided by the light of the lanterns, disclosed the hoof prints of Butlers horse, which led off to the left, and which were followed until the searchers found themselves on the borders of an extensive pine wood growing on hard, steeply rising ground over which it was impossible to trace further the trail in the darkness. This impossibility once realised, the search was abandoned for the night, and Harry very reluctantly gave the word for a return to camp, which was reached about nine o'clock.

At daybreak the next morning the camp was roused, breakfast prepared and eaten, and, taking with them rations to last until nightfall, the search party again set out upon their quest, making their way direct to the spot where the trail had been lost on the previous night, where it was again picked up without much trouble. It led in straight toward the heart of the wood, and was followed, with ever-increasing difficulty, for a distance of about three-quarters of a mile until it was lost on hard, shaley ground, nor were the utmost efforts of the party equal to finding it again. After carefully considering the situation, therefore, Escombe detailed one man, an Indian, to accompany him, and, placing the remainder of the peons in charge of a man whom he believed he could trust, with instructions to search the wood thoroughly, returned to the outskirts of the timber, and, beginning at the spot where the trail entered it, proceeded, with the assistance of the Indian, to encircle the wood, carefully examining every foot of the ground as they went, in the hope that, if Butler and his party had passed through the timber and emerged on its other side, the Indian would succeed in picking up the spoor. But the hope was vain, for the wood was completely encircled—the task occupying the entire day—without the discovery of the faintest trace or sign of the passage of the missing party, which was not at all surprising, for when the far side of the wood was reached the soil proved to be of so stony a character, thickly interspersed with great outcrops of rock, that even the most skilled and keen-eyed of trackers might have been excused for failing in the search for footprints on so unyielding a surface. It was a little puzzling to Harry that not even the horse had left any trace behind him; but this was accounted for when, upon rejoining the party who had been detailed to search the interior of the wood, it was discovered that the animal had been found by them, still saddled and bridled, wandering aimlessly about in search of such scanty herbage as the soil there afforded. Upon the horse being brought to him, the young Englishman—mindful of the scarcely concealed hatred which Butler had, almost wantonly, as it seemed, aroused in the breasts of the peons—immediately subjected the animal and his trappings to a most rigorous examination in search of any sign of possible violence, but nothing of the kind could be found, and the only result of the examination was the conclusion, to which everything pointed, that Butler had, for some reason, voluntarily dismounted and at least temporarily abandoned the animal.

Butler and his party had now been missing for full twenty-four hours, and Harry speedily arrived at two conclusions which inexorably led him to a third. The first conclusion at which he arrived was that the peons who had accompanied his chief, accustomed as they had been from their earliest childhood to make their way about the country, were so little likely to have lost their way that that theory might be unhesitatingly abandoned; the second was that Butler would certainly not have absented himself purposely from the camp for a whole night and a day, and that therefore—this was the third conclusion—something had gone very seriously wrong. The next problem that presented itself for solution was: What was it that had gone wrong? Had the entire party met with an accident? It was most unlikely. There were seven of them altogether, and in the event of an accident, surely at least one of the seven would have escaped and returned to the camp for help. Had they been seized and carried off by brigands? When Harry put this question to the peons who remained with him he was laughed at good-naturedly and assured that, in the first place, there were no brigands in Peru, so far as they were aware; and, in the second place, that if perchance there were they would probably not have contented themselves with simply carrying off seven men, six of whom would be only an encumbrance to them, but would almost certainly have attacked and sacked the camp some time during the hours of daylight, when it was left comparatively unprotected. There was but one other probable alternative of which Harry could think, and that was that Butler's peons, exasperated at length beyond endurance by some fresh piece of petty tyranny on the white man's part, had deserted, carrying off their employer with them, either with the purpose of being revenged upon him, or in the hope that by holding him as a hostage they might be able to secure payment of the amount of wages due to them. But when Escombe submitted this alternative to his peons for their consideration and opinion, they shook their heads and emphatically declared that they did not believe that any such thing had happened. And when further asked for their opinion as to what had happened, they simply answered that they did not know what to think. But to Harry it seemed that there was a certain lack of spontaneity in this reply, which caused him to doubt whether the speakers were quite sincere in so saying.

With a very heavy load of responsibility thus unexpectedly thrown upon his shoulders, the young Englishman spent several anxious hours in camp that night pondering upon what was the proper course for him now to pursue, and he finally came to the conclusion that, having ascertained beyond much possibility of doubt that his chief had been abducted, the next thing to be done was to discover whither and under what circumstances he had been carried off, and then to take the necessary steps to effect his rescue. On the following morning, therefore, he mustered the peons who still remained with him, and briefly explaining to them his theory of an abduction, dispatched six of them in as many different directions to seek for traces of the missing party, offering a substantial reward to the one who should bring him such information as should lead to the recovery of the missing white man; and then, taking a couple of sure-footed mules, set off in company with an Indian tracker to scour the entire neighbourhood, in the hope of obtaining some clue to the whereabouts of the missing party from some of the people by whom that particular part of the country was sparsely inhabited. And in order to avoid the loss of time which would be entailed by returning to camp at night, he took with him three days' provisions for himself and his guide, intending to carry out as exhaustive a search as possible in that space of time.

Thus far the search had been prosecuted entirely in a forward direction; but at the last moment, before setting out upon his three days' quest, it suddenly occurred to Escombe that the missing ones might possibly have doubled back and be making their way toward the sea coast, so in order to test the value of this theory he determined to return a few miles along the line of the survey and see whether he could discover any traces of them in that direction.

At this time the surveyors were in the heart of an exceptionally difficult tract of country, where the obstacles to rapid work were such that, since Harry's return to duty after his adventures in the *quebrada*, they had not advanced very much more than twenty miles from that spot; thus it was still early in the afternoon of the first day when he found himself gazing down into the abyss, wherein he had so narrowly escaped a terrible death. By a natural association of ideas he no sooner beheld the scene so indelibly engraven upon his memory than his thoughts reverted to Cachama, his kind-hearted old Indian nurse, and her son Yupanqui, and he vaguely wondered whether perhaps either of these might be able to afford him any information or suggestion that would assist him in his quest. The more he thought of it the more did the idea grow upon his mind, and at length he came to the decision that he might as well prosecute his search in the direction of their cave as in any other, and he forthwith communicated his decision to his guide, who, somewhat to Escombe's surprise, at once admitted that he was well acquainted with Cachama and her son, and offered to conduct the young Englishman to the cave in which the two resided, by a short route, if Harry would consent to be blindfolded during their passage of certain portions of the way. To this the lad readily agreed—for he was by this time becoming exceedingly anxious on Butler's account—and thereupon the Indian, having hobbled the mules, demanded Harry's pocket—handkerchief and immediately proceeded to blindfold the owner therewith, after which, with joined hands, the pair resumed their way, travelling for two full hours or more over exceedingly broken and difficult ground. Then the pocket-handkerchief was removed, and Harry found himself standing in the midst of a number of enormous fallen boulders at the foot of a stupendous cliff, and facing an opening in the latter which had all the appearance of being the mouth of a cavern. But by what route he had arrived at the spot he could not tell, for he was so completely hemmed in on every side by the boulders in the midst of which he stood that the surrounding landscape was completely shut out, nothing being visible save the boulders and the face of the cliff with the opening in it. That he was correct in his surmise that this opening was a cavern was now demonstrated by his Indian guide, who said:

"Be pleased to take my hand again, Señor, and follow me without fear. This is one of several entrances to the cavern in which Cachama dwells. You will find the ground smooth and even for almost the entire distance, and presently we shall find torches by which to light our way."

And so, as a matter of fact, they did; for after traversing some ten or fifteen yards the Indian halted and, releasing Escombe's hand, was heard groping about in the darkness, and a moment later the rattling of dry branches reached the lad's ears.

"Now, Señor," came the voice of the Indian out of the darkness, "if you will graciously condescend to produce fire by means of those small sticks which you call 'matches' we shall soon have light to guide our steps."

So said, so done; and as the torch kindled and blazed up the pair found themselves standing in a rugged rock passage some five feet wide and about eight feet high, with a perfectly smooth floor which, in the flickering, uncertain light of the torch, presented the appearance of having been brought into this condition by human agency. It was not only smooth, but also level at the point where they stood. But even as they started to resume their journey—the Indian bearing the torch and leading the way—Harry saw that it almost immediately began to dip, and ere they had advanced many paces the dip became so pronounced that the smooth floor gave place to a long flight of roughly hewn steps, at first broad and shallow, but rapidly steepening, until they became so narrow and deep as to necessitate a considerable amount of care in the negotiation of them. To Harry this flight seemed interminable; there must have been hundreds of steps, for—although the lad did not time himself—the descent appeared to have occupied considerably more than half an hour; but at length they once more reached level ground and, leaving the steps behind them, proceeded to traverse a narrow and winding passage, the air in which smelt stale and musty, while here and there they were obliged to squeeze their painful way between long, spiky stalactites and stalagmites until they came to more steps—this time leading upward. Harry counted these; there were only one hundred and twenty-three of them, and they were not nearly so steep as the others; and then they ceased, and the pair came to a gently rising floor, along which they passed for about half a mile, finally entering a spacious chamber or cavern, where, very much to the young Englishman's surprise, they found Cachama awaiting them with a torch in her hand.

It was perfectly evident that the old lady was intensely angry, for upon the appearance of her visitors she darted toward them and, shaking her fist furiously in the face of the Indian—whom, by the way, she addressed as Arima—she poured out upon him a torrent of strange words, the virulence of which could be pretty accurately estimated by the effect which they produced upon their recipient, for poor Arima writhed under them as though they had been the lash of a whip. For fully ten minutes the old woman stormed relentlessly before she was reduced to silence through want of breath, and then the Indian got his chance to reply, and apparently vindicate himself, for, as he proceeded with what appeared to Escombe to be his explanation, Cachama's wrath gradually subsided until she became sufficiently mistress of herself to greet the young white man, which she did with more cordiality than her previous outburst had led him to expect.

"Welcome back to my poor home, Señor!" she exclaimed. "I knew that you were coming, and am glad to see you; but that dolt Arima enraged me, for he brought you by the secret way, although he knew that it is forbidden to reveal that way, or even the fact of its existence, to strangers. He tells me, however, that the matter is urgent, and that he adopted the precaution of blindfolding you so that you might not learn the secret of the approach, therefore I will let the matter pass, especially as I feel certain that I have but to express the wish and you will forget that such a way exists."

"Certainly I will, Mama Cachama," answered Harry cheerfully. "You saved my life not long ago, and I should be an ingrate indeed if I refused to conform to your wishes in so simple a matter as that. But I understood you to say that you knew I was coming to you! How on earth could you possibly know that? I didn't know it myself until a few hours ago!"

"Did not I tell you that I possess the gift of foreknowledge?" remarked Cachama somewhat impatiently. "You had no sooner conceived the idea of coming to me than I became aware of it; nay, I even knew the way by which you were coming, and it was that knowledge which angered me, for I knew that you could not visit the cave by the secret approach except with the help of one of us! But let that pass. Follow me to my living room, where I have provided a meal for you; and while you are partaking of it you may tell me in what manner you think I can assist you."

Ten minutes later Escombe once more found himself in the cavern which he knew so well, partaking of a most excellent stew, and detailing to his hostess between mouthfuls all the particulars relating to the disappearance of Butler and his party of peons. He brought his recital to a close by enquiring whether Cachama or Yupanqui had chanced to see any of the missing ones.

"No," said Cachama. "They have not passed near here, or Yupanqui would certainly have seen something of them and mentioned the fact to me. But you have done well to come to me, for it will be strange indeed if I cannot help you. You wish to know what has become of the Señor whom you call Butler; is not that so? Very well. Seat yourself there before me, hold my two hands in yours, and recall to your mind as vividly as possible all the circumstances, be they ever so trivial, that you can remember relating to the doings of the day upon which the Señor disappeared, beginning with the moment of your awakening. Now begin, for I am ready."

While the old creature spoke she was arranging matters in such a way that she and Escombe could sit facing each other, knee to knee and with their hands clasped, she leaning slightly back in a reclining posture, with her eyes upturned toward the invisible roof of the cavern. As she finished speaking the young Englishman directed his thoughts backward to the morning of two days ago, mentally reproducing every incident of the day, beginning with the moment when he arose from his camp bed, and intending to continue, if need were, to that other moment when, after the long fruitless search in the pine wood, he cast himself on that same bed at the end of the day and, completely exhausted, sank to sleep.

But when he had reached this latter point of retrospection Mama Cachama's eyes were closed and, to Harry's chagrin, she appeared to have fallen into a deep sleep. Before, however, his disappointment had found time to express itself in words the old Indian woman began to speak in a low tone, as though soliloquising.

"Yes," she murmured, "I see it all quite distinctly, the white tents gleaming in the brilliant sunshine of early morning, with their ropes strained tight by the dew that has fallen heavily during the night; the peons moving hither and thither, shivering in the keen air as they make their preparations for the day's work; the horses and mules feeding eagerly; the fires blazing cheerily and the blue smoke streaming straight up in the still air. Yes, and I see the two Englishmen, the old and the young one, sitting at breakfast in their tents. The elder man is tall and thin, with black hair touched here and there with grey, and a close-clipped moustache. He is dressed in dark-grey woollen clothing, and wears brown boots reaching to the knee. He is glancing through a little book as he eats, writing in it from time to time. Now he rises and, taking a whip in his hand, puts on a soft cloth cap and goes to the tent door. He calls to one named José to bring him his horse, and then gives the young *Inglés* certain instructions, speaking sharply as though in anger.

"Now the horse is brought, and the elder *Inglés* mounts him somewhat awkwardly, as though he were not accustomed to life in the saddle, and rides off, accompanied by six peons who carry long poles with small flags on them, also heavy hammers, axes, machetes, ropes, and bundles of wooden stakes. The young *Inglés* also prepares to leave the camp, and busies himself in examining certain strange instruments that are packed in boxes of polished wood. But it is the elder *Inglés* that I must follow. He leads the way over rising ground, riding toward a snow-clad peak that gleams like silver in the far distance, pausing occasionally while his peons drive a stake into the ground where directed by him. They proceed thus until they find themselves facing a bare rocky slope so steep that scarcely might a llama climb it; and here they pause for a time while the *Inglés* looks about him. Then they move off to the left, skirting the precipice until they come to a great wood growing on a steep spur of the mountain. They enter this wood and penetrate it for a considerable distance, the ground ever rising more steeply and becoming looser and more difficult as they go. Here the horse finds it so hard to keep his feet, and is in such constant danger of falling, that at length the rider dismounts and, leaving the horse standing, presses forward as though anxious to get to the other side of the wood, his peons following and whispering eagerly together. They are encumbered with the various articles which they carry, and consequently cannot travel over that steep, loose ground so rapidly as the Englishman, who carries nothing but his riding whip and one of the poles with a flag on it, which he uses to help him over the rough ground, and he turns upon them from time to time with angry words, urging them to greater exertion. At first they answer nothing; but at length the strictures of the *Inglés* goad them to retort, humbly in the beginning, but soon with such heat that he lifts his whip and strikes one of them savagely with it across the face. And at that, as though the blow were a signal, every peon flings from him his burden, and the whole of them hurl themselves upon the white man and bear him to the ground, the one who was struck raising his machete as though to split the skull of his enemy."

Chapter Six
Found!

At this point Mama Cachama became greatly agitated, and struggled violently in an endeavour to wrench her hands out of Escombe's grasp, crying that they were going to murder the Englishman, and that she would not remain to see it. But the vision which she had thus far described was of so extraordinary a character, and impressed the young man so strongly with a sense of its reality and truth, that he was determined to follow up the clue as far as possible; he therefore resolutely retained his grip upon the old woman's hands, under the impression that, if he released them, the vision would pass, possibly beyond recall.

But suddenly Cachama's struggles ceased, and she sighed as though relieved of some great fear.

"Ah!" she exclaimed, "they will not kill him after all; one of the peons intervenes, pointing out that if the Englishman is killed, none of them may dare to again show their faces in the towns, for information of the murder will be given, and the Peruvian Corporation—who have employed the Englishman to do this work for them—will never rest until every one of the murderers is brought to justice. The others understand this at once, and agree that there shall be no murder; but they are binding the Englishman's hands and feet, so that he cannot escape; and now they are asking each other what will be best to do with him. There is much talk—some urge one thing, some another—now José, the man who prevented the murder, speaks—he proposes that the prisoner shall be carried to a certain place and there detained until the whole of their wages be paid them, after which they are to release their prisoner, and each man will go his way, working no more for the Englishman. Now they are pondering on the proposal—yes, they have all agreed to it; and now they are releasing the Englishman's feet, in order that he may walk with them, but his hands remain tied behind him, and one of the peons holds the end of the rope, to make sure that their prisoner shall not escape. Two others grasp him, one by either arm, to help him, for the ground is rough and steep, and the going bad. They move forward again, following an easterly direction—their progress is slow, for the Englishman stumbles at almost every step, his hands being tied. He declares that walking, under such circumstances, is impossible, and angrily demands to be released—but they laugh and jeer at him. He struggles on, falling frequently despite the assistance of the two men who are holding him, and at length the party emerge from the wood on its far side and find themselves on the spur of the mountain, on barren, rocky, open ground. Now they reach the crest of the spur, and, passing over it, still travelling in an easterly direction, descend into the valley beyond until they reach the margin of a small stream flowing northward. Here they pause in the shadow of an enormous granite rock of very remarkable appearance, for it bears a most extraordinary resemblance to the head and neck of an Indian—I know it well; and among us it is called 'The Inca's Head'. They sit down beneath this rock and proceed to eat and drink—for it is now two hours past midday—binding the Englishman's feet and releasing his hands to enable him to feed himself. Now the meal is over, and the party resume their march, going northward along the western bank of the stream and plunging ever deeper into the valley. The soil here is once more rich and fertile, being overgrown with long, rank grass—through which they leave a trail easy to follow—and dense masses of mimosa and other bush. Now it is evening, the valley grows dark, and the party prepare to camp for the night; they have found a suitable spot, quite close to the river bank, and are lighting a large fire. They eat and drink again. Now they have finished, and are disposing themselves to rest, one man of the party undertaking to remain awake for a certain time to watch the prisoner, until relieved by another who will perform the same service.

"The night passes; the light of dawn sweeps down the steep mountain slopes into the valley, and the peon who is watching the prisoner awakes his fellows. Again they eat and drink. Now they have finished their meal and resume their march, still following the western bank of the stream. I go with them as they plod on, hour after hour, until they reach a point where the stream turns westward, and here they take advantage of a shallow spot which enables them to cross to the other side. They are now marching eastward up the slope of the valley, and at length they emerge upon a great plateau, thickly dotted with extensive clumps of bush, interspersed here and there with wide belts of timber through which they pass. For many miles they plod onward, winding hither and thither among the clumps of bush and through the belts of forest trees, but all the while holding steadily toward the east. Night comes again; a fire is lighted, as on the preceding night, they eat and drink, and once more dispose themselves to sleep, one man again undertaking to watch the prisoner. For a time—how long I know not, but it appears to be about an hour—this man remains faithful to his duty; but, as the moments pass and the prisoner appears to be sleeping heavily, the watcher's vigilance relaxes, he grows drowsy, his eyelids close, he dozes, awakes, dozes again, once more awakes, and finally succumbs to sleep.

"Meanwhile the prisoner, who has to all appearance been sleeping heavily, has remained very wide awake, and, observing that his guard is not over watchful, proceeds to strain stealthily upon his bonds, which, he has noticed, are not drawn quite so tight as usual. Gradually he succeeds in loosening them to such an extent that eventually he is able to free one hand. To free the other at once becomes easy, and, this done, the prisoner very cautiously raises himself sufficiently to assure himself that his captors are all soundly sleeping. Satisfied of this, he rolls himself gently over and over, a few inches at a time, until he is outside the circle of his captors, when he rises to his feet and with infinite caution withdraws into the darkness, making for the nearest clump of bush, which, upon reaching, he places between himself and the faint glow of the dying camp fire. Hidden thus from his late captors, should any of them chance to awake and miss him, he now walks rapidly forward, constantly glancing over his shoulder in fear lest he should be pursued; and in this manner he soon places a couple of miles between himself and the sleeping peons. He believes that he is now returning toward the camp over the ground which he has already traversed, and he hastens onward as fast as the uneven nature of the ground will permit. But the night is dark, the stars are obscured by heavy masses of threatening rain-cloud; there is therefore no beacon by which he can guide his footsteps, and, unsuspected by himself, he has gradually swung round until he is heading south-east. And now the gathering storm breaks, the rain falls heavily, and in a few minutes the unhappy fugitive is drenched to the skin, and chilled to the marrow by the fierce and bitter wind which comes swooping down from the snowfields and glaciers of the higher Andes; yet he dares not take shelter from the storm, even in the recesses of a clump of scrub, for he fears that by dawn at the latest, his enemies will be on his track, and—forgetful or ignorant of the fact that the storm will obliterate his trail from all but dogs or experienced trackers—of which the peons have none— the fugitive is madly anxious to put as many miles as possible between himself and his pursuers. On he staggers, blindly and breathlessly, whipped by the pelting rain, buffeted by the furious wind, half-fainting already from exhaustion, yet spurred on by unreasoning terror—I think that unless he is quickly rescued the Englishman will die."

Escombe shuddered and went white to the lips. This man, whose every wandering footstep had been faithfully traced through Mama Cachama's marvellous clairvoyant gift, was a remorseless tyrant in his petty way, so curiously constituted that his one idea of pleasure appeared to be the making miserable the lives of all about him, even to going out of his way to do so, to such extent, indeed, that men had been heard to say bitterly that, as in the case of some noxious animal or reptile, the world would be the better for his death. The young Englishman could recall without effort many an occasion when he had been so harassed and worried, and his existence so embittered by the impish spite of this same Butler that even he, gentle and kindly as was his disposition in general, believed he could have contemplated the demise of the other with a feeling not far removed from equanimity. Yet, now that the man was in actual peril, all that was forgotten, every generous instinct in the lad sprang at once to the surface, his one idea was to hurry to the rescue, and he cried eagerly:

"Tell me exactly where to find him and I will go at once and bring him in."

"Wait, *muchacho*, wait!" exclaimed Cachama impatiently. "Let me follow him first as far as I may, lest I lose him, for now his way is growing erratic, his mind and body are becoming numb with the misery of his plight, and he no longer has any clear knowledge of anything, the one conviction which haunts him being that he must press onward anywhere—no matter where—otherwise his pursuers will overtake him and put him to a terrible death. Ah! now the dawn breaks, and the storm is subsiding; but the Englishman takes no note of this. He seems quite incapable of noticing anything now, but runs on aimlessly, panting and gasping, his breath bursting from his labouring lungs in great sobs, his eyes staring unseeingly before him, his limbs quivering and staggering beneath him, his thin clothing clinging in saturated tatters to his body, which is streaked here and there with blood where the thorns have torn him, as he burst through them in his headlong flight. Aha! the end must surely now be drawing near, for see, the foam upon his lips is tinged with blood, and rapidly grows a deeper crimson; he reels and stumbles as he runs—he is down—no—yes—he is up again—and staggers onwards for a few yards—now he is down again, falling with a crash—and, rolling over on his back with outstretched arms, lies motionless, his eyes closed, and the blood trickling out of the corners of his mouth."

"Is he dead, Mama Cachama? is he dead?" gasped Escombe, his grievances all forgotten now, and his sense of pity stirred to its uttermost depths by the shocking plight of his chief, so graphically painted by the words of the old Indian woman.

"Nay," answered Cachama, "he still lives, for his chest heaves and he now and then gasps for breath; but his flight is ended, for the present at least, and if you would find him with the life still in his body you must surely hasten."

"But how shall I find him?" demanded Harry. "You must direct me how to go straight to where he lies; for should it be necessary for us to pick up his trail and follow that, he would be dead long ere we could reach him."

"Where is Arima?" demanded Cachama. "Let him come to me."

"I am here," answered the Indian, drawing near to the old woman.

"Then listen attentively, Arima, and mark well what I say," commanded the Mama. She spoke to him for a full minute or more in the Indian tongue, of which Escombe comprehended enough to understand that she was describing what might be termed the bearings of the spot where Butler lay exhausted and senseless, Arima nodding his head understanding and murmuring here and there a word of comprehension as she went on. Her description ended, she paused for a few seconds, then murmured: "It is enough. Now let me awake, for I am old. I have wandered afar, and the journey has wearied me."

Whereupon, after an interval of a minute or two, she slowly opened her eyes, stared about her vacantly for a little, and finally said: "Ah, yes, I remember! I was to tell you something, Señor. Have you learned what you desired to know?"

"Yes, thanks," answered Harry, "always provided, of course, that—that,"—he was about to say—"that your information is reliable"; but substituted for those somewhat ungracious words—"that Arima can find the spot which you have described to him."

"Think you that you can find it, Arima?" demanded the old woman.

"Yes, Mama Cachama," answered Arima, "I shall find it without doubt; for I have listened attentively to all that you have said, and already know the direction generally, in which to seek it, while the particulars which you have given me are so explicit that I can scarcely miss the exact spot."

"That is well," approved Cachama. Then, turning to Escombe, she said: "And now, Señor, if you will remain with me for the rest of the day and the coming night it will give me pleasure, and I will do my best for your comfort; the afternoon is wellnigh spent, and if, as I understood you to say, you started from your camp shortly after daybreak this morning, you can scarcely return to it ere nightfall, and the way is a rough and dangerous one to travel in the darkness."

"Nevertheless, with many thanks for your hospitable offer, I must go," answered Harry, "for the matter is urgent, as you must know, for your last words to me were that if I would find my—friend with the life still in him I must hasten."

"Nay, *amigo*, I know nothing of what I told you while in my state of trance," answered the old woman; "but, whatever it may have been, you may depend that it was true; therefore if I bade you hasten, it is certain that hasten you must, and in that case it would be no kindness in me to urge you to stay. Yet you will not go until you have again eaten and drank."

"Thanks again, Mama," answered Harry, "but I fear we must. As you have said, the afternoon is far advanced, and there is therefore all the more reason why we should make the best possible use of every remaining moment of daylight. If you will excuse us, therefore, we will bid you adios and go forthwith. You have rendered me an inestimable service, Mama, for which mere words of thanks seem a very inadequate recompense, yet I will not offend you by offering any other reward. Still, if there is a way—"

"There is none—at present—*amigo mio*" interrupted the old woman; "nor do I wish any recompense beyond your thanks. If, as you say, I have been able to help you I am glad, and shall be glad to help you again whenever and as often as you may need my assistance. Nevertheless,"—looking with sudden intentness into the young Englishman's eyes—"I think—nay, I am certain—that a time is coming when, if you care to remember them, Mama Cachama and Yupanqui will be glad that they befriended you."

"Rest assured, then, Mama, that when that time arrives, you will not be forgotten," answered Harry. "And now, *adios*, until we meet again. Remember me to Yupanqui, and say that I am sorry I could not stay to see him. Are you ready, Arima? Then march!"

It was close upon midnight when Escombe and his Indian guide rode into camp, after a fatiguing and somewhat adventurous journey; for as Mama Cachama had said, the way was rough and by no means devoid of danger even in the daytime, while at night those dangers were multiplied a hundredfold. Enquiry revealed that none of the six peons whom Harry had that morning despatched to seek for traces of the missing party had returned, and the young man therefore gave Arima instructions to make all necessary preparations to start with him at daybreak, in search of the spot at which Cachama had described Butler as falling exhausted after his terrible flight through the night and storm. Of course Harry scarcely expected to find Butler there, and still less did he hope it, for in that event it would only too probably mean that the missing man was dead, whereas Harry hoped that, after lying exhausted for perhaps some hours, his chief would recover strength enough to make a further effort to return to camp; but he knew that in any case the search must necessarily start from the spot indicated by Cachama, and for that spot, therefore, he must make in the first instance.

It was broad daylight, but the sun had not yet risen above the snow-capped Andes when Escombe, accompanied by Arima, each of them mounted upon a sturdy mule, and the Indian leading Butler's saddled and bridled horse, rode out of camp the next morning on their quest for the missing man, taking with them a week's rations for each, and a similar quantity for Butler's use—should they be fortunate enough to find him—as well as a small supply of medical comforts, the whole contained in a pack securely strapped upon the saddle of the led horse.

For the first hour the route followed by Arima was identical with that described by Mama Cachama while in her clairvoyant state; but when they reached the wood wherein Butler's horse had been found straying, the Indian bore away to the right, and, skirting the belt of timber for some distance, cut through it near its southern extremity, emerging upon the mountain spur some three miles from, and much higher than, the spot where the first search party had come out. The crest of the spur now lay about half a mile in front of them, and upon reaching it the travellers beheld a magnificent prospect before them. The mountain spur sloped away steeply from their feet, plunging down until it was lost in a wide, densely wooded ravine about a mile in width, beyond which the ground again rose somewhat irregularly in a wide sweep of upland, gradually merging into foothills which, viewed from that distance, appeared to be the advance guard of the towering Andes. The atmosphere was exquisitely clear, revealing every object in the landscape with photographic sharpness, and Arima paused for a few minutes, with the double object of breathing the animals and taking a good, long, comprehensive view of the scene before him. For some minutes he gazed intently at the many landmarks, that stretched away before him and on either hand, and at length turned to Escombe and said, pointing:

"You see those twin peaks yonder, Señor?"

"Assuredly," assented Harry.

"And you also see that hill between them and us—the one, I mean, with the cloud shadow resting upon it which causes it to tell up dark against the sunlit mountain slopes beyond?"

"Certainly," again assented Harry.

"It is a few miles on the other side of that hill that we shall find the spot of which Mama Cachama spoke," explained Arima.

"Then you recognise the various marks which she described for your guidance, do you, and believe that she actually saw them in her trance?"

"Without doubt, Señor," answered the Indian in a tone of surprise, as though he wondered at the slight hint of incredulity suggested by the question.

"And do you think that, when we arrive, we shall find the chief there?" asked Harry.

"Nay, Señor, that I cannot say," answered Arima. "But this I know, that if he is still there when we reach the spot he will be dead."

"Yes," assented Escombe, "I fear you are right. And how long will it take us to reach the spot?"

"We shall do well if we get there before the sun sinks half-way down the heavens to-morrow," was the answer.

"To-morrow!" ejaculated Harry incredulously. "How far, then, is it from where we now stand?"

"If we could ride straight to it we might reach it to-day some two hours before sunset," answered Arima. "But that is impossible, Señor; our road lies off yonder to the right, along the slope of the mountain, to the nearest point at which it will be possible for us to cross the ravine; and when we have accomplished that, there will still be a toilsome ride of some three hours before us, ere we can hope to emerge from the ravine on the other side. We shall be fortunate if we accomplish so much before we are overtaken by the darkness."

"Is that so?" questioned Harry. "Then in that case we had better press forward without further delay." And, digging his heels into the ribs of his mule, the young Englishman resumed his march.

It was shortly after three o'clock on the following afternoon when Arima, who for the previous half-hour had been riding slowly and studying the ground intently, suddenly reined up his mule, and, leaping lightly to the ground, knelt down and carefully examined the long, coarse grass that thickly carpeted the soil. For a full minute he remained thus, delicately fingering the blades and gently pushing them aside, then he rose to his feet, and, with a sigh of satisfaction, pointed with his finger, saying:

"Here is the trail of the chief, Señor; he came from yonder and went in that direction."

"Are you sure, Arima?" demanded Harry. "I can see no sign of the passage of a man through this grass."

"Very possibly not, Señor," answered Arima dryly, "because, you see, you are not accustomed to tracking; moreover, this trail is some days old, and was made while the grass was wet and beaten down by the rain. But it is there, nevertheless, for practised eyes to read, and, being found, can now be easily followed. When the chief passed here he was in a terribly exhausted state, and staggered as he ran, exactly as Mama Cachama described, for just here he stumbled—if your honour will take the trouble to dismount you can see the mark where the toe of his boot dug into the soil—and I think the spot where he fell finally cannot be very far from here."

"In that case," said Harry, "let us press on as quickly as possible, for even minutes may be of inestimable value now. As to dismounting and examining the marks for myself, we have no time for that at present, Arima, and I am quite content to take your word for it that matters are as you say. Can you follow the trail mounted, or must you proceed on foot?"

"I can follow it mounted, Señor, seeing that I was mounted when I found it," answered Arima. "But it will be well that you should ride a few yards behind me, lest the trail should swerve suddenly to right or left and be crossed by your mule." So saying, the Indian sprang into his saddle and, turning the head of his animal, rode forward at a foot pace, his eyes intently searching the sea of waving grass before him. For a quarter of an hour he rode on thus, with Harry, leading Butler's horse, following a yard or two in his rear; then he suddenly reined his mule aside and, pointing to a barely perceptible depression in the grass, said:

"See, Señor, there is where the chief first fell, as described by Mama Cachama—yes—and,"—as his keen eyes roved hither and thither—"yonder is the spot where he fell and lay."

A few paces brought them to the spot indicated, and here the signs were clear enough for even Escombe's untrained eyes to read, the grass being still depressed sufficiently to show that a human form had lain there motionless and stretched at length for several hours; moreover, at that part of the depression where the man's head had rested, the grass blades were still flecked here and there with dried, ruddy froth, beneath which lay a little patch of coagulated blood, from which a swarm of flies arose as Arima bent over it and pointed it out to Harry. But the fugitive had disappeared, and the Indian gave it as his opinion that the chief had revived after lying insensible for about six hours, and had immediately resumed his interrupted flight. As to the direction in which he had gone, there was no difficulty in determining that, for, leading away toward the eastward there were two wavering lines, close together, traced through the long grass by the feet of the wanderer, and still distinct enough to be followed by even so inexperienced a tracker as the young Englishman.

"Now, Arima," exclaimed Harry, "is there anything worth knowing to be gained by a prolonged examination of this 'form'? Because, if not, we will press on at once, since time is precious. The chief went in that direction, of course—even I can see that—and the trail is so clear that we ought to be able to follow it at a canter."

"Yes, quite easily, Señor," acquiesced Arima. "There is nothing to be learned here beyond the fact that the Señor Butler fell at this spot, and lay absolutely motionless for so long a time that he must have been in a swoon. Then he revived, sat up, rose to his knees—see, there are the impressions of his two knees, and of the toes of his boots behind them—then he stood for several minutes, as though uncertain whither he would go, and finally struck off to the eastward. But see how the trail wavers this way and that way, even in the short length of it that we can trace from here. He moved quite aimlessly, not knowing whither he would go; and I think that, if he is still alive when we find him, Señor, he will be quite crazy."

"So much the greater reason for finding him as quickly as possible. Mount and ride, Arima," exclaimed Harry, pressing his heels into his mule's sides, and urging the animal into a canter along the plainly marked trail until he was taught better by the Indian.

"Never ride immediately over a trail which you are following, Señor, but close beside it, on one side or the other of it, so that the trail itself is left quite undisturbed. One never can tell when it may be necessary to study the trail carefully in search of some bit of information which might easily be obliterated if it were ridden or walked over."

Harry at once pulled his mule to one side of the trail, Arima following it on the opposite side, and the pair pushed on, winding hither and thither as the track of the fugitive swerved this way and that, until they had travelled a further distance of some nine or ten miles, when they came upon another "form", where Butler had laid himself down to rest for—as Arima estimated—a space of about two hours. There was nothing of importance to be learned here; they therefore pushed forward again with all possible speed, for the sun was now rapidly declining toward the western horizon, and Escombe was anxious to find the wanderer before nightfall, if possible, since another night's exposure in the keen air of that elevated plain might very well prove fatal to a man in Butler's terribly exhausted condition.

For the last hour of the pursuit the track had led over rising ground, and it soon became pretty evident that the fugitive had been making his uncertain way toward a gorge between two mountains, which had gradually been opening out ahead of the pursuers. Meanwhile the spoor had been growing fresher with every stride of the cantering mules, showing that the trackers were rapidly gaining upon the chase, and that the latter was now in the very last stage of exhaustion, for the "forms" where he had paused to rest were ever becoming more frequent and closer together. The Indian, therefore, after attentively studying the last form which was encountered, gave it as his opinion that the hunted man could not now be more than a mile or two ahead, and suggested that Harry should push straight on for the entrance of the gorge, in the hope of sighting the fugitive and running him down, while he (Arima), with the led horse, should continue to follow the trail, for if Butler should gain the gorge before being overtaken, his pursuit over the rocky ground might be slow and difficult. Accordingly, Harry turned his mule slightly aside from the trail, and made straight for a landmark indicated by the Indian, pressing his beast forward at its best pace. He had ridden thus about a quarter of an hour, and was rapidly approaching the entrance of the gorge, when he suddenly caught sight of a moving object ahead, winding its way among a number of masses of granite outcrop; and urging his exhausted mule to a final effort, Escombe presently had the satisfaction of identifying the moving object as a man—a white man—attired in a few tattered remnants of what had once been civilised clothing. That the man was Butler there could be no shadow of doubt, and a few strides farther enabled Harry to recognise him. As he did so, the stumbling, staggering figure paused for a moment, glanced behind him, and saw that he was pursued; whereupon he flung his arms above his head, emitted a most horrible, eldritch scream, started to run forward again, staggered a few paces, and fell forward prone upon the ground, where he lay motionless.

Chapter Seven
The Jewel

Reining up his mule, Escombe at once glanced behind him to ascertain whether Arima happened to be within sight. Yes, there he was, about a mile distant, pushing along at a trot and winding hither and thither, as he persistently followed the erratic twistings and turnings of the pursued man's spoor. Harry therefore drew his revolver from his belt, and, pointing the muzzle of the weapon upward, discharged two shots in rapid succession to attract the Indian's attention, and then waved his white pocket handkerchief in the air as a sign that the lost man had been found, and that the pursuit was at an end. The Indian immediately uttered a peculiar shrill whoop by way of reply, and turned his beast's head directly toward the spot where the young Englishman could be seen sitting motionless in his saddle; whereupon Harry at once sprang to the ground and, throwing his mule's bridle upon the grass—a sign which the animal had been trained to obey by standing perfectly still—rushed toward the prostrate figure, and, turning it gently over, raised it to a sitting posture, passing his arm round the neck as a support to the drooping head.

Yes, the man was Butler, there could be no doubt about that; but oh! what a dreadful change had been wrought by those few days of flight and exposure! Butler had always been a man of somewhat spare build, but now he was emaciated to an extent almost past belief—his cheeks were so hollow that it seemed as though an incautiously rough touch would cause the protruding cheek-bones to burst through the skin; his closed eyes were sunk so deep in their sockets that the eyeballs appeared to have dwindled to the size of small marbles; while the lips had contracted to such an extent as to leave the tightly clenched teeth clearly visible, the general effect being that of a grinning, fleshless skull with a covering of shrivelled skin drawn tightly over it. The once immaculate suit of white clothing was now deeply soiled and stained by contact with the earth and grass, and was a mere wrapping of scarcely recognisable rags, the coat being missing altogether, while great rents in the remaining garments revealed the protruding ribs and the shrunken limbs, the colour of the yellowish-brown skin being almost completely obscured by the latticing of long and deep blood-smeared scratches that mutely told how desperately the man had fought his way through all obstacles in his headlong, panic-stricken flight; his finger nails were broken and ragged; his boots were cut and torn to pieces to such an extent that they afforded scarcely any protection to his feet; and his once iron-grey hair and moustache, as well as his short growth of stubbly beard, were almost perfectly white.

With a quick slash of his knife Escombe severed the filthy wisp of silk that had once been a smart necktie, as it had somehow become tightly knotted round the unconscious man's throat, and then impatiently awaited the coming of Arima, who was leading the horse on the saddle of which were strapped the small supply of medical comforts which had been brought along to meet just such a contingency as this; and a few minutes later the Indian cantered up and, flinging himself from the back of his mule, came forward to render assistance.

Bidding the man kneel down and support the unconscious Butler's head, Harry sprang to the saddle bags and drew forth a flask of brandy, which he held to the sick man's lips, allowing a few drops of the liquid to find their way between the clenched teeth. For fully ten minutes he strove to coax a small quantity of the spirit down his chiefs throat, and at length had the satisfaction of seeing that some at least had been swallowed. The almost immediate result of this was a groan and a slight, spasmodic movement of the emaciated limbs; and presently, after a few minutes of further persistent effort, Butler opened his eyes.

"Ah, that's better!" ejaculated the amateur physician with a sigh of extreme satisfaction. "You will soon be all right now, sir. Let me give you just another spoonful and you will feel like a new man. No, no, please don't keep your teeth clenched like that; open your mouth, Mr Butler, and let me pour a little more down your throat. Do please," — in a most insinuating tone of voice — "it will do you no end of good. Arima, take hold of his chin and see if you can force his lower jaw open, but be as gentle as you can. There, that's right! Now then!"

With a deft touch and no apparent violence the Indian succeeded in getting the locked jaws apart, and Escombe promptly availed himself of the opportunity to pour about a tablespoonful of spirits into the partially open mouth. For a moment there was no result, then a cough and a splutter on the part of the sick man showed that the potent elixir was making its way down his throat, and, with another groan, the patient made a feeble effort to struggle to his feet. But the attempt was a failure, the last particle of strength had already been spent, and, sighing heavily, Butler subsided back upon the supporting arm of the Indian, and lay staring vacantly at the rich sapphire sky that arched above him. Then Harry took him by the hand, and, calling him by name, endeavoured to win some sign of recognition from him, but all in vain. The utmost that he could accomplish was to extract from his patient a few meaningless, incoherent mumblings, which conveyed nothing save the fact that the speaker's mind was, at least for the moment, a perfect blank. At length, convinced that he could do no more until he had got his patient settled in camp, he called upon Arima to help him, and between the two they soon had the unfortunate man comfortably stretched upon a blanket under the lee of an enormous granite rock, which would at least partially shield him from the keen wind of the fast approaching night. Then, with the help of a few stout saplings cut from a clump of bush close at hand, they contrived to rig a small, makeshift kind of tent over the upper half of his body, as a further protection from the cold, and lighted their camp fire close to his feet. Then, while the Indian, with gentle touch, cut away the soiled rags of clothing from the wasted body and limbs, and swathed them in a waterproof rug, Escombe unsaddled and hobbled the horse and mules, and turned them loose to graze. Next he unpacked the saddle bags and camp equipage, and proceeded to prepare a small quantity of hot, nourishing soup, which, with infinite difficulty, he at length induced his patient to swallow, a few drops at a time; and finally, with a makeshift pillow beneath his head, the invalid was gently laid down in a comfortable posture, when he soon sank into a refreshing sleep. The weary pair seized the opportunity thus afforded them to attend to their own most pressing needs; but neither of them closed their eyes in sleep that night, for they had scarcely finished their supper when Butler awoke and again demanded their most unremitting care and attention, as he evinced great uneasiness and perturbation of mind which speedily developed into a state of such violent delirium, that it was only with the utmost difficulty the combined efforts of the pair were able to restrain him from doing either himself or them some serious injury.

For more than forty hours did that dreadful delirium continue, the patient being extraordinarily violent during almost the entire period; then his unnatural strength suddenly collapsed, leaving him weak as an infant and in an almost continuous state of lethargy, so profound that it was with great difficulty that his two nurses were able to arouse him sufficiently to administer small quantities of liquid nourishment. It was by this time evident, even to Harry's inexperienced eye, that Butler's condition was desperate, even if not altogether hopeless, and he consulted Arima as to the possibility of procuring the services of a qualified physician; but the Indian had no encouragement to offer. Cerro de Pasco, the nearest town in which one might hope to find a doctor, was some fifty miles distant, as the crow flies, but the difficulties of the way were such that, using the utmost expedition, it would take a messenger at least four days to reach the place, and as many to return—assuming that the messenger were fortunate enough to find a doctor who could be persuaded to set out forthwith—by which time, Harry knew instinctively, the patient would be long past all human aid. Besides, there was no messenger to send, save Arima; and, in view of the possible recurrence of delirium, the lad felt that he would not be justified in sending the Indian away. While the two were still engaged in debating the question of what was best to be done under the distressing circumstances, Butler ended the difficulty by quietly breathing his last, crossing the borderland between life and death without a struggle, and without recovering consciousness. Indeed so perfectly quiet and peaceful was the end that it was some time before young Escombe could convince himself that his chief was really dead; but when at length there could no longer be any question as to the fact, the body was at once wrapped in the waterproof sheet which had formed a makeshift tent for the shelter of the sick man, and packed, with as much reverence as the circumstances would allow, upon the deceased man's horse, for conveyance back to camp for interment, the pair having with them no implements wherewith to dig a grave. Moreover, Harry considered that, taking the somewhat peculiar circumstances of the case into consideration, it was very desirable that the body should be seen and identified by the other members of the survey party before burial took place.

This event occurred on the evening of the third day after death, Escombe himself reading the burial service; and he afterwards fashioned with his own hands, and placed at the head of the grave, a wooden cross, upon which he roughly but deeply cut with his pocket knife the name of the dead man and the date of his death. He also, as a matter of precaution, took a very careful set of astronomical observations for the determination of the exact position of the grave, recording the result in his diary at the end of the long entry detailing all the circumstances connected with the sad event.

Escombe now suddenly found his young shoulders burdened with a heavy load of responsibility, for not only did Butler's death leave the lad in sole charge of the survey party, with the task of carrying on unaided the exceedingly important work upon which that party was engaged, until assistance could be sent out to him from England; but it also became his immediate duty to report all the circumstances of the death of his leader to the British Consul at Lima—who would doubtless put in motion the necessary machinery for the capture and punishment of the men who were responsible for the events which had brought about Butler's death—and also to Sir Philip Swinburne, who would, of course, in turn, communicate the sad intelligence to the deceased man's family. And there were also all Butler's private effects to be packed up and sent home forthwith.

Yet, taking everything into consideration, the death of his chief was a relief rather than otherwise to the lad, unfeeling though the statement may appear at the first blush. Butler was a man for whom it was quite impossible for anyone to acquire a friendly feeling; Harry therefore felt that when he had committed his chief's body to the earth with as much respectful observance as the circumstances permitted, had carefully and scrupulously collected together and dispatched to England all the dead man's personal belongings, and had taken such steps as were possible for the capture and punishment of the men who were primarily responsible for Butler's death, he had done everything that a strict sense of duty claimed from him, and was not called upon to feign and outwardly manifest a sorrow which had no place in his heart. Besides, he was now the responsible head of the survey party; upon him depended—for at least the next three months—the conduct of an important and highly scientific operation; and upon the manner in which he conducted it depended very serious issues involving the expenditure of exceedingly large sums of money. This was his opportunity to demonstrate to all concerned the stuff of which he was made; it was an opportunity so splendid that many a young fellow of his age would cheerfully give half a dozen years of his life to obtain such another; for Harry fully realised that if he could carry his task to a successful conclusion his fortune, from the professional point of view, was made. And he felt that he could—ay, and would—do this. The experience which he had already gained since his arrival in Peru had been of inestimable value to him, and he had made the very utmost of it; he therefore felt confident of his ability to carry through his task to the satisfaction of his employers and with credit to himself, and he entered upon it with avidity and keen enjoyment. Moreover, he was tactful, and possessed the happy knack of managing those under him in such a way that he was able to extract the very last ounce of work from them without offending their susceptibilities, or causing them to feel that he was making undue demands upon them.

Under these circumstances, and with the perpetual galling irritation of Butler's presence and influence removed, the survey made rapid and very satisfactory progress, the party arriving at Cerro de Pasco in a trifle under six weeks from the date of Butler's death, thus completing the second section of the survey. The third section was very much longer and more difficult in every respect than either of the two completed, since it extended from Nanucaca—already connected by rail with Cerro de Pasco—along the shore of Lake Chinchaycocha to Ayacucho and Cuzco, and thence on to Santa Rosa, the distance being some four hundred and seventy miles as the crow flies, while the difficulties of the route might possibly increase that distance by nearly one-third. But Escombe was by no means dismayed by the formidable character of the obstacles that lay before him; he had come to realise that, to the man who would achieve success, obstacles exist only that they may be overcome, and he was gaining experience daily in the overcoming of obstacles. He therefore attacked this third and very formidable section, not only without any anxiety or fear, but with a keen zest that instantly communicated itself to his little band of followers, welding them together into a perfectly harmonious, smooth-working whole.

It must not be thought, however, that Escombe allowed himself to become so completely absorbed in his work that he could think of nothing else. On the contrary, he understood perfectly the meaning of the word "recreation" and the value of the thing itself. He knew that no man can work for ever without wearing himself out, and he looked upon recreation as—what its name implied—a re-creation or rebuilding of those forces, mental and physical, which labour wears away, and valued it accordingly, taking it whenever he felt that he really needed it, even as he took food or medicine.

Now it chanced that fishing was one of Escombe's favourite recreations; and no sooner had he started the third section of the survey—which began by skirting the eastern shore of Lake Chinchaycocha—than he made a practice of indulging in an hour or two's fishing whenever the opportunity offered. It was this practice that led to an occurrence which was destined to culminate in an adventure so startling and extraordinary as to be scarcely credible in these prosaic twentieth-century days.

It happened on a Saturday afternoon.

On the day in question, the survey party being then encamped on the shore of Lake Chinchaycocha, as soon as he had squared up his week's work, and snatched a hasty luncheon, the young Englishman brought forth his fishing tackle, and, getting aboard a balsa, or light raft, which Arima had constructed for him, proceeded to paddle some distance out from the shore to a spot which he had already ascertained afforded him a fair prospect of sport. Arrived there he dropped his keeleg—a large stone serving the purpose of an anchor—overboard and settled down comfortably to enjoy his favourite pastime, and also provide an exceedingly welcome addition to the somewhat monotonous fare of camp life.

The sport that afternoon was not so good as Harry had expected, and it was drawing well on toward evening before the fish began to bite at all freely—he was trying especially for a certain particularly delicious kind of fish, something between a trout and a mullet, which was only to be captured by allowing the hook to rest at the very bottom of the lake. Suddenly he felt a smart tug at his line and at once began to haul it in, but he had scarcely got it fairly taut when the tremulous jerk which denoted the presence of a fish at the other end was exchanged for a steady strain, and it soon became perfectly evident that the hook had become entangled in something at the bottom. Now Escombe's stock of fishing tackle was of exceedingly modest proportions, so much so, indeed, that the loss of even a solitary hook was a matter not to be contemplated with indifference, therefore he brought all his skill to bear upon the delicate task of releasing the hook from its entanglement.

But at the end of half an hour he was no nearer to success than at the beginning of his endeavours, while the sun was within a hand's breadth of the horizon, and he had no fancy for being caught by the darkness while on the lake, therefore he adopted other tactics, and strove to bring the object, whatever it might be, to the surface by means of a steady yet not dangerously powerful strain. Ah, that was better! At the very first tug Escombe felt the resistance yield by the merest hairs-breadth, and presently a faint jerk told him that he had gained another fraction of an inch, which success was repeated every few seconds until he was able to lift and drop the line a clear foot. Then the sun's lower limb touched and rested for an instant upon the ridge of the Western Cordilleras before it began to sink behind them, and Harry realised that the moment for energetic measures had arrived; for he was a good two miles from the shore, and it would take him the best part of an hour to paddle his clumsy craft that distance. Therefore he steadily increased the strain upon his line, determined to release himself one way or another, even though at the cost of a hook. But it proved unnecessary for him to make so great a sacrifice, it was the unknown object that yielded, with little momentary jerks and an ever decreasing resistance until it finally let go its hold of the bottom altogether and came to the surface securely entangled with the hook. Upon its emergence from the water Harry gazed at his catch in astonishment; he had expected to see the water-logged branch of a tree, a bunch of weed, or something of that sort, but as it dangled, dripping with sandy ooze in the last rays of the setting sun, certain ruddy-yellow gleams that flashed from it told its finder that he had fished up something metallic from the bottom of the lake. The next moment Escombe was busily engaged in disentangling his find from the fish hook, but long ere he had succeeded in doing so the young man had made the interesting discovery that he had been fortunate enough to retrieve a most remarkable jewel, in the form of a gold and emerald collar, from the depths of the lake. Methodical even in the midst of his excitement at having made so valuable a find, the young Englishman carefully disentangled his hook and line from the jewel, neatly wound up the former, and then proceeded patiently to wash away from the latter the ooze with which it was thickly coated, having done which he found himself in possession of an ornament so massive in material and so elaborate and unique in workmanship that he felt certain it must be worth quite a little fortune to any curio collector. It was, or appeared to be, a collar or necklace, a trifle over two feet in length, the ends united by a massive ring supporting a medallion. The links, so to speak, of the necklace consisted of twelve magnificent emeralds, each engraved upon one side with certain cabalistic characters, the meaning of which Escombe could not guess at, and upon the other with a symbol which was easily identifiable as that of the sun; these emeralds were massively set—framed would be almost the more appropriate word—in most elaborately sculptured gold, and joined together by heavy gold links also very elaborately cut. The pendant was likewise composed of a superb emerald of fully three inches diameter set in a gold frame, chiselled to represent the rays of the sun, the emerald itself being engraved with the representation of a human face, which, oddly enough, Harry recognised, even at the first glance, to be extraordinarily, astoundingly like his own. This was a find worth having, the young man told himself, and might prove worth several hundreds of pounds if judiciously advertised and offered for sale at Christie's upon his return home; for safety's sake, therefore, he put it round his neck, tucking it inside his shirt, snugly out of sight, and, heaving up his keeleg, proceeded to paddle thoughtfully back to the shore.

It was some three months after this occurrence—and in the interim young Escombe had pushed forward the survey so rapidly, despite all difficulties, that he had covered more than half the distance between Nanucaca and Ayacucho—when, as he returned to camp at the end of his day's work, he observed two strange mules tethered near his tent; and presently a stranger emerged from the tent and advanced toward him. The stranger, although deeply tanned by the sun, was unmistakably an Englishman, some twenty-eight years of age, rather above middle height, and with a pleasant though resolute expression stamped upon his good—looking features. Approaching Harry, he held out his hand and smilingly remarked:

"Mr Escombe, I presume. My name is Bannister—John Bannister—and I come from Sir Philip Swinburne to act as your colleague in the completion of the survey upon which you are engaged. These,"—producing a packet of papers—"are my credentials. Grand country this,"—casting an admiring glance at the magnificent scenery amid which the camp was pitched—"but, my word, you must have had some tough bits of work, even before reaching this spot."

"You are right, we have," answered Harry as he cordially returned Bannister's grasp. "I am right glad to see you, and to bid you welcome to our camp, for I have been pretty badly in want of intelligent help lately. These fellows,"—indicating the native helpers who were now scattered about the camp busily preparing for the evening meal—"are all well enough in their way, and since poor Butler's death I have managed to drill them into something like decent, useful shape; but I have often been badly hampered for the want of another surveyor who could work with me in surmounting some of the especially bad places. Now that you have come we shall be able to get ahead nearly twice as fast. I suppose you came out by the last mail, eh? And how are things going in the dear old country?"

Harry led the new arrival into his tent, and proceeded forthwith to discard his working clothes and divest himself of the stains of his day's toil as he chatted animatedly, asking questions for the most part, as is the wont of the old hand—and Escombe had by this time grown to quite regard himself as such—when he foregathers with somebody fresh from "home". Bannister, having arrived at the camp pretty early in the afternoon, had already bathed and changed; he therefore had nothing to do but to sit still and answer Harry's questions, jerking in one or two himself occasionally, until the younger man's toilet was completed, when they sat down to dinner together. By the time that the meal was over each felt perfectly satisfied that he would be able to get on well with the other, and was looking forward to a quite pleasant time up there among the stupendous mountains.

Upon first seeing Bannister, and learning that he had come out from Sir Philip, Harry naturally thought that the new arrival had been dispatched to fill the position of chief of the survey party, rendered vacant by the death of the unfortunate Butler; but upon opening the credentials which Bannister had presented, he found that it was actually as the bearer had stated, that he and Harry were to act as colleagues, not as chief and subordinate, in the completion of the survey, thus making the pair jointly responsible for the work, while they would share equally the credit upon its completion. They spent an exceedingly pleasant evening together, chatting mostly over the work that still lay before them, Harry producing his plans and explaining what had already been done, while Bannister sat listening gravely to the recital of sundry hairbreadth escapes from death in the execution of duty, and of the manner in which a few of the more than ordinarily difficult bits of work had been accomplished; and when the pair again sat chatting together, twenty-four hours later, at the end of their first day together, each felt absolutely satisfied with the comrade with which fortune had brought him into touch. Under these agreeable circumstances the survey progressed with greater rapidity than ever, the two Englishmen conquering obstacle after obstacle, and meeting with plenty of thrilling adventures in the process, until in the fullness of time they reached first Ayacucho and then Cuzco, when the worst of their troubles were over. For there was a road—of sorts—between the ancient capital and Santa Rosa, and the two Englishmen, after riding over it in company, agreed that, for a considerable part of the way at least, the best route for a railway would be found contiguous to the highroad, by following which the surveyors would derive many substantial advantages, in addition to finding a comparatively easy route to survey.

Chapter Eight
The Abduction

The survey party had traversed about half the distance between Cuzco and Santa Rosa when the two Englishmen, following their invariable custom of indulging in a swim as often as opportunity afforded, made their way, at the end of a hard day's work, to a most romantic spot which they had encountered. Here a small stream, flowing through a rocky gorge, fell over a granite ledge on to a large flat slab of rock some nine feet below, from which in turn it poured into a noble basin almost perfectly circular in shape, about twenty feet deep, and nearly or quite a hundred feet in diameter, ere it continued its course down the ravine. To stand on the slab of rock beneath the fall was to enjoy an ideal shower bath; and to dive from that same slab into the deep, pellucid pool and thereafter swim across the pool and back three or four times was a luxury worth riding several miles to enjoy; small wonder, therefore, was it that the two Englishmen resolved to make the most of their opportunity, and continue to use this perfect natural swimming bath so long as their work kept them within reach of it.

The camp was situated some two miles back from the pool, the bathers therefore, fatigued with a long day's work, decided to ride to and from the spot, instead of walking, and Arima, the Indian—who had by this time constituted himself Escombe's especial henchman—was directed to accompany them to look after the horses while the riders were enjoying their dip.

Arrived at the pool, the two friends dismounted and proceeded to undress on a small space of rich, lush grass in close proximity to the basin, the Indian meanwhile squatting upon his heels and holding the horses' bridles while the animals eagerly grazed.

Now, Arima's devotion to Harry, originating at the time when the two had made their memorable journey together to Mama Cachama's cave, and very greatly strengthened during the adventurous hunt for the missing Butler, had steadily developed until it had become almost if not quite as strong as that of a parent for an idolised child. The Indian could not bear his young master to be out of his sight for a moment, and was always most unhappy whenever the exigencies of work necessitated a separation of the two. He had been known to resort to the most extraordinary devices to prevent such an occurrence, and when the two were together Arima never allowed his gaze to wander for a moment from his master's form if he could help it. Yet, singularly enough, it was not until this particular evening that the Indian had become aware of Escombe's possession of the jewel so strangely fished up from the depths of Lake Chinchaycocha, or had ever caught sight of it. But he saw it now, as Escombe undressed at a few yards' distance, the light falling strongly upon the dull red gold and the emeralds, as the lad carefully removed it from his neck and laid it upon the top of his clothes ere he rushed, with a joyous shout, and placed himself immediately beneath the foaming water of the fall. The sight appeared to arouse a feeling of very powerful curiosity in the breast of the Indian, for it was only with the utmost difficulty that he contrived to retain his attitude of passivity until the more deliberately moving Bannister had joined his friend upon the slab beneath the fall; but no sooner had this happened than, abandoning the horses to their own devices, Arima crept cautiously forward until he reached Escombe's heap of clothing, and, availing himself of the preoccupation of the bathers, took the jewel in his hand and examined it with the most rapt attention and care. For a space of nearly five minutes he continued his examination, after which he slowly and thoughtfully made his way back to the horses, which were too busily feeding upon the luscious grass to stray far. For the remainder of the evening the Indian seemed to be plunged in a state of meditation so profound as to be quite oblivious of all outward things save his young master, his conduct toward whom was marked by a new and yet subtle attitude of almost worshipping reverence. But when the hands were mustered for work on the following morning, Arima was nowhere to be found; he had vanished some time during the night, saying nothing to anyone, and leaving no trace behind.

Harry was very much upset at this sudden and inexplicable disappearance of the servant who, in a thousand little unobtrusive ways, had ministered so effectually to his comfort that his loss was at once felt as a serious misfortune, and he devoted two whole days to a search for the missing man, fearing that the fellow had strayed away from the camp and that something untoward had befallen him. But the search was quite unavailing, and on the third day it was abandoned, the only conclusion at which Escombe could arrive being that the Indian had deserted under the influence of pique at some unintentional affront and gone back to his own people.

It was some two months later—by which time the party was drawing near to Santa Rosa, and the great railway survey was approaching completion—that in the dead of a dark and starless night three Indians stealthily approached the surveyors' camp and, having first reconnoitred the ground as carefully as the pitch darkness would permit, made their way, noiseless as shadows, to the tent occupied by young Escombe. The leading Indian was Arima, the two who followed were very old men, their scanty locks, white as snow, hanging to their shoulders, their ascetic, clean-cut features sharp and shrunken, yet they carried themselves as upright as though they had been in the heyday of youth, and their sunken eyes glowed and sparkled with undiminished fire. They wore sleeveless shirts of pure white, finely woven of vicuña wool, reaching to the knee, the opening at the throat and arms, and also the hem of the garment, being richly ornamented with embroidery in heavy gold thread. This garment was confined at the waist by a massive belt of solid gold composed of square placques hinged together, and each elaborately sculptured with conventional representations of the sun. Over this was worn a long cloak, dyed blue, also woven of vicuña wool, but without ornament of any description. Their heads were bare, and the lobe of each ear was pierced and distended to receive a gold medallion nearly four inches in diameter, also heavily sculptured with a representation of the sun. Their legs were bare, but each wore sandals bound to the feet and ankles by thongs of leather. To judge from the travel-stained appearance of their garments they must have come a considerable distance, and have been exposed to many vicissitudes of weather.

Entering Escombe's tent, which was dimly lighted by a hanging lamp turned low, Arima noiselessly moved aside and silently, with outstretched hand, indicated to his two companions the form of the sleeping lad, who lay stretched at length upon his camp bed, breathing the long, deep breath of profound slumber. Nodding silently, one of the two withdrew from a pouch which hung suspended from his belt a soft cloth and a small phial. Extracting the stopper from the latter, he emptied the contents of the phial upon the cloth, which he then very gradually approached to the nostrils of the sleeper until it was within an inch of them. He held the cloth thus for about five minutes, allowing the fumes of the liquid to enter the sleeper's nostrils, while his companion very gently laid his fingers upon the pulse of Escombe's right hand, which happened to be lying outside the coverlet. At length the second Indian—he who held Harry's wrist—nodded to the first, saying, in a low voice, in the ancient Quichua language: "It is enough; nothing will now awaken him,"—whereupon the holder of the cloth returned it and the phial to his pouch and stepped back from the side of the bed. Then, turning to Arima, he said, in the same language:

"Say you, Arima, that this youth always wears the collar upon his person, night and day?"

"Even so, Lord," answered Arima. "At least," he modified his statement, "so I surmise; for I have never seen the jewel save the once whereof I told you, and again on that same night when I stole into his tent while he slept, and found that he was wearing it then. Whereupon I hastened to you with my momentous news."

"You have done well, friend," answered the first speaker. "Should all prove to be as you say, you shall be richly rewarded. And now," —he caught his breath with sudden excitement—"to settle the question." Then, turning to his companion, he said:

THE PRIESTS IN HARRY'S TENT

"Approach, brother, and look with me. It is meet that we should both gaze upon the sacred emblem—if so it should prove—at the self-same moment." He signed to Arima, who turned up the flame of the lamp, whereupon the two Inca priests—for such the strangers actually were—bent over Escombe's sleeping figure, one on each side of the bed, and while one drew down the coverlet the other unbuttoned the lad's sleeping jacket, exposing to view the jewel which he had fished up from Lake Chinchaycocha, and which, for safety, he always wore round his neck.

Eagerly the two priests bent down and scrutinised the magnificent ornament as it lay upon the gently heaving breast of the sleeper; and as their eyes hungrily took in the several peculiarities of the jewel a thrill of excitement visibly swept over them. Finally, he who appeared to be the elder of the two said to the other:

"There can scarcely be a doubt that Arima's surmise is correct; nevertheless, brother, pass your hand beneath the young man's shoulder and raise him slightly that I may remove the collar and examine it."

The priest addressed at once obeyed the request of the other, who thereupon gently passed the ornament over the sleeper's head and, taking it immediately beneath the lamp, proceeded to examine every part of it with the closest scrutiny, his companion allowing Escombe's limp body to subside back on the pillow before he, too, joined in the inspection. Every link, almost every mark of the chisel, was subjected to the most careful examination, and apparently certain of the engraved marks were recognised as bearing a definite meaning; for on more than one occasion the elder of the two priests pointed to such a mark, saying, "Behold, Motahuana, here is, unmistakably, the secret sign," while the other would nod his head solemnly and respond, "Even so, Tiahuana; I see it." Finally he who had been addressed by the other as Tiahuana turned the jewel over in his hand and examined the back of it. His gaze instantly fell upon the cabalistic characters engraved upon the backs of the emeralds, which had puzzled Escombe, and, laying the jewel gently down upon the bed, he prostrated himself before it, Motahuana immediately following his example, as also did Arima.

For a space of some three or four minutes the trio appeared to be absorbed in some act of silent devotion, then Tiahuana rose to his feet and fixed his gaze on the jewel which lay upon the coverlet of Escombe's bed. Meditatively his eyes rested upon the great emerald pendant with its engraved representation of a human face, and from thence they wandered to the calm features of the sleeping lad. Suddenly he started, and his gaze became alert, almost startled. He bent down and scrutinised the engraved features intently, then quickly diverted his gaze to those on the pillow. Was it some trick of light, he asked himself, or were the two sets of features identical?

"Look, Motahuana, look!" he whispered in tense accents; "see you the resemblance? I have but observed it this instant. Nay, man, you can scarcely see it from where you stand, for that side of his face is in shadow. Come to this side of the couch—or, stay, I will move the lamp."

He did so, holding the lamp so that its light fell full upon the sleeper's face, while with the other hand he rearranged the collar so that the pendant lay upright upon Escombe's breast. In this position, and in the stronger light, the likeness was even more startlingly striking than before, and for two long minutes the aged pair bent intently over the object of their scrutiny with an ever-growing expression of wonder and awe upon their attenuated features.

"Well, brother," at length demanded Tiahuana, somewhat sharply, "see you what I mean, or is it merely my fancy—a figment of my over-heated imagination?"

"Nay, Lord," answered Motahuana in an awestruck whisper, "it is no figment, no fancy; the likeness is wonderful, marvellous, perfect; the features are identical, curve for curve and line for line, save that those engraved on the emerald bear the impress of a few more years of life. That, however, is immaterial, and in no wise affects the fact that in this sleeping youth we behold the reincarnation of him who first wore the sacred jewel, the lord and father of our people, Manco Capac!"

"Even so; you say truly, Motahuana," agreed Tiahuana in tones of exultation. "The revelation is complete and indisputable past all doubt; the mighty Manco Capac has returned to earth from his home among the stars, and soon now shall Peru resume its former glorious position as the greatest and most powerful nation in the world. It is true that the great Manco returns to us in the guise of a young Englishman, for which circumstance I was scarcely prepared; but what of that? It is better so; for England is to-day the wisest and most mighty nation on the face of the earth, and doubtless the Inca brings with with him a rich store of the knowledge of England. Come, there is no occasion for further delay; let us be going, for we must be far hence and beyond the reach of pursuit ere our father the Sun awakens his children and discloses the fact of our Lord's disappearance. Go thou, Arima, and summon hither the litter bearers and the others."

In a perfect ecstasy of pride and delight that it should have fallen to his lot to become the humble instrument whereby had been made known to his people the glorious fact of the great Inca's reincarnation in the person of Escombe—as he never for a moment doubted was the case—Arima hurried out to where the remainder of the party lay patiently in ambush, briefly announced to them that all was well, and bade them follow him in perfect silence to the tent in which Harry still lay plunged in a deathlike yet quite harmless sleep. The litter—a light but strong structure, framed of bamboos and covered with vicuña cloth, so arranged that it could be completely closed—was carried right into the tent, the covering thrown back, and Escombe was lifted, on his mattress and still covered with the bedclothes, off the little iron camp bedstead and carefully placed in the litter, the jewel was replaced about his neck, the pillow under his head was comfortably arranged by Arima, the litter was closed, and then a little procession, consisting of the litter and its four bearers, with the eight other men who acted as reliefs, headed by the two priests, filed silently out into the darkness, leaving Arima, with six men, armed to the teeth with bows and arrows—the latter tipped with copper—lances of hardwood sharpened by fire, and short swords, the copper blades of which were hardened and tempered almost to the consistency of steel by a process known only to the Peruvians themselves. The duty of these men was to collect together and pack, under Arima's supervision, the whole of Escombe's private and personal belongings; and this they did with such expedition that, in less than half an hour from the involuntary departure of its owner, the tent was almost entirely stripped of its contents and left deserted.

Under the anaesthetic influence of the vapour which he had unconsciously inhaled, Escombe continued to sleep soundly until close upon midday, by which time the effect had almost entirely passed off, and he began to awake very gradually to the consciousness that something very much out of the ordinary course of things was happening. The first thing to impress itself upon his slowly awakening senses was the fact that the bed upon which he was lying was in motion, a gentle, easy, rhythmic, swaying motion, unlike any movement that he had ever before experienced. Yet the bed seemed to be the same as that upon which he had retired to rest upon the preceding night, so far as he could judge; the mattress had the old familiar feel, and—yes, certainly, he was still under the shelter of the bedclothes, and his head still rested upon the familiar pillow—he could feel the lumps in it where the flock filling had become matted together. But why the mysterious motion? Could it be that he was experiencing for the first time the effects of a Peruvian earthquake? Slowly and reluctantly he opened his eyes, and saw that his bed was indeed the same, yet with a certain difference, the precise nature of which he was at first unable to define. But presently he saw that the bed or couch upon which he was lying was closely encompassed by a soft blanket-like cloth, tightly strained over a light bamboo framework, forming a sort of canopy. And the motion? He was by this time sufficiently awake to understand that it was real; nor was it due to earthquake, as he had at first been inclined to think it might be; no, it was the regular, rhythmic movement of men marching and keeping step; he was being carried!

With a rush his senses came fully back to him, and he started up into a sitting posture. It was high time for him to get to the bottom of this mystery, he told himself. He saw that midway in their length the side curtains which enclosed him were divided and overlapped, and, stretching out his hand, he wrenched them apart, at the same time, in his forgetfulness, calling loudly for Arima.

In an instant the Indian was by the side of the litter and peering in through the opening between the parted curtains, to his masters intense astonishment.

"You called, Señor—my Lord, I mean?" exclaimed the man submissively.

"I did!" answered Escombe incisively. "What has happened, Arima? Where have you been? Where am I? Why am I being carried off in this outrageous manner? Answer me quickly."

"My Lord," answered the Indian deprecatingly, "I implore you not to be disturbed or alarmed in the least. We are all your slaves, and are prepared to lay down our lives in your service. No harm is intended you; but it is necessary that you accompany us to the place whither we are going. Here is my Lord Tiahuana. He will perhaps explain further."

Meanwhile, during this brief colloquy, the cortege had come to a halt, and now the elder of the two priests presented himself as Arima retired, and, with a profound obeisance, said:

"Let my Lord pardon his servants, and let not his anger be kindled against them. What we have done has been done of necessity and because there seemed to be no other way. But my Lord need have no fear that evil is meditated against him; on the contrary, a position of great power and glory will be his at the end of his journey; and meanwhile every possible provision has been made for the comfort and wellbeing of my Lord during his passage through the mountains."

"But—but—I don't understand," stammered Harry. "Who are you, why do you address me as Lord, and what do you mean by talking about a passage through the mountains? There is a ridiculous mistake."

"Nay, Lord, be assured that there is no mistake," answered Tiahuana impressively. "The matter has been most carefully investigated, and the fact has been conclusively established that my Lord is he whom we want. The jewel which my Lord even now wears about his neck proves it. Further than that—"

"The jewel that I am wearing about my neck—this thing?" exclaimed Harry, drawing it forth. "Why, man, I fished this up from the bottom of Lake Chinchaycocha, and am simply wearing it because it appeared valuable and I did not wish to lose it."

"Even so, Lord," answered Tiahuana soothingly, and with even increased reverence, if that were possible. "The circumstance that my Lord drew the collar of the great Manco Capac from the depths of Chinchaycocha is but an added proof—if such were needed—that my Lord is he whom we have believed him to be, and that no mistake has been made."

"But, my good man, I tell you that a mistake *has* been made—a very stupid mistake—which I must insist that you rectify at once," exclaimed Escombe, who was beginning to grow a trifle exasperated at what he inwardly termed the fellow's stupid persistence. "Look here," he continued, "I don't in the least know whom you suppose me to be, but I will tell you who I am. My name is Escombe—Henry Escombe. I am an Englishman, and I only came to Peru—"

"My Lord," interposed Tiahuana with deep humility, yet with a certain inflection of firmness in his voice, "all that you would say is perfectly well known to us your servants; it has been told to us by the man Arima. But nothing can alter the fact that my Lord is the man referred to in the prophecy pronounced by the great High Priest Titucocha on the awful night when the Inca Atahuallpa was strangled by the Spaniards in the great square of Caxamalca. From that moment the ancient Peruvian people have looked for the coming of my lord to free them from the yoke of the foreign oppressor, to give them back their country, and to restore them to the proud position which they occupied ere the coming of the cruel Spaniard; and now that my lord has deigned to appear we should be foolish indeed to permit anything—anything, Lord—to stand in the way of the realisation of our long-deferred hopes."

Harry began to realise that the misunderstanding was more serious than he had at first thought. It must be put right without any further delay. But he could not sit there in that ridiculous palankeen affair and argue with a man who stood with his head thrust between the curtains; he must get up and dress. Moreover, he was ravenously hungry, and felt certain that the breakfast hour must have long gone past. So, instead of replying to Tiahuana's last remarks, he simply said: "Send Arima to me."

The old priest instantly withdrew, and in his place appeared Arima again, who had been standing within earshot, quite expecting a summons at any moment.

"Behold, I am here, Lord," remarked the Indian with a deep obeisance. "What is my Lord's will with the least of his servants?"

"My will," answered Harry, "is to dress and have breakfast at once. When you and your friends kidnapped me last night, did you by any chance have the sense to bring my clothes along?"

"We have brought everything with us, Lord," answered Arima. "Nothing that I know to be my Lord's property has been left behind."

"Um!" thought Harry, "the beggar has been altogether too faithful for my liking. He has brought everything of mine, has he? That means that if I cannot persuade these idiots to take me back to the camp, and it becomes necessary for me to make my escape, I shall have to go off with just what I stand up in, leaving the rest of my belongings in their hands!" Aloud he said: "Very well, then please bring me the clothes that I wore while at work yesterday."

With breathless haste the clothes required were brought forth from a bundle into which they had been hastily thrust, and presented to their owner; the litter was gently deposited upon the ground, and Harry, lightly clad in his pyjama suit, scrambled out, to find himself in the midst of an extensive pine wood, with his escort, consisting of twenty-one persons all told, prostrate on their faces around him! Evidently, he told himself, he was a personage of such dignity and consequence that he must not be looked at by profane eyes while dressing. Smiling to himself at the absurdity of the whole adventure, he quickly proceeded with his toilet, obsequiously assisted by the faithful Arima; and when at length he was dressed, a word from Arima caused the escort to rise to their feet. Then, while some of them proceeded to gather branches and light a fire, others set to work to open certain bundles from which they rapidly extracted bread, chocolate, sugar, and, in short, all the ingredients required to furnish forth an appetising and satisfying breakfast. Finally, about half an hour later, the young Englishman, in a frame of mind about equally divided between annoyance at his abduction and amazement at the unaccountable behaviour of his abductors, found himself partaking of the said breakfast, presented to him in a service of solid gold of curious but most elaborate design and workmanship, and waited upon by his entire suite with as much ceremony and obsequiousness as though he were a king.

Chapter Nine
Tiahuana Tells a Strange Story

Escombe's appetite was good, the food delicious, the cooking perfection, the service irreproachable, if somewhat elaborate. It is not to be wondered at, therefore, that the young man made an excellent meal, and that at its conclusion he should feel himself in admirable form for tackling his captors upon the subject of their outrageous abduction of him. Therefore, after performing his post-prandial ablutions in a basin of solid gold, held before him by a kneeling man, and drying himself upon an immaculate towel woven of cotton which was a perfect miracle of absorbent softness, tendered to him by another kneeling man, he resolutely seated himself upon a moss-grown rock which happened to conveniently protrude itself from the soil close at hand, and proceeded to deal with the matter. He had no difficulty in recognising that Tiahuana and Motahuana were the two wielders of authority in his escort—which, by the way, he noticed had a persistent trick of arranging itself about him in a tolerably close circle of which he was the centre—he therefore opened the proceedings by remarking:

"Now, before I go another step I insist upon having a full and explicit explanation of your unwarrantable behaviour in entering my camp last night and abducting me, to the serious detriment of the exceedingly important work upon which I am engaged. You have assured me that I have nothing to fear at your hands, and you appear to be quite satisfied that in abducting me you have got the man you want; but I am as far as ever from understanding what your motive can be. Which of you two men is responsible for the outrage?"

"I am the responsible one, Lord," answered Tiahuana. "I, the high priest of the remnant of the ancient Peruvian race, now and for many long years established in the city of the Sun which, unknown to any but ourselves, lies hidden far away among the mountains. You demand an explanation of what you have termed my unwarrantable action in taking possession of your august person. It is a just and reasonable demand, Lord; moreover, it is necessary that you should have it. Therefore, let my Lord deign to listen to what to him may seem a wild and incredible story, but which is strictly true in every particular.

"When in the dim and remote past our Lord and Father the Sun took compassion upon us his people, he sent two of his children—Manco Capac and Mama Oello Huaco—to earth in order that they might form us into a united and consolidated nation. These two established themselves in a certain spot, the locality of which had been divinely revealed to them by a certain sign—even as your identity, Lord, has been revealed to us; and our forefathers gathering about them, the ancient and royal city of Cuzco was built, wherein Manco Capac took up his abode as our first Inca. Now, Manco Capac, being of divine origin, was endowed with marvellous wisdom and knowledge, even to the foreseeing of future events; and among the events which he foretold was that of the conquest of our country by the Spaniard. He also formulated many wise and righteous laws for the government of the people, which laws were further added to by his successors.

"Now, with the building of the city of Cuzco and his establishment therein as Inca, Manco assumed royal dignity, and inaugurated a code of stately ceremonial for all those who formed his court and might have occasion to come to it. He also arrayed himself in regal garments and adorned his person with certain regal ornaments, of which the collar now worn by you, Lord, was the most important next to the imperial borla, or tasselled fringe of scarlet, adorned with coraquenque feathers, which was the distinguishing insignia of royalty.

"When in the fullness of time Manco was called home to the mansions of his father the Sun, he gave minute instructions, before his departure, as to the disposal of everything belonging to him, including his royal jewels. Some of these he ordained were to be deposited with his body in the great temple of the Sun at Cuzco. But the jewel which you are now wearing, Lord, he decreed was to be handed down from Inca to Inca, even unto the last of the race; and it was so. Atahuallpa wore it as he entered the city of Caxamalca at the head of his vassals and retinue on the afternoon of that fatal day when he fell into the hands of the treacherous Spaniards and, helpless to prevent it, beheld thousands of his unarmed followers slaughtered like sheep in the great square. But he did not wear it on the night when, at the command of the false and treacherous Pizarro, he was haled forth himself to die in the great square where so many of his followers had previously perished. Nor did it fall into the hands of his captors, thus much was ascertained beyond all possibility of doubt. What became of it nobody could—or would—say; but on the night of Atahuallpa's murder the High Priest Titucocha suddenly emerged from the great temple of the Sun in Cuzco and, standing before the entrance, summoned the inhabitants of the city to assemble before him. Then he told them that Atahuallpa was dead, that the Inca dynasty was at an end, and that the great Peruvian nation was doomed to pass under the rule of the *Conquistadors*, and be swallowed up by them and their descendants. 'But not for all time, my children,' he cried. 'We have sinned in that we have permitted the Spaniards to overrun our country without opposition, instead of utterly destroying them as we might have done; and this is our punishment for not defending the land which our Father the Sun gave us for our sustenance and enjoyment. But be not dismayed; a remnant of you shall survive, and under my leadership shall retire to a certain place the locality of which has been revealed to me, and there will we build a new City of the Sun, the glory of which shall exceed that of Cuzco, even as the glory of our Lord and Father the Sun exceeds that of his consort the Moon. And in the fullness of time it shall come to pass that Manco Capac, the founder of our nation, shall be reincarnated and shall appear among us, and he will become our Inca, to reign over us as aforetime, and restore the Peruvian nation to its pristine power and glory by virtue of his own wisdom and the power of the wealth which we will accumulate for his use. And when he appears ye shall know him from the fact that he will wear about his neck the great emerald collar worn first by himself and afterward by all the Incas.'

"And behold, Lord, as Titucocha spake, so hath it all happened. A remnant of the ancient Peruvian race survives to this day, untainted by any admixture with the blood of aliens; and while many of them are scattered abroad over the face of the country watching ever for the reappearance of Manco Capac, the lesser part are gathered together in the City of the Sun, founded by Titucocha, and now in the very zenith of its magnificence, awaiting the coming of my Lord."

"So that is the yarn, is it?" exclaimed Harry, as Tiahuana came to a halt in his narrative. "And a very extraordinary story it is; never heard anything like it in all my life! And I suppose, friend Tiahuana, that because I happen to have fished up this collar out of Lake Chinchaycocha, and am wearing it round my neck because I do not wish to lose it, you identify me as the reincarnated Manco Capac, eh?"

"Assuredly, Lord," answered Tiahuana. "He would indeed be a sceptic who should venture to entertain the shadow of a doubt in the face of proof so complete in all respects as that which has been vouchsafed to us."

"Ah!" ejaculated Harry, bracing himself to demolish this absurd fable, and secure his release at a stroke. "Now, I don't understand very much about the doctrine of reincarnation, but I suppose, if I were really Manco Capac come to earth again, I should have some recollection of my former state of existence, shouldn't I? Well, will it surprise you to learn that I have nothing of the sort—not the feeblest glimmer?"

"Nay, Lord," answered Tiahuana, "that is not in the least surprising. It often happens that the reincarnated one has no recollection of his former existence until he finds himself amid surroundings similar to those with which he was familiar in his past state; and even then remembrance often comes but slowly. Your lack of recollection does not in the least alter facts; and of those facts we have all the proof that can possibly be required. And now, Lord, will it please you that we resume our journey? There are many difficulties to be surmounted before we reach the spot at which we must encamp to-night, and it is high time that our march should be resumed."

"No," answered Harry, "it does not please me that we resume our journey. On the contrary, I refuse to accompany you another step unless you will undertake to convey me back to the camp whence you brought me. If you will do this I am willing to overlook the outrage which you have perpetrated in abducting me, and promise that you shall hear nothing more about it. But if you persist in keeping me a prisoner, I warn you that the British Consul will be speedily made acquainted with the facts, and he will never rest until I have been released and every one of you severely punished; and that punishment, let me tell you, will be no joke; for he will take care that it is adequate to the offence. You will be made to understand that even a solitary young Englishman like myself cannot be kidnapped with impunity!"

"Pardon, Lord," answered Tiahuana with a deprecatory gesture. "I am overwhelmed with distress at having incurred my Lord's displeasure; but I must not permit even that to interfere with the discharge of my duty. It is imperative that my Lord should accompany us. Were we to fail to convey him to the hidden City of the Sun we should all be justly put to death; my Lord will therefore see that we have no choice in the matter. The only one who has a choice is my Lord himself, who can choose whether he will accompany us willingly, or whether we must resort to something in the nature of coercion."

As Tiahuana spoke the last words he made a sign with his hand, upon which the little band of attendants contracted themselves into a circle of considerably smaller diameter than before, yet still preserving an attitude of the most profound respect. Escombe saw at once that the moment was by no means favourable for an attempt to escape; he therefore quickly decided to make the best of things and to submit *pro tem*, with a good grace to what was unavoidable. He accordingly said:

"Very well; since you are absolutely determined to carry me off, I prefer to accompany you voluntarily. But I warn you that you will all suffer severely for this outrage."

It is most regrettable to be obliged to record it, but Escombe's threatened invocation of Britain's might and majesty seemed to discompose those obstinate Indians not at all; to use his own expression when talking of it afterwards, his threats glanced off them as harmlessly as water off a duck's back, and all that they seemed in the least concerned about was his welfare and comfort during the journey. With much solicitude Tiahuana enquired whether it would please him to walk or to be carried in the litter. "We would have brought your horse with us for your use, Lord," the High Priest explained apologetically, "but much of the road before us is impassable for horses or mules—nay, even a llama might scarcely pass it."

"Oh, that's all right!" answered Harry cheerily; "I dare say I can walk as fast and as far as you people can."

Nevertheless he deeply regretted that they had not thought fit to bring his horse, for he felt that, mounted, he would have had a much better chance of escape than on foot; and this conviction was greatly strengthened when, as the day wore on toward evening and the stiff ascents which they were frequently obliged to negotiate began to tell upon him, he observed how the Indians, with their short, quick step, covered mile after mile of the uneven, rocky road, without the slightest apparent effort or any visible sign of distress. Then it began to dawn upon him gradually that, even should he find a suitable opportunity to give his custodians the slip, they could easily run him down and recapture him. Besides, he was by no means certain that he could now find his way back to the camp. He had not the remotest notion of the direction in which the camp lay, for during many hours of his journey he had been asleep, and the Indians were not only continually changing the direction of their travel, but were apparently taking a constant succession of short cuts across country, now winding their way for a mile or two along the face of some dizzy precipice by means of a ledge only a foot or two in width, anon clambering some hundreds of feet up or down an almost vertical rock face, where a slip or a false step meant instant death; now crossing some ghastly chasm by means of a frail and dilapidated suspension bridge constructed of cables of maguey fibres and floored with rotten planking, which swung to the tread until the oscillation threatened to precipitate the entire party into the terrible abyss that yawned beneath them, and perhaps half an hour later forcing their way, slowly and with infinite labour and difficulty, up the boulder-strewn bed of some half-dry mountain stream that was liable at any moment—if there happened to be rain higher up among the hills—to become swollen into a raging, foaming, irresistible torrent, against the impetuous fury of which no man could stand for an instant. To do the Indians no more than the barest justice, they were to the last degree solicitous to spare their prisoner the least fatigue, and repeatedly assured him that there was not the slightest necessity for him to walk a single step of the way, while whenever there was the barest possibility of danger there was always a sufficient number of them within arm's reach to render him every required assistance, and to ensure that no harm should possibly befall him. But although continuous travelling hour after hour over such very difficult ground became at last most horribly fatiguing, Harry set his teeth and plodded grimly on. He was not going to let "those copper-coloured chaps" suppose that they could tire an Englishman out, not he! Besides, he wished to become accustomed to the work against the time when the opportunity should come for him to break away successfully and effect his escape. For that he would escape he was resolutely determined. The prospect of being an Inca—an absolute monarch whose lightest word was law—had, at that precise moment, no attraction for him. He had not a particle of ambition to become the regenerator of a nation; or, if a scarce-heard whisper reached his mental ear that to become such would be an exceedingly grand thing, he promptly replied that his genius did not lie in that direction, and that any attempt on his part to regenerate anybody must inevitably result in dismal and utter failure. No, he had been sent out to Peru by Sir Philip Swinburne to execute certain work, and he would carry out his contract with Sir Philip in spite of all the Indians in the South American continent. As to that story about his being the reincarnated Inca, Manco Capac, Harry Escombe was one of those estimable persons whose most valued asset is their sound, sterling common sense. He flattered himself that he had not an ounce of romance in his entire composition; and it did not take him a moment to make up his mind that the yarn, from end to end, was the veriest nonsense imaginable. He laughed aloud—a laugh of mingled scorn and pity for the stupendous ignorance of these poor savages, isolated from all the rest of the world, and evidently priding themselves, as such isolated communities are apt to do, upon their immeasurable superiority to everybody else. Then he happened to think of the exquisitely wrought service of gold plate off which he had fed that day, and the wonderfully fine quality of the material of the priests' clothing; and he began to modify his opinion somewhat. A people with the taste and skill needed to produce such superb goldsmith's work and such beautiful cloth—soft and smooth as silk, yet as warm as and very much finer than any woollen material that he had ever seen—could scarcely be classed as mere savages; they must certainly possess some at least of the elements of civilisation. And then those "second thoughts", which are proverbially best, or more just, gradually usurped in young Escombe's mind his first crude ideas relative to the ignorance and benighted condition generally of the inhabitants of the unknown City of the Sun. And as they did so, a feeling of curiosity to see for himself that wonderful city gradually took root, and began to spring up and strengthen within him. Why should he not? he asked himself. The only obstacle which stood in the way was his duty to Sir Philip Swinburne to complete the work which he had been sent out to do. But after all, when he came to consider the matter dispassionately, his absence—his enforced absence—was not likely to prejudice appreciably Sir Philip's interests; for the railway survey was very nearly completed, and what remained to be done was simple in the extreme compared with what had already been accomplished, and there was Bannister—a thoroughly capable man—to do it. And as to the soundings on Lake Titicaca, they were simply child's play—anybody could take them! No, it was only his own conceit that had caused him to think that his absence, especially at the existing state of the survey, would be in the least inimical to Sir Philip's interests; it would be nothing of the kind. Bannister could finish the work as satisfactorily as he—Escombe—could, probably much more so!

It will be seen, from these arguments—which were in the main perfectly sound—that Mr Henry Escombe, having conceived the idea that he would like to have a peep at the mysterious City of the Sun, was now endeavouring to reconcile himself as thoroughly as might be to what was rapidly assuming to him the appearance of the inevitable; for with every step that the party took, it was being borne with increasing clearness upon his inner consciousness that to escape was already impossible. For, first of all, their route had been over such trackless wastes that, despite the keenness with which he had noted the appearance of every conspicuous object passed, they were all so very much alike that he had the gravest doubts as to his ability to find his way back to the camp without a guide. And if he were to attempt it and should lose his way, there could be very little doubt that he would perish miserably of exposure and starvation in that wilderness, where not even so much as a solitary hut had been sighted throughout the day. But, apart from this, and granting for the moment that his memory might be trusted to guided him aright, there were places to be passed and obstacles to be overcome which he admitted to himself he would not care to attempt unaided unless he were in actual peril of his life, and the assurances of Tiahuana had completely set his mind at rest on that score. The thought of invoking Arima's assistance came to him for a moment, only to be dismissed the next, however; for, faithful and devoted as the Indian had proved himself in the past, Harry remembered that it was through his instrumentality and direct intervention that all the pother had arisen. Arima seemed to be as completely convinced as any of the others that Harry was the person foreordained to restore the ancient Peruvian nation to its former power and splendour, and Escombe knew enough of the fellow's character to feel certain that he would not permit personal feeling to interfere with so glorious a consummation. It seemed, then, as though fate, or destiny, or whatever one pleased to call it, willed that he—Harry Escombe—should see the mysterious city; and he finally concluded that, taking everything into consideration, perhaps the wisest thing would be to go quietly and with as much semblance of goodwill as possible, since it appeared that no other course was open to him.

This thought naturally suggested others, each more wild and extravagant than the last, until by the time that the party at length reached the camping ground that had been their objective all through the day, the young Englishman discovered, to his unqualified amazement, that not only did there exist within him a strong vein of hitherto entirely unsuspected romance—awakened and brought to light by the extraordinary nature of the adventure of which he was the hero—but also that, quite unconsciously to himself, his views relative to the exigency and binding character of his engagement to Sir Philip Swinburne had become so far modified that it no longer appeared imperatively necessary for him to jeopardise his life in a practically hopeless endeavour to escape.

The journey had been an up-and-down one all day, that is to say, the party had been either climbing or descending almost the whole of the time; the general tendency, however, had been distinctly upward, and when at length a bare, rocky plateau was reached about sunset, affording ample space upon which to camp, the greatly increased keenness of the atmosphere indicated a net rise of probably some two or three thousand feet. The scene was one of almost indescribable but dreary grandeur, titanic peaks crowned with snow and ice towering high on every hand, divided by gorges of immeasurable depth, their sides for the most part shaggy with pine forests, and never a sign of human habitation to be seen, nor indeed any sign of life in any form, save where, here and there, a small moving blotch on the distant landscape indicated the presence of a flock of huanacos or vicuñas; but even these were but few, for the travellers had not yet reached the lofty frozen wastes where alone the ychu grass is found, which is therefore the favoured habitat of those animals.

Escombe now had fresh evidence of the foresight exercised by his escort in providing for his comfort and welfare; for no sooner had the precise spot been selected upon which to camp than from among the baggage borne by the attendants a small tent made of cloth woven from vicuña wool was produced and erected upon jointed bamboo poles; and in a few minutes, with his litter placed inside it to serve as a bed, and a lighted talc lantern suspended from the ridge pole, the young man was able to enter and make himself quite at home.

Nor was he at all sorry; for although he had now been accustomed for several months to be on his feet all day long, day after day, and up to that moment had regarded himself as in the very pink of condition as to toughness and wiriness, the past day's journey had been a revelation to him in the matter of endurance. He had never before in his life experienced anything like the intense fatigue which now racked every joint in his body; and, ravenously hungry as he was, he felt that it would scarcely be possible for him to remain awake long enough to get a meal. But those wonderful Indians appeared to have foreseen everything. Loaded as most of them were with heavy burdens in addition, to their weapons, they had each gradually accumulated a very respectable bundle of firewood during the progress of their march; and while one party had been erecting the tent and arranging its interior for Harry's occupation, a second had been busily engaged in lighting a roaring fire, while a third had been still more busily occupied in preparing the wherewithal to furnish forth a most appetising and acceptable evening meal, which, when placed before the prospective Inca, was found to consist of broiled vicuña chops, delicious bread, mountain honey, fruit, and chocolate. By the time that the meal was ready night had completely fallen, a bitterly keen and piercing wind from the eastward had arisen and came swooping down from the frozen wastes above in savage gusts that momentarily threatened to whirl the frail tent and its occupant into space, and hurl them into one of the many unfathomable abysses that yawned around the party, while, to add to the general discomfort, the wind brought with it a dank, chilling fog, thick as a blanket, that penetrated everywhere and left on everything great beads of icy moisture like copious dew. But Escombe was too unutterably weary to let any of these things trouble him. Sleep was what every fibre of his body was crying aloud for; and he had no sooner finished his meal than, leaving all responsibility for the safety and welfare of the party in the hands of the two priests, he hurriedly divested himself of his clothing, and snuggling into his warm and comfortable bed-litter, instantly sank into absolute unconsciousness, his last coherent thought being a vague wonder how he would fare in such a place and on such a night if, instead of being under the care and protection of the Indians, he had chanced to be a lonely and houseless fugitive from them.

Chapter Ten
The Valley of Mystery

When young Escombe next morning awoke from the soundest sleep that he had ever enjoyed in his life he at once became aware, from the motion of the litter, that his Indian friends were already on the move; and when, in obedience to his command, they halted to enable him to dress and partake of breakfast, a single glance, as he stepped forth from the litter into the keen air, sufficed to assure him that they must have been in motion for at least three or four hours, for the sun had already topped the peaks of the Andes, and the aspect of the landscape surrounding him was entirely unfamiliar. Not a trace of the spot where they had camped during the preceding night was to be seen, and there was no indication of the direction in which it lay; which fact tended still further to drive home to the young man a conviction of the folly of attempting to find his way back to the survey party alone and unaided.

The journey that day was in all essential respects a counterpart of that of the day before. Tiahuana, who was evidently the leader of the expedition in a double sense, chose his own route, making use of the regular roads only at very infrequent intervals, and then for comparatively short distances, soon abandoning them again for long stretches across country where no semblance of a path of any description was to be found. As on the preceding day, he skirted, climbed, or descended precipices without hesitation, crossing ravines, ascending gorges, and, in fact, he took the country pretty much as it came, guiding the party apparently by means of landmarks known only to himself, but, on the whole, steadily ascending and steadily forcing his way ever deeper into the heart of the stupendous mountain labyrinth that lay to the eastward. And ever as they went the air grew keener and more biting, the aspect of the country wilder and more desolate, the *quebradas* more appalling in their fathomless depth. The precipices became more lofty and difficult to scale, the mountain torrents more impetuous and dangerous to cross, the primitive suspension bridges more dilapidated and precarious, the patches of timber and vegetation more tenuous, the flocks of huanaco and vicuña larger and more frequent, the way more savage and forbidding, the storms more frequent and terrible, until at length it began to appear to

Escombe as though the party had become entangled in a wilderness from which escape in any direction was impossible, and wherein they must all quickly perish in consequence of the unendurable rigours of the climate. Yet Tiahuana still pushed indomitably forward, overcoming obstacle after obstacle that, to anyone less experienced than himself in the peculiarities of the country and the mode of travel in it, must have seemed unconquerable. For ten more days—which to the Indians must have seemed endless by reason of the awful toil, the frightful suffering, and the intense misery that were concentrated in them, although, thanks to the sublime self sacrifice of his escort, Escombe was permitted to feel very little of them — the priest led the way over vast glaciers, across unfathomable crevasses, and up apparently unscalable heights, battling all the time with whirling snow storms that darkened the air, blinded the eyes, and obliterated every landmark, and buffeted by furious winds that came roaring and shrieking along the mountain side and momentarily threatened to snatch the party from their precarious hold and hurl them to destruction on the great gaunt rocks far below, while the cold was at times so terrible that to continue to live in it seemed impossible.

About the middle of the afternoon of the twelfth day after leaving the survey camp, the party topped a ridge and saw before them a long, steep, smooth slope of snow, frozen hard by a night of almost deadly frost; and a sigh of intense relief and thankfulness broke from the breasts of the utterly exhausted Indians. Without wasting a moment, they proceeded to open and unpack a certain bale which formed part of the baggage which they had brought with them, and drew from it a number of llama skins. These they spread out flat on the crest of the snow slope, with the hair side upward, and then the entire party carefully seated themselves upon them—two men to each skin, one behind the other—when, with a little assistance from the hands of the occupants, the skins started to glide smoothly over the surface of the snow, slowly at first, but with swiftly increasing velocity, until the descent of the party became a sweeping, breathless, exhilarating flight, speedy as that of a falcon swooping upon its prey. The riders sat cross-legged upon the skins, and to Escombe—who was piloted by Tiahuana— it seemed that the slightest inclination, right or left as the case might be, throwing a trifle more weight on one knee than the other, and thus causing one part of the skin to press more hardly than another upon the snow, was all that was needed for steering purposes; for the toboggan-like skins swept downward straight as the flight of an arrow, save when some black fang of rock protruded through the snow fair in the track, when a slight slope of the body sufficed to cause a swerve that carried the adventurous riders safely clear of the obstacle. To Escombe this headlong, breathless swoop down the slope seemed to last but a few seconds, yet during those few seconds the party had travelled nearly three miles and descended some three thousand feet. The slide terminated at last upon the very edge of the snow-line, where it met a mile-wide meadow thickly clothed with lush grass and bountifully spangled with lovely flowers, many of which were quite new to the young Englishman.

For some minutes the entire party, as with one consent, remained sitting motionless just where their impromptu toboggans had come to a halt; for they felt that they needed a certain amount of time in which to become accustomed to the glorious change that had been wrought by that three-mile glissade. Above and behind them were furious tempest, deadly cold, and never-ceasing danger; while here was perfect safety, cloudless sunshine, grateful warmth, and surroundings of surpassing beauty. The meadow upon which they rested sloped gently away before them for about a mile, where it appeared to plunge abruptly down into a thickly wooded ravine, beyond which shot up a long, rocky ridge, the slopes of which appeared to be absolutely inaccessible; for, search as Escombe might with the aid of his telescope, nowhere could he detect so much as a single speck of snow to indicate the presence of even the smallest ledge or inequality in the face of the rock. This ridge, or range, stretched away to right and left of the spot where the party had come to a halt, retiring to the eastward, as it went, in a tolerably regular curve, until the cusps, if such there were, swept out of sight behind the nearer ridge.

At length Escombe rose from his llama skin and, with an ejaculation of inexpressible relief, began to slap his still benumbed hands together, and vigorously rub his stiffened limbs, in order to restore feeling and warmth to them; whereupon Tiahuana also rose and gave the order to re-pack the skins prior to resuming the journey. A few minutes later the entire party were once more on the march, moving rapidly athwart the meadow toward the ravine, and within a quarter of an hour they were in the ravine itself, clambering down the steep slope of its hither side toward where the sound of rushing water began to make itself heard with increasing distinctness. Another ten minutes, after a wild and breathless downward scramble among the trunks of thick-growing pine trees, brought them to the margin of a wide and turbulent mountain torrent that in the course of ages had scored a deep channel for itself right down the centre of the ravine. The bed of the stream was thickly strewed with enormous boulders, moss-grown upon their upper surfaces where drenched with the everlasting spray, and between these the turbid waters from the melting snow on the heights above leapt and foamed with a clamour and fury that rendered conversation impossible, and threatened instant death to the foolhardy adventurer who should attempt to cross them.

Yet those indomitable Indians somehow contrived to win a passage across; and half an hour later the entire party stood safely on the opposite side.

Then followed a long and toilsome scramble up the other side of the ravine, the top of which was not reached until the sun had set and darkness had fallen upon the scene. But, at the top of the ravine and clear of the trees, they found themselves on a grassy slope very similar in character to that which they had encountered on the other side of the stream, and there, fatigued to the point of exhaustion by their long and arduous day's travel, they went into camp, prepared and partook of their evening meal, and at once resigned themselves to a long night of repose under conditions of infinitely greater comfort than they had enjoyed for many days past.

Escombe's sleep that night was unusually sound, even after making every allowance for the excessive fatigue of the past day; in fact he had not slept so soundly and so long since the night of his abduction from the survey camp. When at length he awoke he found himself labouring under the same feeling of puzzlement that had oppressed him on that eventful morning; for when consciousness again returned to him and, opening his eyes, he looked about him, he at once became aware that his surroundings were very different from what he had expected. It is true that he still occupied the litter in which he had retired to rest on the previous evening, but a single glance was sufficient to show him that the litter was no longer in the little tent which had then sheltered it; the tent was gone, and the litter, or couch, upon which he lay comfortably stretched now stood in a room lighted by a single window in the wall, facing the foot of the couch. The window was unglazed, and apparently had no window frame; it seemed in fact to be no more than a mere rectangular aperture in a thick stone wall through which the sun, already some hours high in the sky, was pouring his genial rays into the room. The couch stood so low on the floor that from it nothing could be seen of the landscape outside save a glimpse of a range of serrated peaks, touched here and there with snow that gleamed dazzlingly white in the brilliant sunshine. Urged therefore by surprise at the mysterious change that had been wrought in his surroundings while he slept, and curious to ascertain where he now was, Harry sprang from his couch and went to the open window, out of which he gazed in an ecstasy of astonishment and admiration. For his eyes rested upon the most glorious landscape that he had ever beheld. He discovered that the building in which he so strangely found himself stood at one extremity of an enormous, basin-like valley, roughly oval in shape, some thirty miles long by twenty miles in width, completely hemmed in on every side by a range of lofty hills averaging, according to his estimate, from three to four thousand feet in height. The centre of the valley was occupied by a most lovely lake about fifteen miles long by perhaps ten miles wide, dotted here and there with fairy-like islets, some of which were crowned by little clumps of trees, while others appeared to be covered with handsome buildings. But that was only a part of the wonder! At the far end of the lake he could distinctly see—so exquisitely clear and transparent was that crystalline atmosphere—the general outline and formation of a large and doubtless populous town built on the margin of the lake, his attention being at once attracted to it by the strong flash and gleam of the sun upon several of the roofs of the buildings, which had all the appearance of being covered with sheets of gold! From this city broad white roads shaded by handsome trees ran right round the margin of the lake, and for a mile or two on either side of the city, glimpses could be had of detached buildings embosomed in spacious gardens, forming a kind of suburb of the city; while the entire remainder of the valley, and the sides of the hills for a distance of about one-third of their height, were entirely laid out as orchards, pasture, and cultivated land, the appearance of the whole strongly suggesting that the utmost had been made of every inch of available space.

As Escombe stood gazing, enraptured at the surpassing beauty of the panorama thus spread out before him, the sound of approaching footsteps reached his ear, and, turning round, he beheld Arima entering the room. The Indian made the profound obeisance usual with him upon entering Harry's presence, and enquired:

"Is it the will of my Lord that he now bathe, dress, and partake of breakfast?"

"Yes, by all means," answered Harry, "for I have somehow managed to oversleep myself again, and am ravenously hungry. But, Arima, what means this? How do I come to be here? And what town is that which I see yonder at the far end of the lake?"

"As my Lord has truly said, he slept long this morning, being doubtless greatly fatigued with the toilsome journey of yesterday," answered Arima smoothly, with another profound bow. "Therefore, when the hour arrived to break camp and resume our march it was Tiahuana's order that my Lord should not be disturbed, but should be allowed to sleep on and take a full measure of rest; and therefore was my Lord brought hither to this house, there to sojourn and recruit himself after the fatigues and hardships of his long journey, while Tiahuana went forward to the City of the Sun—which my Lord sees yonder at the head of the valley—to acquaint the Council with the success of our expedition, and to make the necessary arrangements for my Lord's reception by the inhabitants of the city. If it be my Lord's will, I will now conduct him to the bath, which I have made ready for him."

"So that is the City of the Sun, is it?" remarked Harry, still gazing admiringly at the enchanting view from the window. "I guessed as much; and it appears to be fully worthy of its name. All right, Arima," he continued, tearing himself reluctantly away; "yes, I will have my bath now. Where is it?"

"If my Lord will be pleased to follow I will show it him," answered the Indian, with the inevitable bow, as he led the way out of the room.

They passed into a long stone corridor, lighted at each end by an unglazed window, and, traversing the length of it, entered another room, much larger than the first, stone paved, and having a large plunge-bath full of crystal-clear water, sunk into the floor at one end. The room was unfurnished, save for a plain wooden bench, or seat, a soft woollen mat for the bather to stand on when emerging from the bath, and a few pegs along the wall, from which Harry's own clothes and three or four very large bath towels depended. This room also was illuminated by a large, unglazed window through which the sun-rays streamed, warming the atmosphere of the apartment to a most delightful temperature. Harry therefore made no delay, but forthwith discarded his pyjama suit and at once plunged headlong into the cool, refreshing water. To dress and take breakfast were the next things in order; and half an hour later Escombe rose from the table like a giant refreshed, amid the obsequious bows of his attendants. Then Motahuana stepped forward and, prefacing his speech with another bow, said:

"Lord, I have been commanded by Tiahuana to say that, knowing well how anxious the inhabitants of the City of the Sun will be to learn the issue of this expedition, he has presumed to hasten forward to apprise them that all is well, without waiting until my Lord awoke to mention his intention and crave my Lord's permission to absent himself; for the way is long, and my Lord slept late this morning. The High Priest also bade me say that he will probably be absent at least four days, for there are many preparations to be made in connection with my Lord's triumphal entrance into his city, and his reception by his rejoicing people. My Lord will therefore have time to rest and recover his strength after the fatigue of his arduous journey; and it is the prayer of Tiahuana that he will do so, since there will be much to fatigue my Lord in the various ceremonies attendant upon his ascent of the throne of the ancient Incas."

"Thanks, Motahuana," answered Harry; "but I am not in the least fatigued by what I have gone through during the last twelve days. If anyone were suffering from fatigue it should be yourself and Tiahuana, for you are both well advanced in years, while I am young and strong, and, so far from being fatigued, I feel quite fresh after my long and refreshing night's sleep; so much so, indeed, that I was just thinking how much I should enjoy a walk down into that lovely valley. I suppose there is no objection to my doing so?"

"My Lord is monarch of the valley and all within it," answered Motahuana with another bow and an expressive throwing apart of the hands. "All is his; his will is absolute in all things; he has but to express a wish, and we his slaves will gladly do our best to gratify it. If my Lord desires to go forth into the open, either on foot or in his litter, he has but to say so, and we his slaves will make the path smooth for him or bear him upon our shoulders, as may seem best to him. But it will be well that my Lord should not venture too far into the valley, for he is a stranger; and it is undesirable, on many accounts, that he should be seen by the inhabitants of the valley until all preparations have been made for his public reception."

"Oh, very well!" returned Escombe. "I have no desire to go very far; a walk of a mile or two from the house, and back, with Arima as my only attendant, to show me the way and answer questions, will satisfy me."

Whereupon Motahuana, with another bow, turned away and addressed a few quick words to Arima in a tongue which was strange to Escombe, after which the Indian fetched the young Englishman's hat and signified his readiness to attend the latter whithersoever he might be pleased to go.

Harry's first act, upon getting outside the house, was to walk away from it some fifty feet, and then turn round and stare at the building to which he had been so mysteriously conveyed while asleep. He saw before him simply a solid, rectangular, stone—built structure, plain almost to the point of ugliness, for it had not a single projection of any kind to mitigate the severity of its simplicity, not even so much as a window sill; and it was thatched!—not with the trim neatness characteristic of some of our charmingly picturesque country cottages in England, but in a slovenly, happy-go-lucky style, that seemed to convey the idea that, so long as a roof was weather-proof, it did not in the least matter what it looked like. The windows were simply rectangular holes in the thick stone walls, unglazed, and without even a frame; but now that Escombe was outside he was able to see that each window was provided with a shutter, something like the jalousies fitted to the houses in most tropical and sub-tropical countries, to keep out the rain. The only thing remarkable about the house, apart from its extreme plainness, was the fact that it appeared to be cut out of a single enormous block of stone; and it was not until he went close up to it, and examined it minutely, that he discovered it to be built of blocks of stone dressed to fit each other with such marvellous precision that the joints were practically invisible.

Having satisfied his curiosity thus far, Escombe looked about him at his surroundings generally. He found that the house to which he had been brought stood at the extreme end of the extraordinary basin-like valley, immediately opposite to the City of the Sun, which occupied the other end, and he naturally concluded that the entrance to the valley must be somewhere not very far distant from the spot on which he stood. But, look as he would, he could see nothing in the remotest degree resembling a pass through those encircling sierras, the upper portion of the sides of which appeared to be everywhere practically vertical, without even as much projection or ledge anywhere as would afford foothold to a goat. Nor was there the least semblance of a road or path of any description leading to the house, save a narrow and scarcely perceptible footpath leading down to the great road which encompassed the lake. Harry turned to the Indian.

"Those hills appear to be everywhere quite impassable, Arima," he said. "Where is the road by which we came over them?"

"It is not permitted to me to say, Lord," answered Arima with a deprecatory bow. "There is but one known way of passing to and from the outside world, and that way is a jealously guarded secret, communicated to but few, who are solemnly sworn to secrecy. It is regarded by the Council as of the first importance that the secret should be preserved intact, as it is known that rumours of the existence of the City of the Sun have reached the outer world, and more than one attempt has been made to find it. But we are all pure-blooded Peruvians of the ancient race here, and it is a tradition with us to keep ourselves uncontaminated by any admixture of alien blood, therefore every possible precaution is taken to maintain the most absolute secrecy as to the way by which the Valley of the Sun is entered and left."

"But if that is so, why has Tiahuana brought me here?" demanded Harry. "I am an alien, you know; yet, as I understand it, I have been brought here to rule over you all!"

"Yes, it is even so, Lord," answered Arima. "But my Lord is an alien only by an accident of birth, which must not be allowed to interfere with the fact that my Lord is in very truth the reincarnation of Manco Capac, our first Inca and the founder of the Peruvian nation."

"In that case," said Harry, "it is but meet and right that I should know the secret way into the outer world. Surely what is known to several of my subjects should also be known to me?"

"Undoubtedly, Lord," answered the Indian; "and the information will certainly be imparted to my Lord in due time, when he has been accepted and proclaimed Inca by the Council of Seven. But I have no authority to impart that information, and I implore my Lord that he will not urge me to do so and thus break the solemn oath of secrecy which I have sworn."

"Very well, Arima, let it be so," answered Harry. "Doubtless, as you say, I shall be informed in due time; and meanwhile you are perfectly right to remain true to the oath which you have sworn. Now, let us get down into the valley. After scrambling up and down mountain sides for so many days, I have a longing to walk on a smooth and level road once more."

The footpath from the house to the main road sloped obliquely along the face of the hill, descending by a tolerably easy gradient for a distance of about a mile before it joined the road at a depth of some three hundred feet below the level of the house. Upon reaching the road, which, be it remembered, completely encircled the lake, Escombe had yet another opportunity to note the thoroughness with which the Peruvians did their work, and the inexhaustible patience which they brought to bear upon it. For this road, approximating to one hundred miles in length, was constructed of a uniform width of about one hundred feet, apparently also of uniform gradient—for in some parts it was raised on a low embankment, while in others it passed through more or less shallow cuttings—and with just the right amount of camber to quickly throw off the rainwater into the broad gutters or watercourses that were built on either side of it. The most remarkable feature of the road, however, was that it was paved throughout with broad flags of stone, which, like the blocks of which the house was built, were so accurately fitted together that the joints could only be found with difficulty.

The young Englishman spent some three hours sauntering along that magnificent road, enjoying the pure air, the genial temperature, and the sight of the superb panorama that hemmed him in on every side, pausing often to note the clever system of irrigation adopted by the inhabitants, whereby every square inch of cultivable soil could at any moment receive precisely the right quantity of water to satisfy its requirements; admiring, with the eye of an engineer, the workmanship displayed in the construction of the ample culverts whereby all excess of water was promptly discharged into the lake; and marvelling at the varied nature of the agricultural products of the valley; for it seemed to him that, in the comparatively circumscribed space between the margin of the lake and the highest point on the mountain slope to which the barest handful of soil could be induced to cling, there were to be found examples of every vegetable product known to the sub-tropical and temperate zones, while it was a never-ceasing source of astonishment to him that such enormous numbers of cattle and sheep were apparently able to find ample sustenance on the proportionately small quantity of land allotted to pasture. What seemed to him somewhat remarkable was that, while cattle, sheep, and even horses were apparently plentiful in the valley, he saw no llamas; but it was afterwards explained to him that the climate there was altogether too mild for them, and that the enormous herds owned by the inhabitants were kept in the highlands on the other side of the encircling mountains.

Chapter Eleven
The City of the Sun

On the afternoon of the fourth day following Tiahuana's departure, about an hour before sunset, as Escombe was about to enter the house after a somewhat longer walk than usual in the valley, he paused for a moment at the head of the footpath to take a last, long look at the lovely landscape, with the leading features of which he was now becoming tolerably familiar, when his wandering gaze was arrested by the glint of the sunlight upon what had the appearance of a number of rapidly moving objects indistinctly seen about a mile distant among the low spreading branches of the trees which lined the great road leading from the City of the Sun.

"Hillo, Arima," he said to the Indian who was his sole attendant, "who comes here? Are they soldiers? Do you see that flash and glitter yonder among the trees? To me it has the appearance of sun-glint upon spear points and military accoutrements."

Arima looked for a moment, and then replied:

"Without question it is so, Lord. Doubtless it is Tiahuana returning with the bodyguard which is to escort my Lord the Inca on the occasion of his triumphal entry into the City of the Sun."

"But those fellows are surely mounted, Arima!" said Escombe. "The movement is that of cavalry; and—listen!—unless I am greatly mistaken, I can hear the clatter of hoofs on the stone pavement of the road."

"It is even so, Lord," answered the Indian. "The bodyguard of my Lord the Inca consists of a thousand picked men, mounted on the finest horses that it is possible to breed in the valley."

"But I have always understood," said Harry, "that you Peruvians did not believe in mounted men, and that it was, in fact, as much due to your terror of the mounted Spaniards as anything else that you were vanquished in the old days. But I am forgetting; you knew nothing of horses then, did you?"

"My Lord says truth," answered Arima. "We had no horses in Peru until the Spaniards brought them. But since then we have learned the value of horses, and I understand that the inhabitants of the valley have devoted especial attention to the breeding of them, even from the date of the foundation of the city."

"And with a marvellous success, I should say, if one may judge from the appearance of the animals yonder," remarked Harry enthusiastically, as he watched the approaching horsemen.

The cavalcade had by this time reached the junction of the footpath with the road, and, debouching on to the former, or rather on to the hillside which it traversed, breasted the slope at a gallop, presenting as it did so a superb and inspiriting picture of eager, prancing, satin-skinned, gaily caparisoned, foam-flecked horses, bestridden by lithe, sinewy forms gorgeous in their blue and gold uniforms, and a-glitter with their burnished copper shields, swords, maces, and lance-heads. At their head rode Tiahuana in his long, white, gold-embroidered robe and mitre-like head—dress as Chief Priest, gallantly holding his own with the magnificently attired commander of the regiment; and in the centre of the cortege there appeared an open litter - somewhat similar to a sedan chair with the top part removed— entirely covered with burnished plates of gold and silver, hammered into a bold but very intricate pattern, while the interior was lined with richly coloured feathers also arranged in a very elaborate design. This structure was supported before and behind by a pair of long, springy poles or shafts, to which were harnessed six white horses, three abreast, the harness and trappings of the animals being blue, elaborately embroidered with gold, while the headstall of each horse was decorated with a plume of half a dozen long blue feathers. The middle horse of each trio—that which ran between the shafts—was ridden by a postilion, who guided and controlled all three of the horses under his charge.

While the gorgeous cavalcade was still some distance away, Motahuana came running out of the house, babbling the most earnest and urgent entreaties that Harry would be graciously pleased to enter the house forthwith, as it was not meet that the members of the Inca's bodyguard should set eyes upon their sovereign lord until the latter should be attired in the robes of his regal rank; and Harry, already painfully aware of the dilapidated condition of the jacket and knickers in which he had accomplished the march from the survey camp, fully agreeing with him, hastily retreated to the interior of the building and, standing well back from the window, where he was concealed in the deep shadow, interestedly watched the movements of his regiment as it went into camp on a little plateau at the rear of the house.

But the troopers had scarcely begun to unsaddle before Tiahuana, still hot and dusty from his long ride, entered the house, followed by a servant bearing a large bundle. And a few minutes later the old fellow entered the room where Harry was standing and, having first made his obeisances, respectfully invited the young Englishman to retire to his sleeping room, there to don certain garments more suitable to his rank and state than those which he was wearing, in order that he might be ready to receive the Lord Umu, commander of the royal bodyguard, who was represented to be dying of impatience to do homage to his Sovereign Lord. With another glance at his ragged and disreputable garments, Harry smilingly admitted the desirability of the change, and followed Tiahuana into the chamber where Arima, now formally confirmed in his rank and position of chief valet and body servant of the new Inca, awaited his master. Ten minutes later, attired in white skin-tight pantaloons which were also stockings; a shirt of white wool, of so marvellously fine a texture that it was thin, soft, and light as silk; a fine white wool sleeveless tunic, the material of which was stiff and almost completely hidden by an elaborately embroidered pattern in heavy gold thread, and which was confined to the waist by a broad white leather belt, also heavily embroidered in gold and fastened by a massive and exquisitely chased gold clasp; with soft, white, gold-embroidered boots on his feet, reaching halfway up to the knee; with the royal borla, or tasselled fringe of scarlet adorned with two feathers from the coraquenque bound round his temples, and the emerald collar of Manco Capac—which he had fished up from the mud of Lake Chinchaycocha—round his neck and hanging down over the breast of his tunic, young Escombe was led by Tiahuana into the largest room in the house. Here, seated upon an extemporised throne, and with his feet resting upon a footstool of solid gold, massively chiselled in an elaborate and particularly graceful scroll-work pattern, hastily brought in from the imperial litter, he presently received not only Umu, the captain of the royal bodyguard, but also some half-dozen other nobles who had come from the City of the Sun to pay their homage to their re-incarnated Lord and Sovereign, Manco Capac.

These individuals were introduced, one by one, by Tiahuana, who, as each person presented himself in the doorway, loudly proclaimed the rank and titles of the visitor, who then, barefooted, and carrying a light burden upon his shoulders as an act of humility in the presence of his sovereign, slowly advanced, with head and body humbly bent, until he reached the footstool, when he knelt down on the bare stone floor and kissed, first the hands and then the feet of the young Inca; after which, still kneeling, he murmured a few words expressive of joy, gratitude, and devotion at the condescension of the great Manco in deigning to return to earth for the purpose of regenerating the ancient Peruvian nation. Then he rose to his feet and, with more bows, retired to make way for the next. The whole ceremony was exceedingly brief, not occupying much more than a quarter of an hour altogether; but, brief as it was, it constituted in itself an education for Harry, who, as he witnessed the almost slavish humility of the demeanour of these proud and haughty nobles toward him, now began to realise, for the first time, the tremendous power to which he had been raised by a most unique and extravagant freak of fortune. And it did him good; for it set him to think seriously of the enormous responsibility which he had almost unwittingly incurred when he so light-heartedly allowed himself to become enmeshed in the toils of the adventure, and caused him to make many very excellent resolutions as to the manner in which he would discharge that responsibility.

With the coming of dawn on the following morning the camp of the royal bodyguard suddenly awoke to strenuous life and activity. The troopers, attired only in thin shirts, riding their barebacked horses down to the lake, where the animals were watered and bathed in preparation for the return journey to the City of the Sun. Then, having returned to the camp, the horses were carefully groomed and fed, after which the troopers spent a busy hour in examining and burnishing their arms and accoutrements. For this was the great day upon which the re-incarnated Inca was to make his triumphal entry into his capital, the new holy and royal city which, during a period of over three hundred and fifty years, his people had been patiently building and extending and decorating and enriching in order that it might be worthy the reception of the monarch when it should please him to return to earth. It was to be the day of days, the first day in the history of a great, glorious, regenerated nation, in which much was to be done, and that in a manner which would becomingly adorn the first page of that history. Then everybody, including Harry—who, meanwhile had bathed and dressed— partook of breakfast; after which the final preparations for the journey were completed. Then Tiahuana and Umu, having first craved audience of their Lord, presented themselves before Harry to intimate respectfully that there were two alternative methods of travel open to him, namely by horse litter or on horseback, and to crave humbly that he would be pleased to indicate which of the two he would choose. To which Harry, who was by this time beginning to enter thoroughly into the spirit of the adventure, replied that, since the task had been laid upon him of restoring the ancient Peruvian race to its former power and splendour, and that, before this could be accomplished it would be necessary for him to lead his troops many times to battle, it was his will to make his first appearance among his subjects on horseback, as a warrior, at the head of his own bodyguard; a reply which created a perfect furore of enthusiasm among the other nobles, and the troopers of the royal bodyguard, when it was communicated to them by Tiahuana and Umu.

That the possibility of such a choice on the part of their new Inca had not been altogether unanticipated was soon apparent; for Umu presently returned to the house, bearing on a cushion of azure blue—which it appeared was the royal colour—trimmed with a heavy cord of bullion and with a bullion tassel at each corner, a sword of hardened and burnished copper, with a hilt of solid gold elaborately chased, and encased in a scabbard of solid gold, also most magnificently chased. This he presented on bended knees to Tiahuana, who, in his capacity of High Priest, then knelt before Harry and girded the weapon to his side, after which Arima came forward with a long roll of extraordinarily fine silk-like cloth woven in bands of many different colours in which, however, scarlet and azure predominated. This was the llautu, or turban, which the Indian at once proceeded with deft fingers to bind about his royal master's head in such a manner as to afford complete protection from the ardent rays of the sun while leaving the borla, or tasselled fringe of scarlet, which was really the royal diadem, fully exposed to view. A woollen mantle of almost silken texture, azure blue in colour, with a very broad border of gold embroidery, and with more gold embroidery on the shoulders and halfway down the back, was next laid upon his shoulders and secured at the throat by a pair of massive gold clasps and chain, and Escombe was fully equipped for the road. And a very handsome and gallant figure he looked as, tall, lithe, and slim, and clad in all his barbaric finery, he stepped out of the house into the dazzling sunshine, to be greeted with a deafening shout of welcome from the officers and troopers of his bodyguard, who were already mounted and drawn up in a double line for his inspection. So obviously was this expected of him that Harry needed no hint to that effect, but, vaulting lightly into the saddle of the magnificent white stallion that, gorgeously caparisoned, chafed and fretted under the restraint of his bridle, held by two of the nobles, while two more held the heavy gold stirrups for the royal rider's feet, wheeled his steed and cantered gaily off to where Umu, sitting bolt upright in his saddle with drawn sword, waited in the centre, and some few paces in front of the regiment, to receive him. That the military usages of the more civilised nations had not been permitted to pass altogether unnoticed now became apparent; for as Harry approached Umu uttered a loud shout of command, and at the word every sword flashed up in salute in the most approved fashion, while a band of mounted musicians blared forth certain weird strains which, the young Inca subsequently learned, was the national anthem of the ancient Peruvians.

Accompanied by Umu, Harry now rode to the right flank of the regiment, from whence he proceeded slowly along the front rank and finally the rear, noting critically the appearance and bearing of the men, and gauging the breed and quality of the horses as he went. The horses were, without exception, splendid animals, while the men were, for the most part, fine, stalwart fellows, well set up; but, accustomed as Escombe had been to the sight of the Life Guards and other crack cavalry regiments in London, he could not avoid seeing that there was plenty of room for improvement in the appearance and discipline generally of his own bodyguard. Yet it was glaringly apparent to him that Umu, their captain, was inordinately proud of his regiment; and the new Inca was by no means untactful. Wherefore, having completed his inspection, Harry spoke a few well-considered words of praise that rang sufficiently true to make Umu his devoted slave henceforward, while the faint suggestion conveyed that the praise was not quite unqualified impressed the Indian noble with a sense of the high standard of perfection that must exist in the young monarch's mind, and caused him there and then to register a silent vow that the regiment should be brought up to that standard, even though he should be obliged to kill every man of it in the process.

By the time that the inspection was completed the priests and nobles had climbed into their saddles, and everything was ready for the commencement of the march. Harry therefore gave the word to Umu, who in turn uttered a few sharp orders to the men, whereupon the ranks closed up. The horses pranced and tossed their heads as they wheeled into line, and the cavalcade proceeded, the band leading the way, followed by a solitary horseman in gorgeous array who bore proudly aloft the Inca's banner—a blue silk flag embroidered in gold and coloured thread with an image of the rainbow, which was the symbol sacred to the Inca, and trimmed with heavy gold fringe round the three free edges. Harry rode immediately behind, surrounded by a little group consisting of the two priests and the nobles who had come out to meet him, and followed by Umu, who led his glittering and imposing regiment.

It was rather a trying ride in some respects for the young Inca, at least at the outset, for Escombe's knowledge of the Quichua, or ancient Peruvian, language was extremely restricted, while the nobles, with the exception of Tiahuana and Umu, were apparently ignorant of Spanish. Anything in the nature of conversation was therefore extremely difficult, quite apart from the fact that everybody excepting Tiahuana seemed altogether too shy to address the Inca, unless first spoken to by him. Harry very quickly realised that his ignorance of the Quichua was likely to handicap him most seriously, and he there and then ordered Tiahuana to make the necessary arrangements to have himself taught without delay.

But although for the first few miles of the journey the young Inca suffered from a certain feeling of constraint, he did not allow it to trouble him long, for if conversation lagged there was plenty apart from it to interest and delight him. There was his horse, for instance. Harry had alway been particularly fond of horses, and was an excellent rider; as a boy, indeed, he had often followed the staghounds over Dartmoor. He therefore had a very fair idea of what a horse ought to be; but he had not been in the saddle more than five minutes, on this particular morning, before he realised that at length he had come into possession of that rarest of all good things, a perfect horse; perfect in temper, shape, and action, full of fire and courage, yet with a mouth so sensitive that it would be quite possible to control him with a thread for a bridle, while one had but to glance at the great; hard muscles sliding so smoothly beneath the satin skin to be assured of his indomitable endurance and insensibility to fatigue. Then there was plenty to interest and occupy his attention as they swept along the great, smooth road at a hand gallop. First of all, there was the road itself, which was, in its way, a masterpiece of engineering; but, apart from that, Harry could not but marvel at the perfect cleanliness of it, until he learned that it had been traversed throughout the entire length of the route by a whole army of sweepers during the early hours of the morning, since when no living thing had been allowed upon it. Then there was the noble and endless avenue of shade trees which bordered the road on either hand, dividing it from the wide footpaths, which in their turn were shaded by less lofty trees, fruit-bearing for the most part, the fruit being intended for the refreshment of the wayfarer. Then there were neat, orderly, and perfectly cultivated fields of sugar cane, maize, tobacco, indigo, cotton, rice, coca trees, cacao, and other tropical products on the flats immediately adjoining the road, while farther back, toward the hills, were grain of all sorts, interspersed with vast orchards and, at intervals, a stretch of pasture land, with low, squat farmhouses and outbuildings dotted about in the midst. The farmers and their helpers were all busily engaged upon various kinds of labour in their fields, but those who were near enough to the roads to do so no sooner heard the distant hoof-beats of the approaching cavalcade, and beheld the royal banner flaunting its blue and gold in the wind, than they flung down their implements and rushed helter-skelter to the roadside to watch the Inca go by, and acclaim him as he passed.

But with every mile of that exhilarating ride towards the City of the Sun the aspect of the landscape became subtly modified; the farms became more extensive, the farmhouses larger and more elaborate in their style of architecture, ornamental and decorative features became increasingly conspicuous in every building encountered, until finally the aspect became distinctly suburban, the farmhouses gave place to country residences, the farms gradually merged into pleasure gardens, gay with flowers and rich in carefully-cultivated fruit trees; the houses drew closer together, and little groups of people in gala attire were encountered, gradually increasing in numbers until the footpaths on either hand were lined with joyous crowds of cheering people.

Then the white buildings of the city itself swung into view, gleaming like alabaster between the boles of the bordering trees, with here and there a flash of sunlight from the golden roofs of the principal buildings; and finally a great archway, pierced through the lofty and massive wall that enclosed the city, came into view, spanning the road, and at the same moment a great blare of horns stifled the sound of trampling hoof-beats, the jingle of accoutrements, and the frantic shouts of the cheering multitude. Then Umu flung his flashing sword-blade aloft and shouted a word of command, whereupon the panting, sweating horses were pulled into a walking pace, the riders straightened themselves in their saddles, the band of musicians which led the way struck up a weird, barbaric air, the great bronze gates, which had been closed, were flung open, and the cavalcade passed through into the principal street of the City of the Sun. If Escombe had been questioned ten minutes earlier he would, in reply, have expressed the confident opinion that every man, woman, and child had left the city in order to line the road outside the gates by which it was known that he must pass; but he had no sooner traversed the echoing archway in the immensely thick city wall than he saw how greatly mistaken such an opinion would have been. For, starting from the very wall itself, the pavement on either hand, all along the line of route, was simply packed with people—the children in front, the women next, and the men in the rear—frantic with enthusiasm, and shouting themselves hoarse in their eagerness to afford an adequate welcome to the Inca whose coming had been looked forward to by them and their ancestors for more than three hundred years. But they did not confine their demonstrations of welcome to mere acclamations. At frequent intervals triumphal arches of an elaborate character and of great beauty, decorated with banners and flags, and profusely wreathed with flowers, were thrown across the roadway, each being connected with the next by a line of poles, painted blue, surmounted by a banner or flag, twined with flowers, and supporting a heavy festoon of flowers which formed an unbroken floral chain from one triumphal arch to the next. The houses on either hand were also decorated with flowers, banners, and long streamers of many-tinted cloths hung from the eaves and windows, the whole scene strongly reminding the young Englishman of the aspect of London's streets on the occasion of our own gracious King's coronation. But what impressed Escombe more than anything else was the fact that all along the line of route children and young girls, provided with large baskets of flowers, were stationed, and, as the procession approached, these young people stepped forward and strewed the road with the contents of their baskets, thus carpeting the hard pavement with freshly gathered flowers, which exhaled a delightful fragrance as they were trampled under foot by the horses.

The young monarch, bowing right and left in response to the enthusiastic greetings of his subjects, now had an opportunity to observe a few of the more striking characteristics of the people among whom he had been thrown in so extraordinary a fashion, and he was considerably surprised to see how widely the different types varied. The lower orders—or what he deemed to be such, from the fact that they were compelled to take as their viewpoint the pavement of the open street—were, as a rule, of merely medium stature, sturdily built, and not particularly intellectual in expression, while the colour of their skin was something very nearly approaching to ruddy copper, very few even of their womenkind having any pretentions to comeliness, to say nothing of beauty. The occupants of the buildings, however, who viewed the procession from their windows or the flat roofs of their houses, and who might be taken to represent a somewhat better class, were not only lighter in colour and more intelligent in expression, but some of them were distinctly good-looking. And, as a general rule, the larger and more important the building—and presumably, therefore, the higher the rank of the owner—the more strongly marked was the difference, which at length, in the case of the nobles, became so accentuated that they might very easily have been taken to be members of a distinct race, the men being much fairer of complexion, of greater stature, and more finely proportioned, as well as much more intellectual in appearance than their humbler brethren; while the women of the higher classes and nobility were in many cases as fair and as lovely as, say, Spanish or Italian women.

Winding its way slowly through some two miles of wide and handsome streets, the buildings in which became ever more imposing as it advanced, the cavalcade at length arrived before a very large building of two stories in height—as against the single story which appeared to be the vogue in the City of the Sun—planned to form three sides of a square, and standing in the midst of a magnificent garden of some thirty acres in extent, which Escombe rightly judged to be the royal palace. It was not a particularly handsome structure—indeed, the builders of the city seemed to be singularly devoid of architectural taste as it is understood elsewhere—but it was imposing on account of its size and solidity, and the bold and massive character of such ornamentation as it displayed. Contrary to the usual custom, which appeared to favour white marble as a building material, the palace was built throughout of massive blocks of greyish-green granite, so accurately joined together that the joints were almost indistinguishable. It stood upon a solid base of much darker granite, some six feet high, and access to its interior was gained by means of a very wide flight of eighteen steps, each about four inches high and some eighteen inches wide from back to front. The door and window openings were surrounded by broad bands or frames of granite projecting some six inches beyond the general face of the walls, and in these bands were set several large, elaborately sculptured medallions, which had all the appearance of—and, as a matter of fact, actually were—solid gold. And all round the building, between the upper and lower tier of windows, ran a flat band, or string course, of solid gold, about two feet in depth, upon which a graceful pattern of scroll-work was boldly chased. Finally, above the upper row of windows, in the place usually occupied by a cornice in European buildings, there was a massive bull-nose moulding, quite three feet deep, also of solid gold, surmounted by the parapet which guarded the flat roof of the building. The façade of the building was the middle of the three sides, and faced toward the road, while the two wings ran from it at right angles back toward the lake.

So much Escombe was able to note with regard to his new home, as the cavalcade swung in through the magnificent gates of wrought copper which gave access to the grounds, and made its way up a wide path or drive to the main entrance, before which it halted. In an instant the two nobles who had held his horse for him while he mounted some hours earlier were again at the animal's head, and Harry swung himself somewhat stiffly out of the saddle; for the ride had been a long and hot one, and it was now a full fortnight since he had last been on horseback. As his foot touched the ground the band of his bodyguard again struck up the national anthem, and every officer and man raised his sword in salute, after which, as Harry ascended the steps and passed through the wide doorway of the palace, Umu shouted a command, the swords flashed in the glaring afternoon sunshine as they were returned to their scabbards, and the weary horses and their riders trotted soberly off to the cavalry stables. The nobles who had accompanied Harry on his ride, and also Tiahuana, entered the palace with the young Inca, doing the honours of the building, and indicating the character of the various apartments which they passed as they conducted him to a superb bathroom, where they assisted him to disrobe, and where he enjoyed a most welcome "tub" in tepid water, made additionally refreshing by the mingling with it of a certain liquid which imparted to it a most exquisite fragrance. Then, attired in a fresh costume, they conducted him to a small but very handsome room, the chairs and tables in which were made of solid silver, where, waited on by a small army of servants in the royal livery, he partook of a light meal. Tiahuana, who, at Harry's special invitation, joined him at the repast, explaining that there was still much to be done that day, since in little more than an hour a solemn service of thanksgiving was to be held in the great Temple of the Sun to commemorate the return of the great Manco to his long-expectant people, and to inaugurate suitably the commencement of a new and glorious era in that people's history.

Chapter Twelve
Huanacocha is unconvinced

The meal over, it became necessary for Escombe to effect another change of attire, the simple garb that he had assumed upon emerging from the bath being discarded in favour of certain gorgeous garments that had been especially prepared for the solemn service in the great Temple of the Sun. There was only one item in this costume which Harry had worn before, and that was the borla or tasselled fringe of scarlet round the temples, which proclaimed his royal rank. On this occasion also, the ceremony in which he was about to take part being a strictly religious one, he wore no weapons. The great Temple of the Sun being the most important building in the city, not even excepting the royal palace, was built on the crest of a hill which dominated the entire city, and was situated about a mile from the palace; the journey thither, therefore, afforded opportunity for another royal procession, in which Harry was to figure in a sort of litter borne aloft on the shoulders of eight men. This litter consisted of a platform covered with a magnificent carpet woven in a pattern composed of many rich colours, and supported by two pairs of shafts made of some tough, springy wood, the end of each shaft being attached to a kind of yoke which rested upon the shoulders of two of the bearers. Upon the platform, which was carried shoulder-high, was mounted a throne, the woodwork of which was entirely enclosed in gold plates, richly wrought and thickly studded with emeralds; and, seated on this throne and surrounded by an escort of some five hundred foot soldiers gorgeously attired and armed with bows, spears, and maces with heavy spiked heads, the young Inca presently found himself being borne at a rapid trot through another wide and handsome street, which, judging from the character of the buildings bordering it, evidently formed the aristocratic quarter of the town. This street, like those which he had already passed through, was lined on both sides by gaily attired people of both sexes and all ages, who rent the air with their enthusiastic acclamations as the cortege swept past them, the only difference being that the majority at least of these folk were, like himself, hurrying in the direction of the temple.

It was with a somewhat abstracted air that Harry acknowledged the salutations of these people, for, truth to tell, his mind and his conscience were being rather severely exercised upon the subject of the function in which he was about to take part. The one great outstanding fact in relation to it was that it was a pagan rite; and he felt that, regarded from an abstract point of view, it was distinctly wrong for him, a professed Christian, to countenance or abet idolatry in any form. Yet he had not been all those months in Peru without having acquired a certain elementary knowledge of the early history of the country, much of which, by the way, had been gained through his conversations with Arima long before that individual had so much as dreamed of the brilliant destiny that awaited his pleasant-mannered young English master. Thus, for instance, he knew that the Peruvian Indians recognised the existence of a Supreme Being, the Creator and Ruler of the Universe, whom they sometimes named Pachacamac, and at others Viracocha; and he also knew that the attributes of this Being were believed to be of so superlatively divine a character that the simple Indians had never dared to rear more than one temple in his honour, which had long since been destroyed. He was aware also that the Inca was not only an absolute monarch, an autocrat invested with greater powers than any other earthly monarch, but that he was implicitly believed to be of divine origin, and that some of the attributes of divinity still clung to him; he was therefore not only a monarch who wielded absolute power, and whose will was law, but he was also the head of the priesthood. Taking these two facts in conjunction, Escombe, with the extreme assurance of youth, and perhaps not attaching quite enough importance to the fact that the sun was the deity whose worship had been especially inculcated and carefully handed down from generation to generation, thought, as he considered the matter, that he could see his way first to divert the adoration of his subjects from the sun to Pachacamac, and afterwards to explain that Pachacamac and the God of the Christians were one and the same, thus insensibly leading them from the paths of paganism into those of Christianity. And he resolved to do it. It was a grand ambition, and it spoke well for him that this should be the first definite resolution that he had taken in connection with the tremendous powers with which he had become so strangely invested; for, singularly enough, it had never occurred to him until within the last hour that he would be called upon to take any part in the functions and ceremonies of pagan worship. Moreover, it swept away every one of the scruples that had been worrying him as to whether or not he was justified in being present at the impending function; for he felt that, having come to the above resolution, he was justified in being present, otherwise how could he offer any suggestions as to a change in the ceremonial?

By the time that he had thought the matter out thus far, and had arrived at the conclusion that he believed he could see his way pretty clearly before him, he had reached the great open space, in the centre of which stood the temple, and he had time only to run his eye hastily over the enormous building and gather in a general idea of its aspect before his litter was deposited at the foot of the magnificent flight of forty-five broad, shallow steps which ran all round the building, and which gave access to the spacious platform upon which the edifice was raised.

As Harry leisurely dismounted from the litter his escort ran nimbly up the steps and arranged itself—four deep on each step, and the remainder on the platform above—into a wide avenue of spearmen to keep back the crowds that thronged the steps, and thus afford the young Inca a clear space in which to accomplish the ascent to the great main doorway of the building. At the same moment Tiahuana, gorgeously attired in a long flowing robe of white that was stiff with the heavy gold embroidery which almost covered it, with a mitre-like headdress, similarly embroidered, on his head, and a gold wand surmounted by a golden image of the sun in his right hand, emerged from the doorway, followed by apparently the entire staff of the priesthood, and stood at the head of the long flight of steps to receive the Inca.

Contrary to his expectation, instead of being conducted directly into the main body of the building, Escombe, surrounded by fully a hundred priests, was led by Tiahuana into an anteroom, where he found assembled the Council of Seven, under the leadership of one Huanacocha—who, Tiahuana whisperingly mentioned, was the chief and most powerful noble of the entire nation—and some five hundred other nobles, to whom he was now to be presented, and who were thus to be afforded an opportunity of thoroughly satisfying themselves before matters were allowed to proceed any further, that the young man was indeed the re-incarnated Manco, for whose return to earth the nation had been looking forward for over three hundred years.

Upon entering this anteroom Escombe found himself upon a dais occupying one end of, and reaching across the entire width of the apartment. In the centre of the dais, but close up to the front of it, was a throne of solid silver, with a footstool before it, and upon this throne Harry was directed by Tiahuana to seat himself, the body of priests immediately arranging themselves behind and on either side of it. Before him, and on the main floor of the room, which was some eighteen inches below the level of the dais, were arranged several rows of benches upon which the nobles were seated, the Council of Seven, which had governed in the absence of an Inca, with Huanacocha occupying the middle place, being seated on the front bench, or that nearest the dais.

The little stir which had been occasioned by the entrance of Harry and the priests having subsided, Arima—to Escombe's amazement—was mysteriously produced by Tiahuana and led forward to the front of the dais, from which standpoint he was ordered to relate the circumstances under which he first came into contact with the young Englishman; how his suspicions as to the identity of his employer with the expected Inca were first aroused; what steps he took to verify those suspicions, and how he proceeded after those suspicions were confirmed; all of which he told in the Quichua language, not only with a total absence of embarrassment, but with a certain undertone of pride and exultation running through his narrative; for he felt that, as the first discoverer of the returned Manco, he was a person of very great consequence. Then Harry was requested to state where and in what manner he came into possession of the long-lost emerald collar of Manco Capac, which he did in Spanish, Tiahuana afterwards interpreting his brief statement into Quichua. Then came Tiahuana's own turn. He began by reminding his hearers of the terrible happenings of that dreadful day when Atahuallpa, deceived by the treacherous Spaniards, unsuspectingly entered the city of Caxamalca, only to see his followers ruthlessly slaughtered, and to find himself a captive in the hands of the *Conquistadors*. Then he drew a graphic word picture of that still more awful night when Atahuallpa, chained hand and foot, was led out into the great square of the city and ignominiously strangled by his unscrupulous and bloodthirsty betrayers. Warming to his subject, he next very briefly sketched the untoward fate of the Inca Manco, son of Huayna Capac, whom the Spaniards had installed, as their tool and puppet, on the throne vacated by the murder of Atahuallpa; and he concluded this portion of his address by briefly reminding his hearers of the sudden and dramatic appearance of the prophet-priest Titucocha on the night of Atahuallpa's murder, and of the prophecy then uttered by him, which Tiahuana repeated word for word. Then, gathering fresh energy and fire as he proceeded, the High Priest told how, after waiting impatiently all his life long for the reappearance of the great Manco, foretold by Titucocha, until he had begun to despair of living to see that happy day, he had been suddenly startled into new life and hope by the arrival of Arima in the city with the glad news that the divine Manco had actually returned to earth and was even then among the mountains of his beloved Peru. He reminded them of how he, Tiahuana, had conducted Arima into the presence of the Council of Seven and caused him to relate his story to them; of the scepticism with which that story had been received, of the difficulty which he had encountered in persuading the Council that it was their duty to permit him, as High Priest, to sift the story and ascertain how far it was true; and how, having at length secured their somewhat reluctant consent, he had triumphantly accomplished his mission and now had the duty and pleasure to present them to the divine Manco, promised of Heaven as the deliverer and restorer of the Peruvian nation.

"But how are we to be assured beyond all possibility of doubt that this young man is in very deed the reincarnated Manco, whose return was foretold by the prophet Titucocha, and for whom the nation has looked these three hundred years and more?" demanded Huanacocha, the head of the Council of Seven. "He is a white man to begin with; and for my part it has always been in my mind that when the divine Manco should deign to return to us, he would come in the form of a full-blooded Peruvian Indian, even as we are."

A low murmur of concurrence and approval filled the room at these bold words of Huanacocha, and every eye was at once turned upon Tiahuana to see what reply he would give to this apparently unanswerable objection.

"Why should you suppose any such thing?" demanded Tiahuana in a cold, level voice. "There is no word in Titucocha's prophecy, as handed down to us in our records, to justify any such belief. I am prepared to admit, if you like, that such an expectation was natural, but further than that I cannot go. Nay, rather let me say that, taking into consideration the careful minuteness with which Titucocha particularised the several means of identification — every one of which has been literally fulfilled in him whom you now see before you — I am convinced that if our Lord the Sun had intended that his child should return to us as an Indian, born of us and among us, Titucocha would have specifically said so. But, as I have already reminded you, he did not. What he said was that the re-incarnated Manco was to be the deliverer and restorer of the ancient Peruvian nation; and who so fit to undertake and successfully carry through this stupendous task as one born, and who has lived all his life in England, that great nation of which we have all heard, whose empire extends north and south, east and west, to the uttermost parts of the earth, so that it has been said of her that she is the empire upon which the sun never sets. My Lords, I, who am full of years and of the wisdom that comes with many years, tell you that if ever we are to free ourselves from the yoke of the oppressor, and to restore Peru to its ancient position of power and glory, we must be helped and guided in that great, that almost impossible task, by one who unites within himself superlative wisdom and superlative courage; and the crowning proof, to my mind, that heaven has now at last fulfilled its glorious promise is to be found in the fact that it has ordained our new Inca to be born an Englishman, possessed of all that courage, that wisdom, and that knowledge for which Englishmen are famed throughout the world. I have spoken! And now, I pray you, come forward every one of you, from the first unto the last, and see with your own eyes the final proof that the great Manco has indeed returned to us. Thus far you have merely been called upon to believe the testimony of Arima and myself; but now it is for you to look with your own eyes upon the collar which this young man wears, and to say whether in very truth it is or is not the emerald collar of the divine Manco, of which we have so perfect and complete a description, and by the wearing of which he was to be recognised in his re-incarnated form."

As Tiahuana ceased speaking, another low murmur ran round the assembly, but whether of approval or of dissent it was not easy to judge. Then Huanacocha, as chief of the Council of Seven, arose, and, stepping forward to the dais, took in his hand the emerald collar that Tiahuana handed to him—having removed it from Harry's neck for the purposes of inspection—and examined it with the most scrupulous care. He was about to return it to Tiahuana when the latter said:

"Has my Lord Huanacocha compared the features delineated on the pendant with those of him whom I am offering to the nation as its long-looked-for deliverer?"

Huanacocha had not, it seemed, for, taking the pendant in his hand, he studied it intently, and then gazed long and steadily at Harry's features.

"I admit that there certainly is some resemblance," he said coldly, as he handed back the jewel.

Then, one after the other, the remaining members of the assembly came forward one by one, scrutinised the jewel with more or less deliberation, and returned to their seats, until every one in the room had obeyed Tiahuana's summons. Then the High Priest stepped forward to the edge of the dais, and said:

"Nobles of the ancient Peruvian blood-royal, I have now submitted to you the last piece of evidence upon which I base my contention that the young man whom I have brought into your midst—and of whose existence we became aware through a sequence of events that can only be described as miraculous—is in very truth he for whose appearance we and our forefathers have been anxiously looking during a period of more than three hundred years. You are all perfectly acquainted with the words of the prophecy which foretold his appearance; for so important, so vital to the interests of the nation, were those words regarded that it has been our rule throughout the ages to teach them to every child until that child can repeat them by heart. You are therefore perfectly cognisant of all the signs and tokens of identification by which the re-incarnated Manco was to be recognised when in the fulness of time he should again come to us, to execute his great mission of our regeneration. It now rests with you to decide whether those signs and tokens have been fulfilled in the case of this young man so clearly and unmistakably as to justify our acceptance of him as the being whom I claim him to be. Although it is perhaps hardly necessary for me to do so, it is my duty to remind you that never in the history of our nation have the Peruvian nobility been called upon to decide a more momentous question. I now ask you to rise in your places, one by one, beginning with my Lord Huanacocha, and say whether or not you are satisfied that this young man is in very truth the divine Manco returned to earth."

A very perceptible pause followed this appeal, and then Huanacocha rose to his feet.

"Before replying to your question, my Lord Tiahuana," said he, "I should like the young man to tell us what he can remember of his former existence. The history of Manco Capac, our first Inca and the founder of our nation, is well known to all of us, and if your claim be indeed justified there must be many incidents in his career, well known to us but quite unknown to the outer world, which the claimant can recall. Let him mention a few of those incidents, and the most doubting among us will be satisfied."

This speech was delivered in the Quichua language, and it was necessary for Tiahuana to translate to Harry, who at once replied:

"I have already told you, I believe, that I have no recollection whatever of any former state of existence."

"My Lords," said Tiahuana, "the young man asserts, with perfect candour, that he has no recollection whatever of any former state of existence; therefore he is unable to furnish those further proofs demanded by the Lord Huanacocha. But what of that? Does this absence of recollection invalidate all the other proofs that have been given? How many of us remember any of our former states of existence distinctly enough to recall any of their happenings? I confess that I do not. Does my Lord Huanacocha, or do any of you?"

A long and profound silence followed this pointed question. So prolonged, indeed, was it that it at length became evident that no one in that assembly had a reply to it; whereupon Tiahuana, his eyes gleaming with triumph, once more stepped forward and said:

"My Lords, your silence is a complete and sufficient answer to my question, and proves that the objection raised by my Lord Huanacocha was an unreasonable one. I must therefore again call upon him to say whether he is or is not satisfied with the other proofs advanced."

There was no pause or hesitation this time; Huanacocha at once rose and said:

"I have no fault to find with the other proofs; but I contend that they do not go far enough. I am still strongly of opinion that when the divine Manco returns to us he will come in the guise of one of ourselves, an Indian of the blood-royal; and therefore I must refuse to accept the dictum of my Lord Tiahuana that the young white man is the re-incarnation of the first Manco, the founder of our nation." And he resumed his seat.

This bold and defiant speech created, as might be expected, a most tremendous sensation among the other occupants of the hall; but Tiahuana, with a slight gesture of impatience, at once threw up his hand to demand silence, and said:

"You have all heard the objections raised by my Lord Huanacocha, and are as well able as I am to weigh and judge their value. Let now the other lords arise, each in his turn, and express his opinion."

The man on Huanacocha's right at once arose, and said:

"I am quite satisfied with the proofs adduced by the High Priest. To me they are complete and perfectly convincing."

The man on the left of Huanacocha then sprang to his feet and said:

"I find it quite impossible to come to a definite decision, one way or the other. On the one hand, I regard the proofs adduced by my Lord Tiahuana as perfectly satisfactory; but on the other I think there is reason in the objection raised by my Lord Huanacocha that the aspirant is a white man. Notwithstanding what has been said by the High Priest, my conviction is that the true Manco, when he appears, will be born among us and be one of ourselves. I am unconvinced."

Thus the expression of opinion went on until all had given one, when it appeared that Huanacocha had four adherents to his views, the remainder of the nobles being quite unanimous in their conviction that Harry was in very deed the re-incarnation of the first Manco. He was therefore accepted by an overwhelming majority, as Tiahuana had confidently anticipated; and the discomfited Huanacocha and his friends were compelled to waive their objections, which, after recording them, they did with a somewhat better grace than might have been expected.

Then came the ceremony of swearing allegiance to the new sovereign, which was done by every individual present, beginning with Tiahuana, who was followed by Motahuana and the entire body of the priests, who, in their turn, were succeeded by the nobles, beginning with Huanacocha.

By the time that this ceremony was concluded the afternoon was well advanced and it was time to repair to the main body of the temple, where the service of thanksgiving was to be held; and in consideration of the fact that Harry was a stranger, and of course completely ignorant of the religious ritual followed by the worshippers of the Sun, Motahuana was told off to accompany and prompt him. Accordingly, led by the deputy High Priest, the young monarch, followed by the nobles, passed down a long corridor and, wheeling to the left, passed through an enormous archway veiled by great gold-embroidered curtains which, upon being drawn aside at their approach, revealed the whole of the vast interior of the temple proper in which the ceremony was to be held.

When, an hour or two earlier, the young Inca—whose official name was now Manco Capac—had approached the enormous building in which he now found himself, he had promptly come to the conclusion that the edifice owed little or nothing of its imposing character to the skill of the architect; for, so far as architectural beauty was concerned, it was almost as plain and unpretentious as his own palace: it was imposing merely because of its immense dimensions. It consisted of a huge rectangular block of pure white marble, the walls of which were from eight to ten feet thick, without columns, or pediment, or even so much as a few pilasters to break up the monotonous smoothness and regularity of its exterior surface, the only aids in this direction being the great east doorway, or main entrance, which was some thirty feet wide by about sixty feet high, with an immense window opening on either side of it, through which and the doorway entered all the light which illuminated the interior. True, the doorway and window openings were each surrounded by heavy marble borders, or frames, encrusted with great plates of gold elaborately ornamented with a boldly sculptured design. There was also a heavy gold string course and bull-nose moulding similar to that on the palace; but, apart from that and the gold-tiled roof, there was no attempt at exterior decorative effect. Whatever might have been deemed lacking in this direction, however, was more than compensated for by the barbaric splendour and profusion of the interior decorations. The entire west wall of the building was covered with a solid plate of burnished gold emblazoned with a gigantic face from which emanated rays innumerable, representing the sun, the great eyes being reproduced in a perfect blaze of gems; precious stones of all kinds being thickly powdered also all over the plate, which was primarily intended to receive the rays of the rising sun through the great east door in the early morning—at which hour the most impressive ceremony of the day was celebrated—and reflect the light back upon the people. The two side walls were also decorated with great gold plates, about two feet square, richly engraved, and arranged in a chequer pattern, a square of gold alternating with a square of the white marble wall of the building from top to bottom and from end to end, each of the white marble squares having in its centre a gold ornament about the size of one's hand which formed a mount for a precious stone, rubies and emeralds being the most numerous, although diamonds of considerable size gleamed here and there. Had the stones been cut and polished, instead of being set in the rough, the effect would have been gorgeous beyond description. Perhaps the most wonderful part of the whole building, however, was the ceiling. This was composed entirely of white marble slabs supported and divided into panels by great beams of solid marble made up of enormous blocks of the stone the ends of which were so cunningly "scarphed", or fitted together, that the joints were invisible and gripped each other so tightly that neither cement nor bolts were needed to complete the union. And in the centre of each panel of the ceiling, and at each crossing of the beams, was a great golden ornament bearing some resemblance to a full-blown rose. The western wall of the building was decorated like the two side walls, save that in place of the bare marble a silver square alternated with a gold one. And, finally, the great doors in the western wall were of solid silver wrought to represent timber, the grain and knots of the wood being imitated with marvellous fidelity, while the nails were represented in gold.

Chapter Thirteen
The Daughter of Umu

Piloted by Motahuana, Harry presently found himself installed in a marble throne raised on a dais at the western extremity of the building, behind the altars—of which there were three—and facing them and the vast assembly. Immediately on the other side of the altars, and facing them, were the nobles, also occupying marble seats; and a brave show they made in their gala attire, Umu, the captain of the royal bodyguard, in his gorgeous uniform, being a very conspicuous figure among them. And behind the nobles, seated on wooden benches, was the people ranged row after row, until, so vast was the building, the features of those seated near the eastern wall were quite indistinguishable to the young Inca.

The slight stir in that immense assemblage caused by the entrance of the monarch and his train of nobles had scarcely subsided when the strains of distant music were heard, rapidly increasing in power and volume as the musicians drew near; and presently, through an archway immediately opposite that by which Escombe had entered, there filed a small army of priests led by Tiahuana, still in his robes and bearing his wand. Some sixty of these were performing on a variety of wind and string instruments more or less remotely suggestive of those known to civilised nations, while the remainder chanted to their accompaniment a quaint but by no means unpleasing melody, the air of which was quite distinctly suggestive of rejoicing. The words of the song—or hymn, rather—were Quichua, and Escombe was therefore unable to gather the sense of them. In the midst of the priests walked a band of some twenty youths attired in richly embroidered white tunics of soft woollen material, girt about the waist with a gold-embroidered belt; and each youth bore in his arms a mass of beautiful flowers, the delicate perfume of which quickly diffused itself throughout the building. Priests and youths were alike barefooted; and a more careful scrutiny soon revealed to Harry the fact that he was the only individual in the building—so far as he could see—who remained shod.

Led by the instrumentalists, the procession wheeled to the right and passed slowly down the first aisle of the building to its eastern extremity, then right across it, past the great eastern door, up the fourth aisle, down the third, and up the second, which brought them finally to the altar which stood on the right of the main or high altar, as looked at from Escombe's point of view. Then, while the priests continued their chanting, the flower-laden youths piled their fragrant burdens upon the right-hand altar and twined them about it until it was completely hidden from view by the vari-coloured blooms and their delicate foliage. This done, the youths retired, and the High Priest—or Villac Vmu, as he was called—standing before the flower-draped altar, with his back to the people, uttered what appeared to be a short invocation or prayer, during which the worshippers all knelt upon the beautifully tessellated marble pavement. This prayer lasted three or four minutes, and upon its conclusion the people rose and resumed their seats; while Tiahuana, turning and facing them, delivered an address of some twenty minutes' length, after which another hymn was sung by both priests and people, the former slowly filing out of the building during the singing, and so timing their movements that as the last note was sung the last priest disappeared through the arch, and the curtain fell behind him.

Harry not unnaturally concluded that this ended the ceremonial; but he was quickly undeceived by Motahuana, who informed him that one, if not two, burnt sacrifices yet remained to be offered. And indeed, scarcely had this piece of information been conveyed when the music and singing again made themselves heard, and the priests filed into the building once more. But, instead of the band of flower-bearing youths, there appeared a llama, decked with garlands and wreaths of flowers, and led by two young priests. This time the order of procedure was reversed, the procession crossing over to the fourth aisle, passing down it and up the first, down the second, and up the third, which finally brought them opposite the second subsidiary altar, to a golden ring in which the llama was now tethered, the processional hymn lasting long enough to allow this operation to be completed. Then followed another prayer, succeeded by another address, during which the unfortunate llama was bound and trussed up so ingeniously that the unhappy creature was rendered incapable of making the least struggle. Then a number of priests seized the helpless animal and laid it upon the top of the altar, upon which meanwhile a great pile of cedar boughs and other scented wood had been carefully piled. This done, two priests strode forward, one bearing a very formidable-looking copper knife, while the other carried a large and most beautifully wrought basin of solid gold. Seizing the llama by the ears and dragging its head back, the first of these two priests raised his knife on high. There was a yellow flash as the keen and heavy blade descended upon the animal's throat, and the next instant the llama's lifeblood was pouring and smoking into the basin which the second priest held to receive it. And so dexterously was the whole thing done that not a single drop of blood stained the white garment of either priest; had it been otherwise, it would have been regarded as an unfavourable omen.

The moment that the blood ceased to flow, the thongs which confined the poor beast's limbs to its body were released, the carcass was turned upon its back, the belly was ripped open, and the Villac Vmu stepped forward and carefully examined the entrails, during which the people appeared to be held in a state of the most painfully breathless suspense. This, however, was happily not prolonged, for it lasted only a few seconds when Tiahuana, stepping forward and facing the assembly, threw up his hands and shouted:

"Blessed be our Father the Sun, the omens are all exceptionally, marvellously, favourable, and our sovereign Lord the Inca is assured of a long and prosperous reign, during which he will be permitted to accomplish all that was prophesied concerning him."

Instantly the priests burst into a loud paean of praise, which was promptly taken up by the entire people, standing, during the singing of which a priest appeared, bearing a torch kindled at the sacred fire, which was kept alight throughout the year. This torch he presented to Harry, who, at Motahuana's prompting, and with several qualms of conscience, rose to his feet and thrust it in among the pile of wood on the top of the altar, beneath the body of the llama. The crackling of the dry twigs that formed the substructure of the cunningly arranged pile, and the curling wreaths of fragrant smoke, soon showed that the wood was fairly alight; and as the little tongues of yellow flame leapt from twig to twig and gathered power, and the smoke shot upward from the altar in a thin perfectly straight column to the ceiling, the great building fairly resounded with the shouts of jubilation of the enormous congregation, for this was the last and most important omen of all. If the smoke column had bent or wavered in the least it would have foretold trouble—ay, or even disaster, had the wavering been sufficiently pronounced. But, on the contrary, every omen, from first to last, had been of so exceptionally favourable a character that the special sacrifice of thank-offering that was always tentatively arranged for upon such occasions as the present became a foregone conclusion, and the assembly, instead of dispersing, as they would have done had the omens been less eminently favourable, settled again into their seats with a great sigh and shudder of tense expectancy; for this would be the first time that many of them had ever been present at a ceremony of the kind that was now pending.

Escombe, who was by this time beginning to feel very tired, as well as distinctly dissatisfied with himself for taking part in all this mummery, noticed vaguely that something out of the common was evidently toward, but he was too thoroughly distrait to even seek an explanation from

Motahuana, and he watched, as in a dream, the long procession of priests file out of the building to the accompaniment of an unmistakable song of triumph. Presently, with more singing and music, they came filing back again; but in the comparatively brief interval of their absence they had contrived to effect a complete change in their appearance, for, instead of the white garments which they had previously worn, they were now robed in crimson, heavily bordered with gold embroidery, while Tiahuana's robe was so completely covered with gold embroidery, encrusted with gems, that it was as stiff as a board, the crimson colour of the material scarcely showing through it. He still bore his wand in his hands, and the mitre which he now wore blazed with gold and precious stones. On this occasion, instead of leading the procession, he was preceded by a priest, scarcely less gorgeously robed than himself, who held aloft a beautiful banner of crimson cloth emblazoned with the figure of the Sun. Other banners, equally rich and beautiful, about twenty in all, were borne by the main body of the priests.

But no sooner was the procession—singing a peculiarly sweet and plaintive air—fairly inside the body of the temple than Escombe aroused himself with a violent start, for walking in the midst of the priests, attired in a simple white robe, from the hem of which her little bare feet peeped as she walked with downcast eyes, and wreathed and garlanded about with a long chain of magnificent crimson roses, and with her hands bound behind her, there walked the most lovely maiden that the young man had ever seen. Although there was little doubt that she was of pure Indian blood, she was as fair as a Spaniard, but without a vestige of colour—as might well be expected under the circumstances. Her long, dark hair, unbound, clustered in wavy ringlets upon her shoulders and far enough below her waist to completely veil her tied hands. Every eye in the building was instantly turned upon this fair vision as the congregation rose *en masse*, and a loud gasp of what sounded very much like dismay drew Escombe's attention to Umu, who distinctly staggered as he rose to his feet, while his face went a sickly, yellowish-white, and the perspiration poured from his forehead like rain. The poor fellow stared at the girl as though he could scarcely believe his eyes; yet that he did believe them was perfectly evident, while the anguished expression of his countenance made it equally evident that he was very deeply interested in the young lady and her fate. As to what that fate was to be there could be no shadow of doubt, even in the mind of one so ignorant of the details of the religious ceremonial of the Peruvians as was its new monarch. The girl's awful pallor, her very presence in the procession, and the fact of her being garlanded with flowers, each had its own significance, and pointed indubitably to the fact that she was the destined victim in a human sacrifice!

Turning to Motahuana, Harry demanded, in a fierce whisper:

"Who is that girl, and why is she taking part in the procession?" To which Motahuana replied:

"She is Maia, the daughter of Umu, captain of my Lord's bodyguard; and, as the most beautiful maiden in the city, she has been chosen by the Villac Vmu as worthy the great honour of being offered in sacrifice upon the altar of thanksgiving on this most memorable and auspicious occasion. It is a great surprise to Umu, of course, to see his only daughter occupying her present proud position, for by the order of Tiahuana she was taken from her father's house within an hour of his departure to meet my Lord and escort him to the city; and his duties have probably not permitted him to visit his home since his return, hence the sight of his daughter in the procession is the first intimation which he has received of the honour conferred upon her—and him."

The utter indifference to the anguish of those chiefly concerned which Motahuana betrayed in this speech made Escombe fairly writhe with disgust and abhorrence, which feelings were increased a hundredfold by the knowledge that this young maiden was to be forced to lay down her life, and her parent's home was to be made desolate, in order that his—Harry Escombe's—accession to the throne of the Incas might be fitly celebrated! He ground his teeth in impotent fury, and unrestrainedly execrated the stupendous folly which had induced him to enter so light-heartedly into an adventure fraught with elements of such unimaginable horror. True, he had done so with the very best intentions; yes, but how often, even in his comparatively brief experience of life, had he known of actions instigated by "the very best intentions" that had culminated in grim disaster! And now he was adding yet another to the long list!

But stay; was this thing inevitable? He suddenly remembered that many of the good intentions that had determined him to acquiesce passively in the events that had placed him where he now was were based upon the fact that, as Inca, he would be the possessor of absolute power, and would be able to mould events to his will; that, as Inca, he would be superior to everybody, even the priesthood, for the Inca was not only the head of the priesthood but was actually credited with the possession of a certain measure of divinity in his own person. If all this were really true, now was the time to assert his authority and test his power. He would forbid the sacrifice, and see what came of it.

As he arrived at this determination he glanced up, to find Umu's gaze fixed fully upon him, and there was such intensity of unmistakable anguish and entreaty in the gaze that Harry unhesitatingly answered it with a nod and an encouraging smile, which evoked a gasp of almost incredulous joy and relief from its recipient.

The procession had by this time passed down the first aisle and was coming up the second, the paean of triumph and thanksgiving pealing louder and more thrillingly on the ear with every step of its progress. At length it reached the head of the aisle and wheeled to the right with the evident intention of turning into the third aisle, which would have caused it to brush close past the row of benches by which Umu was standing. But a moment before the banner bearer who was leading the procession arrived at the wheeling point, Harry rose from his throne and, standing on his footstool, so that every person in that vast building might see and hear him, flung up his right hand and imperiously called a halt in the proceedings, in response to which the procession came to an abrupt standstill, and the singers and musicians almost as abruptly became silent. Then Harry beckoned Tiahuana to his side, and said:

"Interpret for me; I have a message for the people."

Then, as Tiahuana gazed aghast and speechless at the young man who had resorted to so unheard of a proceeding as to interrupt a ceremony of thanksgiving at its most intensely interesting and dramatic moment, Harry proceeded:

"Children of the ancient Peruvian nation, hearken unto me; for Pachacamac, the Supreme, the Creator and Ruler of the Universe, who made all things, yea even unto the Sun, Moon, and Stars which you adore, each in their several seasons, has this moment put a message into my mouth and bid me deliver it unto you.

"Thus saith Pachacamac, the Great and Only One. 'In the days of old, when the Peruvians were but a few scattered tribes plunged in the depths of ignorance and barbarism, I took pity upon them and sent to them Manco Capac and Mama Oello Huaco, two of my children, to gather together those scattered tribes and form them into communities, to instruct them in the mysteries of my worship, and to teach them the arts whereby they might become a great and civilised nation. And for a time all things went well with the Peruvians, for they listened to the voice of my messengers, and obeyed it, worshipping me and acting in accordance with my commands. Therefore I blessed and prospered them exceedingly, and made of them a glorious and powerful nation, wise in the art of government, and invincible in the field of battle, so that as the years rolled on they conquered all the surrounding tribes and nations and absorbed them into themselves.

"'But with the progress of time my people fell into error. They ceased to worship and honour me, and transferred their adoration to the Sun, which I had made and given unto them as the beneficent source of all their material benefits, from which they derived light and warmth, which caused their streams to flow and their soil to bring forth abundant crops for the sustenance of man and beast, which caused their flocks to increase and multiply greatly, and which is the source of all life, health, and beauty. They gave their gratitude and devotion to that which I had created, and forgot me, the Creator of all things; they built hundreds of temples in honour of the Sun—and one only did they dedicate to me! Therefore was I displeased with them and withdrew from them the light of my countenance. I permitted the *Conquistadors* to land upon their shores and gave them power to triumph over the Peruvians in battle, to destroy Atahuallpa, and to wrest their land from them until, behold, all that is left of that once great nation is this valley and the city that ye have built in it.

"'But my anger burns not for ever, nor will I hide my face from you for all time. Behold, I have given you another Inca, who shall guide your straying feet back into the right path, who shall point out to you the mistakes which you have made and teach you how to correct them. And if ye will obey him it may be that in process of time I will again make you a great and powerful nation, even as you were in the old days ere I hid my face from you and permitted calamity to overtake you.

"'And now, listen, my people, unto this. I have no pleasure in sorrow or suffering; the shedding of blood in sacrifice is an abomination unto me. Therefore do I forbid now and henceforth the sacrifice in burnt offering of any creature that doth breathe the breath of life; for death is a curse that I have sent upon the earth, and not a blessing, as ye shall be taught in due time. Ye may deck my altars with flowers, and make beautiful the houses in which ye worship me, if ye will; but obedience to my laws and precepts is more precious to me than any other thing, and if ye render that unto me ye shall do well.'"

As Harry uttered the last words, and sank back into his seat, it is safe to say that no individual in that great building was more astonished at his behaviour than himself; for he had sprung to his feet without the ghost of a notion of what he meant to say, animated only by the one great and overmastering impulse to save the life of Umu's daughter and rescue a household from a great and terrible grief. But the words had leapt to his lips, and he had spoken as one under the influence of inspiration, without thought, or pause, or hesitation. In the very building devoted to the worship of that object which, ever since Peru became a nation, had been the especial veneration of its inhabitants, he had stood up and boldly denounced the worship of the Sun as idolatry; had told them that their religious beliefs were all wrong, and had unceremoniously broken in upon and put a stop to the most impressive ceremony in their ritual, and had forbidden certain practices hallowed by ages of religious teaching! And now, what was to be the result? Would the priests and the congregation rise up as one man and tear the audacious young innovator limb from limb, or offer him up as a sacrifice on the altar from which he had essayed to snatch its destined victim, to propitiate their outraged deity? The sensation produced on all sides as Tiahuana had translated Escombe's denunciation, sentence by sentence, was tremendous, and grew in intensity as the denunciation proceeded. But whether the emotion excited was that of anger, or of blank astonishment, the young man could not determine; nor, to speak the truth, did he very greatly care, for he felt that he was doing his duty regardless of the possibility of the most ghastly peril to himself. Indeed there are few possibilities more dreadful than those attendant upon the bearding of a multitude of fanatical idolators and the denouncing of the objects of their idolatry. Everything, or almost everything, would depend entirely upon the view which Tiahuana and the priests took of Harry's conduct. If, after that uncompromisingly outspoken attack upon the worship of the Sun—the fundamental principle of their religion—Tiahuana's belief in the theory that Escombe was indeed the re-incarnation of the first Manco, foretold by the prophet Titucocha, remained unshaken, all might yet be well; but if not—!

For some minutes excitement and consternation reigned supreme over that vast assembly, yet there was nothing approaching tumult or disorder in the behaviour of the people; the points raised by the young Inca's message were evidently of such tremendous import that they felt themselves quite unable to deal with them. They recognised, almost from the first moment, that these were matters which must be left in the hands of the priests, and presently the excitement began to die down, and everybody waited to see what would next happen. As for Tiahuana, the denunciation had fallen upon him with such paralysing effect that he had simply translated Escombe's message as nearly word for word as the Quichua language would permit, with the air and aspect of a man speaking under the influence of some fantastically horrible dream. But by the time that the excitement had subsided, and silence again reigned in the great building, he had pulled himself together and, turning to Harry, said:

"Is my Lord quite certain, beyond all possibility of doubt, that the message which he has just delivered has been put into his mouth by Pachacamac, and not by some evil and malignant spirit?"

"Yes," answered Escombe with conviction; "I am. What evil spirit would instruct the Peruvians to worship and adore the Great Pachacamac Himself instead of one of the works of His hands? The very import of the message ought to be convincing testimony of the source from which it comes."

"It may be; it may be; I cannot tell," answered Tiahuana wearily. "If the message comes in very truth from Pachacamac, then have we indeed strayed far from the right path, and much that has troubled and puzzled the wisest heads among us can be accounted for. It would also explain why our forefathers were so blind as to permit the *Conquistadors* to enter their country, and so weak as to be conquered by them! Yes, methinks there are matters of vast moment contained in that message; but they cannot be discussed here and now. Is it my Lord's will that the people be dismissed?"

"Yes," answered Harry, almost breathless with astonishment at the complete success of his intervention. "Tell the people that my appearance among them is the signal for many great and momentous changes decreed by Pachacamac for their advantage, one of the most important of which will be that, henceforth, Pachacamac Himself—the Supreme, the Creator of the Heavens and Earth, and all that are therein, and only He, is to be worshipped in this building. Ye have wandered far astray; but be of good comfort, I— and, later on, others whom Pachacamac will send to you—will point the way of return, and all shall be well with you."

"And the maiden, Lord, who was to have been offered as a thank-offering—what is to be done with her?" demanded Tiahuana.

"Let her be returned with all honour to her home and parent," answered Harry. "Henceforth there are to be no burnt sacrifices, whether human or otherwise."

Then Tiahuana, standing before the central altar, where he could be seen by all, and heard by perhaps about half of the congregation, raising his hand to command the attention of his audience, interpreted Escombe's second message to them, adding the words "Go in peace!" and raising both hands in a gesture of blessing, which he maintained until the last person had passed out through the great eastern door. Meanwhile Maia, the daughter of Umu and the destined victim of the thank-offering, having not only heard but also understood everything that had transpired, had fainted from excess of emotion produced by the revulsion of feeling from that of lofty exaltation to relief and joy at her reprieve from death—even though that death had come, through long usage, to be regarded as more honourable and glorious than anything that this life had to offer—and had been delivered to her father, who had lost not a moment in conveying her back to the shelter of his roof.

"And now, Lord," said Tiahuana, "tell me, I pray you, what is to be done in the matter of conducting the ceremonies in the temple, henceforth; for

Pachacamac's message seems to strike at the very root of our religion, and until I am more fully instructed I know not what to do, or how to proceed."

"Nay," said Harry reassuringly, for he saw that the old man was intensely worried and distressed, "the matter is surely very simple. All that you have to do is to transfer your adoration from the Sun to Pachacamac, offering to him your prayers and praises instead of addressing them to the Sun. Surely it is wiser and more reasonable to worship Him who made all things, than it is to worship one of the things that He has made? Do this, and ye shall do well. And if any doubts should arise in your minds, come to me and I will resolve them. Also I will instruct you from time to time in the truth concerning Pachacamac, until his messengers shall arrive. And now, go in peace; for ye have but to be obedient, and to instruct the people in the truth, even as you yourselves shall be instructed, and all will be well."

Then Harry rose, and, escorted by the nobles, made his way out of the building to the place where his litter and his guard awaited him, whence, mounting into his seat, he was rapidly borne back to the palace amid the enthusiastic acclamations of the populace which lined the streets. But as the bearers trotted smoothly and evenly along the road Escombe detected—or thought that he did—a new note in those acclamations; a note which he could not for the life of him interpret. It was not that the acclamations were less hearty than before. On the contrary, they seemed to be more enthusiastic than ever; yet, mingled with their enthusiasm and joy there seemed to be a certain subtle undertone that thrilled him curiously and caused him to vaguely wonder whether that "message" of his, delivered without forethought on the spur of the moment, would prove to have been a master-stroke of genius—or an irreparable mistake. Anyhow, he had delivered it, and that was the main thing. He had quite determined that he would deliver it at the first fitting and convenient opportunity; he had, therefore, no regrets on that score, and the only thing that worried him was the question whether it had been delivered prematurely; whether, in fact, it would have been more powerful and effective if he had deferred its deliverance until he had taken time to prepare the minds of the people for its reception. But, be the issue what it might, he had accomplished at least one good deed; he had saved a life and given joy to one household in the city, and that was certainly a matter upon which he might unreservedly congratulate himself.

Meditating thus, Harry found himself, he scarcely knew how, back at the palace, where his chamberlain informed him, first, that a grand banquet had been arranged for that same evening, to be given by him to the nobles to celebrate his accession to the throne; and, secondly, that the Lord Umu was in waiting, and craved an audience. Whereupon the young man requested to be conducted to some room in which he could suitably receive the captain of his bodyguard, and directed that functionary to be brought to him.

Flinging himself wearily into the only chair in the room to which he had been conducted, Escombe awaited the arrival of Umu, who was presently ushered into the apartment barefooted, and carrying upon his shoulders a small burden as a badge of his immeasurable inferiority—great and powerful noble though he was—to the Inca. So intense was his emotion upon finding himself in his Lord's presence that, for the moment, he seemed quite incapable of speech; and, to help him out of his difficulty, whatever it might be, Harry extended his hand to him and said:

"Well, Umu, my friend, what is it? Are you in trouble, and can I help you?"

UMU EXPRESSES HIS GRATITUDE

Whereupon Umu, the great and powerful noble, and captain of a thousand picked warriors, flung himself upon his knees before the young Inca, and, clasping the outstretched hand in both of his, pressed it convulsively to his lips, while the tears streamed like rain from his eyes. But he quickly pulled himself together, and, gazing up into Harry's face, answered:

"Gracious Lord, pardon this unseemly emotion, I pray you, and attribute it to the awful ordeal through which I have this day passed. I have presumed to hasten hither, Lord, to express, as well as may be, the heartfelt gratitude of myself and my daughter for your gracious intervention to-day in the temple, but for which my Maia would now be dead and my home desolate. Lord, you are as yet strange among us, and may therefore not know that for a maiden to be chosen to be offered as a thank-offering on the altar of the temple upon such an occasion as that of to-day is regarded by the Peruvian Indians as the highest honour that can be conferred upon her and all who are connected with her; and doubtless it would be so regarded by many. But, Lord, natural affection is not always to be so easily stifled. I am a widower, and Maia my daughter is my only child; the love that exists between us is therefore perhaps unusually strong, and the honour of having given my daughter as a thank-offering would never have compensated me for, or reconciled me to, her loss. The shock which I experienced to-day when I recognised her, bound and decked with flowers for the sacrifice, in the midst of the priests, I shall never forget, for I had not then been to my house, and knew not that she had been chosen. And though, having been chosen, she had wrought herself up to the point of passive submission, she had no wish to die, for she is young, and the best part of her life is still before her; moreover she loves me, and knows that without her my heart and my house would be empty and desolate. Therefore, Lord, I pray you to accept our heartfelt thanks for her deliverance, and to believe my assurance that henceforth, let what will betide, we two are your faithful and devoted slaves unto our lives' end."

"Thanks, Umu, for your assurance of devotion, which, I am convinced, comes from your heart," said Harry, raising the soldier to his feet. "But, Umu, I wish to regard you henceforth not as my 'slave', but as a faithful and devoted friend. Servants who will unhesitatingly do my will I shall doubtless be able to command in plenty; but sincere friends are less easily won, especially by a monarch, and a wise, faithful, devoted friend who will help and advise me in the difficult task that lies before me will be of greater value than many slaves. I shall always remember with especial pleasure that my first official act was to save an innocent life, and that the life of your daughter, whom heaven long spare to be a joy and comfort to you. Go in peace, Umu, and serve me faithfully."

"I will, Lord; I swear it by the great Pachacamac Himself!" answered Umu, raising his right hand as though to register his oath. Then, turning, he went forth from the palace the proudest, and probably the happiest, man in the Valley of the Sun that day.

Chapter Fourteen
The Inca's Treasure Chambers

The fatigue and excitement of the momentous day were by this time beginning to tell upon Escombe. If he could have followed his own inclination he would certainly have called for a light meal, and, having partaken of it, retired forthwith to rest; but he was already beginning to learn the lesson that even an absolute monarch has sometimes to put aside his own inclinations and do that which is politic rather than that which is most pleasing in his own eyes. Here was this banquet, for instance. He would much rather not have been present at it; but it was an official affair, and to absent himself from it would simply be to inflict a gratuitous slight upon every guest present, and sow a seed of unpopularity that might quite possibly, like the fabled dragon's teeth, spring up into a harvest of armed men to hurl him from his throne. With a sigh of resignation, therefore, he summoned Arima, and, resigning himself into that functionary's hands, submitted to be conducted to the bath, and afterwards attired in the festal garments prepared for the occasion. The bath of warm, delicately perfumed water he found to be so wonderfully refreshing that upon emerging from it all sensation of fatigue had vanished; and by the time that he was completely arrayed for the banquet he felt perfectly prepared to do both himself and the occasion full justice.

He was only just ready in the nick of time, for as Arima was completing the adjustment of the imperial borla upon the young monarch's temples, the lord high chamberlain appeared with the intimation that the guests were all assembled, and that nothing now was needed, save the Inca's presence, to enable the banquet to be begun. Whereupon Harry arose, and, preceded by the chamberlain and his satellites, made his way to the banqueting hall, which was an enormous chamber on the upstairs floor of the palace, occupying the entire length and width of that part of the building in which was situated the main entrance. One row of windows overlooked that part of the garden which gave upon the main road, while the windows on the opposite side of the apartment commanded a view of the piece of garden which lay between the two wings and extended down to the shore of the lake.

The decorations of this room, if they could not be accurately described as "artistic", from a European's point of view, were at least impressive on account of the wanton lavishness with which gems and the precious metals were used; for, look where one would, the eye encountered nothing but gold, silver, and precious stones; indeed the impression conveyed was that the architect had exhausted his ingenuity in devices for the employment of the greatest possible quantity of these costly minerals. The huge beams which supported the ceiling were encased in thick plates of gold, the ceiling itself, or at least those portions of it which showed between the beams, consisted of plates of silver, thickly studded with precious stones arranged—as Tiahuana explained—to represent the stars in the night sky over the city. The walls, of enormous thickness, with deep niches or recesses alternating with the windows, were covered with thick gold plates heavily chased into a variety of curious patterns; and each niche contained either a life-size image of an animal—the llama figuring most frequently—in solid gold, wrought with the most marvellous patience and skill, or was a miniature garden in which various native trees and plants, wrought with the same lifelike skill, and of the same precious materials, seemed to flourish luxuriantly. The floor was the only portion of the apartment that had escaped this barbarously magnificent system of treatment, but even that was composed of thick planks of costly, richly tinted native timber of beautiful grain, polished to the brilliancy of a mirror; and, as though this were not sufficient to meet the insatiable craving for extravagance everywhere displayed, the beauties of the highly polished wood were almost completely concealed by thick, richly coloured, woollen rugs of marvellously fine texture, made of the wool of the vicuña. Nor was the furniture of the apartment permitted to fall short of its surroundings in point of extravagance. For the tables and chairs occupied by the guests were of solid silver, while that occupied by the Inca and such of his guests as he chose to especially honour by an invitation to sit with him were of solid gold; and all the table utensils throughout the room were of the same precious metal, most exquisitely and elaborately wrought.

As for the guests, as might be expected, they had taken especial care that their personal appearance should be in keeping with the general scheme of wantonly lavish display that characterised the adornment of the banqueting room. Every one of them, men and women alike, were apparelled in the richest and most brilliantly coloured stuffs procurable, stiffened with great masses of embroidery in heavy gold thread, while they were literally loaded with ornaments of massive gold, encrusted with gems, upon the hair, neck, and arms. And now, for the first time, Harry had leisure to note—and to strongly disapprove of—the characteristic ornament which was adopted to distinguish the Peruvian noble from his plebeian brother. This consisted of a massive circular disc of gold, wrought into the semblance of a wheel, and measuring in some cases three or four inches in diameter, which was inserted into the cartilage of each ear, which, of course, had previously been pierced and gradually distended to receive it. To Harry's unsophisticated eye these so-called ornaments constituted a hideous disfigurement, and he was glad to see that they were worn by men only, the ears of the women being for the most part innocent of artificial adornment, although a few of the ladies wore ear-rings of somewhat similar character to those of their more civilised sisters.

The Inca's table was placed at one end of the room, and raised upon a dais some three feet high, from which elevation he could of course be seen of all, and also command a view of the entire apartment, easily distinguishing the whereabouts of any particular guest whom he desired to honour especially with a summons to his own table; and to this he was conducted by the chamberlain and ushers, the guests rising upon his entrance and remaining standing until he had seated himself. There was at this moment but one guest at the royal table, and that was Tiahuana, whom Harry had commanded to sit beside him to act as a sort of "coach", and generally explain things. And the first communication which the Villac Vmu made to his young monarch was not precisely of a reassuring character. It was to the effect that Huanacocha, and the four friends who had sided with him that afternoon in the expression of a doubt as to the genuine character of Harry's claims to be accepted as Inca, had absented themselves from the feast.

"Yes," said Tiahuana, again casting his eyes carefully over the room, "they are all five absent, Lord; and I like it not. They are men of great power and influence, and they can easily stir up very serious trouble in the city if they choose to do so. We must keep a wary eye upon them; and upon the first sign of a disposition to be troublesome they must be summarily dealt with."

"Yes," said Harry; "I have been raised to the position of Inca by a very remarkable combination of circumstances, in the bringing about of which I have had no part; but, being where I am, I intend to govern firmly and justly, to the best of my ability; and I will certainly not tolerate the presence in the city of turbulent spirits bent upon the stirring up of discord and strife. I have already seen, elsewhere, too much of the evil results of mistaken leniency to permit anything of the kind here. But this is not the moment to discuss politics: you hinted, a short time ago, Tiahuana, that at functions of this kind it is usual for the Inca to show honour to certain individuals by inviting them to his table. Now, of course I know none of those present— except Umu, the captain of my bodyguard, whom I see yonder—so I must look to you for guidance in the matter of making a judicious choice. There is room for ten at this table, beside ourselves; therefore, if it be the proper thing for me to do, choose ten persons, and I will summon them to come to us."

Whereupon Tiahuana, who to the sanctity of the Villac Vmu added the shrewdness and sagacity of a Prime Minister, named those members of the late Council of Seven who had accepted Escombe as Inca, and certain other powerful nobles, completing the list by naming Umu, whom, he rather satirically suggested, was perhaps entitled to some especial consideration in recompense for the distinction which he had that day missed in consequence of the rescue of his daughter from the sacrificial altar. "And, remember, Lord," concluded Tiahuana, "that it is not necessary to keep any of those people at your table during the entire progress of the banquet; let them stay here long enough to taste a single dish, or to drink with you out of your cup, and then dispatch them with instructions to send up someone else in their stead."

Upon this principle, accordingly, Harry acted, arranging matters so judiciously that, under Tiahuana's able guidance, he was able, during the course of the evening, to compliment every guest whom that astute old diplomatist considered it desirable especially to honour, and thus avoid all occasion for jealousy.

It is not necessary to describe the banquet in detail; let it suffice to say that for fully three hours there was placed before the Inca and his guests a constant succession of dishes representing all that was esteemed most choice and dainty in Peruvian culinary art, washed down by copious libations of the wine of the country, prepared from the fermented juice of the maguey, for which, it is deplorable to add, the Peruvians exhibited an inordinate fondness. By the exercise of extreme circumspection, taking merely a taste here and there of such food as especially appealed to him, and merely suffering the wine to moisten his lips when pledging his nobles, the young Inca contrived to emerge from the ordeal of the banquet not a penny the worse.

The next morning Escombe spent in the company of a sort of committee of the chief *amautas* or "wise men", who represented the concentrated essence—so to speak—of all Peruvian wisdom and learning, and who had been embodied for the express purpose of instructing the young Inca in the intricacies—such as they were—of the code of Tavantinsuyu—or "four quarters of the world"—as it then stood. This code was simple, but exceedingly severe, the laws, properly so called, relating almost exclusively to criminal matters and their punishment. The regulations governing the daily life of the Peruvian Indian—where he should live, what should be the character of his work, what should be the distinctive character of his clothing, when and whom he should marry, how much land he should hold and cultivate, and so on, were the result of ages of tentative experiment, and were so numerous and intricate that probably none but the *amautas* themselves thoroughly understood them. The committee, however, which had for nearly a month been preparing itself for the task of initiating the young Inca into the secrets of good government, had arranged a procedure of such a character that even in the course of that one morning's instruction they contrived to give Escombe a sufficiently clear general insight of the subject to enable him to see that, taken altogether, the system of government was admirably designed to secure the prosperity of the nation.

Then, in the afternoon, at the instigation of the Council of Seven, who had now become a sort of cabinet, to control the machinery of government, under the supervision of the Inca, Harry was conducted, by an official who performed the functions of Chief of the Treasury, through the enormous vaults beneath the palace, in order that he might view the treasure, industriously accumulated during more than three hundred years, to form the sinews of war for the regeneration of the race which was Escombe's great predestined task.

If, before visiting these vaults, Harry had been invited to express an opinion upon the subject, he would have confidently asserted the conviction that such treasure as the inhabitants of the Valley of the Sun had been able to accumulate must all, or very nearly all, have been expended in the adornment of the great temple and the royal palace. But that such a conviction would have been absolutely erroneous was speedily demonstrated when the great bronze doors guarding the entrance of the vaults were thrown open. For the first room into which he was conducted—an apartment measuring some twenty feet wide by thirty feet long, and about fourteen feet high—was full of great stacks of silver bars, each bar being about twenty pounds in weight; the stacks, of varying height, being arranged in tiers of three running lengthwise along the room, with two narrow longitudinal passages between them. Escombe, after staring in dumb amazement at this enormous accumulation of dull white metal, drew from his pocket a small memorandum book and pencil which he had found in one of the pockets of his old clothes, and, with the instinct of the engineer rising for a moment to the surface, made a rapid calculation by which he arrived at the astounding result that there must be very nearly eight hundred tons of bar silver in the stacks before him!

From this room he was conducted into another of about the same size, and similarly arranged; but in this case the metal in the stacks was virgin gold, instead of silver, while the bulk of the stacks was, if anything, rather greater than those in the outer rooms. But, for the purposes of a rough estimate, Escombe assumed them to be of only equal bulk, upon the strength of which assumption his figures informed him that the gold in this vault amounted to the not altogether insignificant weight of close upon fourteen hundred tons. The sight of such incredible quantities of the precious metals had so paralysing an effect upon the young Englishman that he could scarcely stammer an enquiry as to where it all came from. The custodian of this fabulous wealth replied, with a smile, that the mountains which hemmed the valley about were enormously rich in both gold and silver, and that some hundreds of men had been kept industriously employed in working the mines almost from the moment when the city had been first founded. "But, Lord," he continued, flinging open a third door, "what you have already seen is by no means all our wealth; the most valuable part of it is to be found in this small room."

Passing through the doorway, which, like the other two, was fitted with massive doors of solid bronze secured by an enormously strong lock of the same metal, the young Inca—who, as one of the results of his having been placed upon the throne, had become the absolute owner of all this wealth, with power to use it in such manner as might seem to him good—found himself in a much smaller room, its dimensions being about ten feet long by the same width, and some twelve feet high. To the sides of the room were fitted large chests of very heavy wood, three chests on each side occupying the entire length of the room, with a passage way about six feet wide between the two rows of chests. Each chest was fitted with a massive wooden cover secured to it by strong bronze hinges, and fastened by a ponderous bronze lock.

The custodian unlocked these chests one at a time, and, raising the heavy cover with difficulty, held the lamp which he carried over the yawning interior, disclosing its contents. The first chest opened was nearly full of what to Escombe appeared to be dull black stones, most of them with at least one smooth surface, ranging in size from that of a walnut to lumps as large as a man's two fists. One of these lumps Harry's conductor took out and handed to the young man for his inspection.

"Well, what do you call this?" demanded Harry, turning the stone about in his hands, and inspecting it curiously.

"That, Lord, is an amethyst," answered the other; "and, as you see, the chest is nearly full of them. But, unless we should happen to discover a new mine, I am afraid we shall get no more of them, for the mine from which those were extracted appears to be exhausted; and it was never very productive even at its best. We did not know what the stones were when they were first discovered, but, as it was suspected that they might possess a certain value, steps were taken to determine the question, with the result that we were told they are amethysts. They are not especially valuable, I believe, but we make a point of never wasting anything, so it was decided to store these until wanted. Now here,"—opening the next chest—"we have another mineral about which we were a bit puzzled at first; but we were in less doubt in this case than we were with regard to the amethysts, as the appearance of the stone seemed to indicate that it possessed a value. We dealt with this as we did with the amethysts, and found that we had chanced upon a particularly rich opal deposit."

The chest of opals was, like the one previously opened, almost full, and Harry took admiringly into his hand the great piece of rock representing the half of a mass of stone that had been accidentally broken in two, and found to contain a considerable quantity of iridescent, many-hued crystal. The next chest contained some very fine specimens of sapphire; but it was little more than half-full, the mine having only been discovered within the last decade, and even then not very industriously worked; but there were in the chest a few specimens that Escombe shrewdly suspected to be practically priceless.

Having completed the inspection of the contents of the coffers on one side of the room, the custodian crossed over to the other side, and threw up the lid of a chest, the interior of which at once began to glow as though each of the stones—looking very much like lumps of ordinary washing soda— contained within it a morsel of phosphorus.

"Aha!" exclaimed Escombe, plunging his hand delightedly into the chest and fishing up two or three of the stones; "no need to ask what these are; there's no possibility of mistaking them. Yes, there's the genuine soapy feel about them all right," as he ran his fingers over the smooth surface of the crystals. "But I didn't know that you had diamonds in Peru."

"There is at all events one mine in the country, Lord, namely that from which these stones came," answered the Indian. "But the existence and locality are known only to the few who work it and who guard the approach to it; for we believe it to be the richest mine in the whole world, and we are naturally anxious to retain possession of it for ourselves exclusively. It is not in this valley; it lies a long three-days' journey from here, in a particularly wild and desolate part of the country which is practically inaccessible, save to the boldest and hardiest mountaineers among us. It has only been known for about twenty years, and the contents of this coffer represent the labour of only six men during that time. But the mine is enormously rich, and, as you may see, the size and quality of the stones improve as the miners penetrate deeper, the largest and finest stones, which are those most recently extracted, being at the top of the others in the chest."

Harry stooped over and picked up a particularly fine specimen, larger than one of his clenched fists, which glowed and scintillated in the light of the lamp as though it were on fire.

"Why," he said, gazing admiringly at the stone as he turned it about in his hand, "The contents of this chest must be of absolutely incalculable value! This stone alone would constitute a very handsome fortune to its lucky possessor, if I am any judge of diamonds."

"True, Lord," answered his companion. "But there are several finer stones than that—this one, and this, for example," as he fished up a couple of superb specimens. "There are probably no diamonds in the world equal to these two in size and purity of colour. And all belong to my Lord."

"Ay," said Harry; "with such enormous and inexhaustible wealth as this at one's command it should not be very difficult to provide the means of reconquering the country and restoring it to its former state of power and glory. What have you in the other two chests?"

"My Lord shall see," answered the Indian, as he unlocked and threw back the lid of the next chest, which proved to be three parts full of rubies, every one of which constituted a little fortune in itself, while many were of such exceptional size and superb colour that the young Englishman could only gasp in speechless amazement and admiration.

"Why, Huatama," he exclaimed at length, "I am at a loss to express my astonishment. Aladdin's cave was nothing to this, nothing at all!"

"Aladdin, did my Lord say?" murmured the Indian, looking enquiringly at Harry. "I do not seem to remember him. Surely he was not a Peruvian? The name does not—"

"No," answered Harry with a laugh. "Aladdin knew nothing of Peru; he was an Eastern—a Chinese fellow, or something like that, if I remember rightly."

"Ah, yes!" remarked Huatama reflectively; "I have seen a few Chinese, down at Lima and Callao, when I had occasion to go there a year ago on business for the Council of Seven. I do not like them; and I hope that when my Lord has subjugated the country he will drive them all out of it."

"Well, we shall see," rejoined Escombe with a laugh. "But it is early days as yet to talk of driving out the Chinese; there is a great deal to be done before we shall find ourselves face to face with that question. And now, what does your last chest contain?"

It contained emeralds, and was more than half-full of stones of surpassing size and purity of colour, every one of them being a picked stone especially selected for its exceptional quality. But Escombe's powers of admiration were by this time completely exhausted, and after having rather perfunctorily examined and expressed his approval of a few of the finest specimens, and commended the treasure as a whole to the unflagging care of Huatama, he returned to his apartments in the palace and flung himself into a chair to endeavour to convince himself that what he had seen in those rock-hewn chambers below was all prosaically real and not the fantasy of a disordered imagination.

As he pictured to himself the great chambers with their heaped-up stacks of silver and gold bars, and the smaller room with its six coffers of uncut gems, his thoughts insensibly floated away across the ocean to the modest little Sydenham home, and he tried to imagine the raptures of his mother and sister, could they but behold the incredible accumulation of priceless gems that his eyes had rested upon that day. Then he remembered that in consequence of this extraordinary adventure of his a mail boat had been permitted to leave for England with no letter on board from him to his mother, and he began to wonder anxiously what would happen at The Limes when its occupants fully realised that the Peruvian mail had arrived, and that there was no letter for them. It was the first time that such a thing had ever been permitted to occur; and, although he had been quite helpless to prevent the accident, Escombe somehow felt that it ought not to have been allowed to happen; that he ought to have remembered in time, and taken steps to ensure that a letter had been despatched by some means or other. What was the use of being an Inca if he could not manage a simple little thing like that? To summon Arima and enquire of that trusty henchman whether, in the hurry of departure from the survey camp, he had remembered to pack up and bring away his master's writing desk was naturally the next thing in order. Upon learning that the desk had not been forgotten, Escombe at once had it brought to him, and sat down and wrote a long letter, addressed jointly to his mother and sister. This letter contained a full account of his abduction and all that had followed thereupon, together with an assurance that not only would he contrive henceforward to communicate with them regularly, but also that if, after the lapse of a certain length of time to allow the process of "settling down" to become complete, it should appear that his scheme of government was likely to prove a success, he would send for them to come out to him. He added that, meanwhile, the enormous wealth represented by the accumulations of more than three hundred years was at his absolute disposal, and that he felt quite justified in awarding himself a salary of one gold bar per calendar month for his services to the state;

also, that since under present circumstances he had no use for a private purse, he should dispatch to them the monthly bar of gold for their own personal use and enjoyment, and that he should expect them to employ it for the purpose named. This somewhat lengthy epistle concluded by giving instructions for the conversion of the gold bar into coin of the realm. Harry also wrote to Sir Philip Swinburne, stating that he had fallen into the hands of the Indians, but was being well-treated by them, and believed he was in no immediate danger, also that at the moment he saw no prospect of being permitted to return to civilisation; he was therefore writing for the purpose of allaying any apprehension that might be experienced on his account. Finally, he wrote to Bannister in somewhat similar terms. Then he sent for Huatama, and gave that functionary instructions to withdraw one gold bar from the treasury vaults and have it securely packed in a suitable box for transmission to Europe.

Chapter Fifteen
The Monsters that haunted the Lake

These matters attended to, Escombe summoned the Council of Seven to the palace, and held what might be considered his first official conference. He began by laying before them his views as to the steps necessary to be taken in order to carry out successfully the desire of the people to become a regenerated nation, instructing them to cause several different kinds of information to be obtained for him, and finally pointing out to them the necessity for free communication with the outside world, and the consequent establishment of something in the nature of a regular postal and transport service between the valley and two or three points on the railway system.

Long before he had finished all that he had to say it was perfectly evident to the young Inca that the members of the Council—or at least some of them—were entirely out of sympathy with many of his views and ideas, and that he would have to contend with a vast amount of ignorance and prejudice. To indicate a few out of many points where this lack of sympathy most strongly manifested itself, Harry had commented upon the necessity for establishing an army and providing it with the most modern and efficient weapons and equipment. To this Huanacocha and his supporters strongly objected, arguing that the State already possessed an army in the shape of the Inca's bodyguard, horse and foot, which, in their opinion, ought to be amply sufficient to reconquer the country in view of the fact that Pizarro's army numbered less than two hundred men when he captured Atahuallpa and thus achieved the conquest of Peru. And, as to the importation of modern weapons, they were altogether opposed to the proposal for many reasons, the chief of which were the difficulty and delay attendant upon the procuring of them and of their introduction into the country, and the further delay involved in training the troops to use them. Moreover, the weapons with which the existing troops were armed were such as they had always been accustomed to, and in the use of which they were already thoroughly skilled. Such a radical change as was proposed must of necessity involve an enormous delay, and for their part they were unable to see any advantage in the proposal. They looked with equal disfavour upon the proposal to establish a postal and transport service, arguing that there was no need for anything of the kind, the fundamental idea governing the settlement of their forefathers in the valley and the founding of the City of the Sun being that its inhabitants and the resources of the valley itself would be amply sufficient to achieve the reconquest of the country. It was not until Harry had very nearly lost his temper in arguing with these men that he learned that not one of them had ever been outside the valley, and that their very meagre knowledge of the outside world had been derived from the few individuals who at rare intervals had been obliged to make short and hasty journeys outside the confines of the encircling mountains upon State business. As soon as Harry had thoroughly grasped this fact he gave them to understand, as politely as possible, that none of them knew in the least what they were talking about, and for that reason he would feel himself compelled to dispense with their advice for the future, forming his own plans in accordance with the knowledge which he had acquired during a residence of several years in the biggest, busiest, and best-informed city in the world; and that henceforth he would ask of them nothing more than loyal wholehearted obedience to his commands. He finally dismissed them with instructions to establish immediately a service of postal runners between the valley and the town of Juliaca on the Santa Rosa, Puno, Arequipa, and Mollendo railway; with further instructions to arrange for the establishment of a thoroughly trustworthy agent at Juliaca, whose sole business it should be to see that all letters for Europe and other parts of the world were duly stamped and posted upon receipt by him; and to the care of whom all letters for the valley might be addressed. This done, Escombe summoned Arima to his presence and, handing him all the coin that he happened to have in his possession, delivered to him the letters which he had written, together with the gold bar—by this time securely packed and ready for posting—and directed him to proceed with all possible speed to Islay—using the railway as far as possible in order to save time—and there post the letters and the box containing the bar. Then he suddenly bethought himself and, before dismissing Arima upon his journey, sat down and wrote a long letter to Mr John Firmin, of Lima, he who had been a fellow-passenger from England with Harry on board the *Rimac*, In this letter he told Firmin as much of his story as he thought it necessary for him to know, and made certain arrangements whereby Firmin was to undertake certain business transactions from time to time, and to supply immediately certain necessaries, for the due delivery of which Harry gave his friend the most minute instructions. This completed what the Inca was pleased to regard as a very excellent and satisfactory day's work.

And now the young Englishman began to find his time very fully occupied, so much so, indeed, that the days seemed not nearly long enough to enable him to accomplish the half of what he wished to do. There was, for instance, the learning of the Quichua language. Harry had not been domiciled in his palace twenty-four hours before it had become patent to him that this was the first task which he must undertake; for very few of the nobles had any knowledge whatever of Spanish, and the inconvenience and loss of time involved in conversing through an interpreter were far too great to be passively endured. And, since he could do very little else as satisfactorily as he would wish until he had mastered this rich and expressive language, he devoted four hours of every day—two in the morning and two in the evening—to its study. Then he soon learned that, exclusive of the inhabitants of the Valley of the Sun, there were some three hundred and fifty thousand Indians scattered up and down the country, at least one in every ten of whom might be counted as a fighting man. These people had to be brought into the valley, housed, fed, disciplined, in preparation for the time when arms should be put into their hands; also—what was more difficult still—matters had to be so arranged that the families of these men, and all dependent upon them, should suffer neither loss nor inconvenience from the drafting of the able-bodied into the valley. Then the arrangements and preparations for the importation of arms and ammunition into the country—everything connected with which had, of course, to be done entirely without the knowledge of the authorities—involved a tremendous amount of hard and intricate work. It is therefore not to be wondered at that during the first six months of his reign the young Inca was unable to spare a single hour for amusement.

But the moment was at hand when Harry was to enjoy some sport of a quite unique character; and the way in which it came about was thus. As he stood one morning in the palace garden, gazing out over the lake, with his faithful henchman Arima close at hand, an idea suddenly occurred to him, and, turning, he remarked:

"The lake looks particularly enticing this morning, Arima. Are there any balsas near at hand? Because, if so, you shall fetch me one, and we will go out together to deep water and indulge in a glorious swim."

"A swim, Lord, in the deep water of the lake?" ejaculated Arima in horror-stricken accents. "Nay, that is impossible."

"Impossible!" repeated Harry. "And why, pray?"

"Because of the monsters, Lord," answered Arima. "Were we to venture to plunge into the lake we should almost certainly be devoured."

"Indeed!" answered Harry. "So there are monsters in the lake, are there? I was not aware of that. And what are those 'monsters'? Are they alligators, or voracious fish, or what are they? I should hardly have supposed that the water of the lake was warm enough for alligators to flourish in it."

"Nay, Lord," answered Arima, "they are not alligators. I have seen alligators in some of the northern rivers, and know them well enough to be able to distinguish between them and the monsters which haunt our lake. Nor are they fish; or if they be, they are quite unlike any other fish that these eyes of mine have ever beheld. We call them 'monsters' because our forefathers did so, and because we have no other name for them; also because of their exceeding size and malevolence."

"Ah!" commented Harry. "Well, what are these creatures—these monsters—like, and how big are they? Have you ever seen them?"

"Yes, Lord," was the answer. "I have seen them no less than three times at close quarters, and always with the same disastrous results. The first time was when, during my passage of the lake on a balsa, one of my companions had the misfortune to fall into the water. Ere the balsa could be stopped and paddled back to where the man was struggling, two of the monsters appeared and tore him limb from limb. The resemblance to an alligator lies chiefly in the shape of the head, which, however, is longer in proportion and more pointed than that of the alligator. Also, our monsters have smooth skins, nearly black in colour, and instead of feet and legs they have fins. The tail also is differently shaped from that of an alligator, being wide and flat at the end."

"By Jove!" exclaimed Harry in astonishment, "they must be queer and formidable-looking creatures indeed; and fins in place of legs and feet! I'll be shot if I can place them at all. Are there many of them?"

"We do not generally see more than two, or three at most, although it is on record that on one occasion, many years ago, four were seen, two of them being obviously young ones," answered Arima.

"Upon my word, this all sounds exceedingly interesting," commented Harry. "I should dearly like to see the creatures myself. Do they often show themselves?"

"Very rarely, Lord, save in the case of such accidents as those of which I have told you," answered Arima. "Yet," he continued, "if my Lord desires to see the monsters it could doubtless be managed. If the carcass of an animal were deposited upon yonder rock,"—the Indian pointed to a rock showing slightly above the water's surface about a mile from the shore—

"and another were cast into the water quite near it, the monsters would doubtless be attracted to the place; and if my Lord were close at hand at the time, upon a large and safe balsa, he would see them when they crawl up on the rock to reach the carcass exposed there."

"Ah!" ejaculated Harry; "you think so? Then let the matter be arranged for to-morrow, Arima. I confess that your description of the creatures has powerfully excited my curiosity, and made me very anxious to see them."

And on the morrow the young Inca's curiosity was fully gratified, and with something to spare.

Oh, those monsters! Harry believed he possessed a passably fair general knowledge of natural history, but these creatures—monsters truly—were entirely new to him. In no natural history had he ever seen a representation of anything like them. And yet, when he came to think of it again, singular and terrifying as was their appearance, it was not altogether unfamiliar. He believed he had seen them portrayed somewhere, although he could not for the moment remember where. Fully forty feet long from the snout to the tip of the tail, with a head shaped midway between that of a pike and a crocodile, with enormous protruding eyes, with a smooth somewhat fish-shaped body almost black above and shading off to a dirty whitish-grey beneath, with a long tail broad and flat at its extremity, and with four seal-like flippers instead of legs and feet, the monsters looked more like nightmare creatures, evolved by reading a book on antediluvian animals after a —. Of course, that was it, Escombe decided, as his thoughts took some such turn as above. He now distinctly remembered having read some years ago a most interesting illustrated magazine article upon extinct animals, and one of the pictures portrayed these identical monsters, labelling them "Plesiosaurus"! Yes, the more Harry thought about it the less room did he find for doubt that these so-called monsters haunting the lake in the Valley of the Sun were actually survivors—most probably the only ones—of the antediluvian plesiosaurus. How they got there was a most interesting problem, yet it seemed by no means a difficult one to solve. The conclusion at which Escombe speedily arrived—rightly or wrongly—was that upon the subsidence of the waters of the Deluge a pair of plesiosauri had found themselves imprisoned in the great basin of the valley, where, the conditions presumably being exceptionally favourable, they had not only survived but had actually contrived to perpetuate their species to a very limited extent. And the reason why the lake was not swarming with them, instead of containing probably only three or four specimens at the utmost, was doubtless that the waters were too circumscribed in extent, and too unproductive in the matter of fish, to support more than that number.

The problem of how they came to be where they were was, however, not one of very great importance; the thing that really mattered was, in Escombe's opinion, that their presence in the lake constituted a horrible danger to those who were obliged to traffic upon its waters, and they must be destroyed. They must not be permitted to exist another day longer than was absolutely necessary. Why, when one came to think of it, how many hundreds of lives might not already have fallen victims to the savage voracity of those creatures? What hope for his life would a man have if he chanced to fall off his balsa at a moment when one of those monsters happened to be close at hand? Positively none. Escombe shuddered as he reflected that, ignorant as he had hitherto been of the presence of the plesiosauri in the lake, it had only been by a series of fortuitous circumstances—or was it the intervention of a merciful Providence?—that he had been from time to time prevented from bathing in the lake, ay, and actually swimming out to the distant rock, as he had several times been strongly tempted to do.

Yes, those implacably ferocious monsters must be destroyed forthwith; and the only point remaining to be settled was, how was the work of destruction to be accomplished?

The plan which first suggested itself to the young Inca was the very obvious one of fishing for them with a baited hook and line, even as sharks were fished for. True, it would need a very big hook and a very strong line to capture a creature of the size and strength of a plesiosaurus; but to manufacture them was surely not beyond the resources of the inhabitants of the valley. Yes; but there was another matter to be considered. What about a craft from which to do the fishing? The largest balsa that Harry had ever seen upon the lake was not nearly big enough for the purpose; a hooked plesiosaurus would drag it under water without an effort, and then what would become of its occupants? The probabilities were too awful for contemplation, and the idea was not to be entertained for a moment. Besides, a balsa was not at all the kind of craft on which to engage in so dangerous a form of sport, even though it were possible to build one big enough; what was needed was a good stanch sturdy boat of, say, twenty tons or so. And, having arrived at this point in his meditations, Escombe was naturally reminded that he had often wished that he possessed a small yacht wherein to disport himself on the lake. Why should he not have one? His will was law; he had but to speak the word and the best and most skilled workers in the valley would be at his disposal for the construction of the vessel. And as to her design, why, he had always been an enthusiastic yacht sailor, and knew, as well as most amateurs, what the shape of such a craft should be, and was quite capable of putting that shape on paper in a form that could be worked from.

Escombe's mind was made up: he would destroy those plesiosauri, and to destroy them a suitable boat was necessary. That boat might be so designed and built as to also afford him a great deal of pleasure, and he would have her. And thereupon he set to work and devoted every minute he could spare to the preparation of her design, which, a week later, was in the hands of a small army of carpenters, eager to show what they could do in a line of work that was entirely new to them.

Chapter Sixteen
The Slaying of the Monsters

"Many hands make light work"; and in just two months from the day of starting work upon the cutter she was complete, rigged, and ready for launching. She was of the most up-to-date type with which Escombe was acquainted; that is to say, beamy, rather shallow of body, with spoon bow, and a fin keel, and her designer felt particularly proud of her as he walked round her and critically surveyed her lines and general shape the last thing before giving the word to put her into the water. Needless to say she was also the object of great and ever-increasing curiosity to the inhabitants of the valley generally, not more than perhaps a dozen of whom had ever seen anything more handy and shipshape than the unwieldy balsa, or raft constructed of reeds, a not very manageable craft at the best of times, and of course quite incapable of being navigated under sail except before the wind. The cutter was got into the water without accident, and after some slight readjustment of her inside ballast, to bring her accurately to her correct water line, her young owner got on board and, a nice sailing breeze happening to be blowing right down the lake, took her for a trial spin from one end of the lake to the other, running down and beating back. The result was eminently satisfactory in every respect, the little vessel developing a fine turn of speed, not only before the wind but also close-hauled, while she was of course, like all craft of similar form, remarkably weatherly; indeed the smartness with which she worked back against the wind, from the lower end of the lake, was regarded by the unsophisticated inhabitants of the valley as nothing short of miraculous.

Meanwhile, Escombe having given instructions for the manufacture of a hardened copper hook, with two fathoms of chain attached, and a stout rope of plaited raw hide, at the same time that he had put the yacht in hand, these articles were now ready. Therefore, after exercising his crew for a week, to get them thoroughly accustomed to the working of the new craft, he made arrangements for a grand plesiosaurus hunt, to which he invited his stanch friend Umu, and three or four other nobles who had manifested a capacity for development into kindred spirits.

On a certain glorious morning this novel fishing party embarked on board the yacht, taking with them, of course, their fishing line and the carcasses of two llamas, cut in half, for bait, together with a formidable battery of bows and arrows, spears, heavy maces, and other weapons for the killing of their quarry when captured; to which armament Escombe added his magazine rifle and two packets of cartridges, which the faithful Arima had been careful to bring away from the survey camp, together with everything else belonging to his young master, on the memorable occasion of that individual's abduction. Starting under easy sail, and heading for the bottom of the lake, the great fishing line—made fast by its inner end to the windlass bitts, and the remainder of it led aft outside and clear of all rigging—was baited and paid out astern as soon as the cutter had run into deep water.

It was not very long before the party, intently on the watch for the approach of the plesiosauri, detected a strong, swirling ripple mingling with that of the yacht's wake, which indicated that at least one of the monsters was at hand, and presently the ripple broke, revealing some six feet of smooth, black, glistening back keeping pace with the little vessel, while occasionally, when the light favoured, an indistinct and momentary glimpse might be caught, through the swirling water, of two enormous, glaring eyes. But the beast, in its eagerness to reach its supposed prey, had apparently passed the baited hook as unworthy of its notice, for the bait was a long way astern of the creature, which seemed intent only on overtaking the yacht, for it now made frequent rushes forward until it was within a few fathoms of the little vessel's counter, and then sank out of sight and dropped astern again, as though it knew not what to make of the moving object ahead of it. But, provokingly enough, from the sportsmen's point of view, it never dropped far enough astern to bring it level with the bait, while, on the other hand, when it approached the yacht it was careful to keep far enough below the surface to render anything like an accurate aim impossible; indeed it behaved as though it instinctively knew that danger threatened it. Although Escombe's companions were eager enough to waste their arrows in obviously futile attempts to hit it, the young leader of the expedition rigorously forbade everything of the nature of chance shooting, lest the creature should happen to receive a more or less slight wound, and thus be driven to flight. And, for the same reason, Escombe himself declined to attempt a shot with his rifle.

But while they were all intently watching the movements of the creature, and standing with weapons in hand, ready to discharge an effective shot at the first favourable opportunity, a sudden, startled yell from Arima, who was tending the fishing line, caused the whole party to wheel round to see what was the matter, and Harry had only bare time to drop his rifle and grip his faithful henchman by the belt, to thus prevent him from being dragged overboard, as the line suddenly tautened out like a bar, flinging up a great shower of spray as it did so, while a terrific plunge in the water far astern revealed the fact that a second monster, whose presence had hitherto been undetected, had taken the bait and become hooked.

"Let go the line, you idiot, let go!" hissed Escombe through his clenched teeth, as he braced his feet against a stanchion and flung himself back, clinging with both hands to Arima's belt, while that individual vainly strove to hold the now frantically struggling reptile—"let go, man, if you don't want to be dragged overboard and eaten alive! Haul down the foresail, there, for'ard!"

The stout raw-hide line twanged like a harp-string as the terrified Arima relaxed his convulsive grip on it and was hauled back inboard to safety by his master, and the yacht's forward progress was checked with an abruptness that threatened to drag the bitts out of her as the strain of the line, with the plunging, struggling monster at the end of it, was suddenly thrown upon them, while the shock sent every individual, fore and aft, sprawling upon the deck, to the uproarious and most undignified amusement of the young Inca, and the mortal terror of his faithful subjects. Then, as all hands scrambled to their feet again and instinctively regained possession of their weapons, the hooked saurian started to "run", in the vain hope, possibly, of breaking away from the restraining influence which had so suddenly and unaccountably seized upon it. The yacht was whirled violently round—almost capsizing in the process—and dragged, with her bows nearly buried in the hissing and curling water, back toward the head of the lake, at a steadily increasing pace, as the now thoroughly terrified plesiosaurus surged forward at headlong speed in its frenzied endeavour to escape, with its companion keeping pace by its side.

The yacht had only travelled a distance of some three miles down the lake when the monster had taken the bait, and on the backward journey this distance was covered in about a quarter of an hour—a fact which bore eloquent testimony to the tremendous strength of the creature. Harry was beginning to feel exceedingly uneasy lest his vessel should be towed into such shallow water that he would be compelled to cut the line in order to save her from being dragged ashore, when the quarry, which probably also objected to shallow water, wheeled suddenly right round and, rushing close past the cutter, in a perfect maelstrom of foam and spray, headed back for the lower end of the lake, with its companion still bearing it company. To thrust the helm hard over, and to shout to everybody to lie down and hang on for their lives, was, with Harry, the work of but a moment; yet the yacht, handy as she was on her helm, had scarcely swept halfway round when the stout line again jerked itself taut, the terrific strain again came upon the bitts, causing them to ominously creak and groan, and once more the little vessel heeled gunwale under as she was whirled violently round, until she righted again and ploughed up a glassy sheet of foam-laced water on either bow as she tore along in the wake of the monster reptiles.

"This cannot possibly last very much longer," remarked Escombe reassuringly to his companions, who had by this time turned a sickly, greenish-yellow with terror at so unaccustomed an adventure—and that, too, on an element to which they were practically strangers—"the brute will soon become exhausted at this rate, and when he does we will haul him alongside and finish him off with our spears and arrows. I don't care how far he runs, so long as he heads as he is now going; it is those sudden twists and turns that are dangerous. If he were to break away we should probably never have a chance to hook him again."

Nevertheless, despite Harry's confident prognostication, they had traversed quite half the length of the lake ere there was the slightest perceptible sign of the creature weakening; and they accomplished another quarter of the distance ere the reptile slackened speed sufficiently to admit of their attempting to haul the yacht up alongside it. Then, when they at length proceeded to make the attempt, the additional strain thrown on the rope, as it was hauled in and coiled down, seemed to exhaust the last remnant of the brute's strength, and, stopping suddenly, it rose to the surface and, throwing its head out of the water, shook it savagely from side to side in a futile endeavour to shake itself free of the hook, emitting a curious grunting kind of roar as it did so.

Yet, even now, the creature was not conquered; for when it found itself being hauled alongside the yacht it suddenly sank, and nearly the whole of the length of rope that had been hauled in was allowed to run out again ere Harry, by taking a quick turn round the bitts, was able to stay its downward progress. And then it became a matter of sheer, downright drag by all hands ere the huge bulk could be brought near enough to the surface to permit of the use of their weapons on it, when it was found that its companion still clung faithfully to its side.

At length, after some fifteen minutes of exhausting labour on the one hand, opposed to stolid dogged resistance on the other, the monster reptile was dragged so close to the surface that the point of its snout was actually raised above the level or the water, and the whole of the gigantic body, right down to the extremity of the broad-ended tail, could be clearly seen hanging suspended vertically in the pellucid depths beneath the yacht, while swimming agitatedly round and round the suspended body could occasionally be seen the creature's mate, now plunging deep, as though, thoroughly terrified, it had at length determined to abandon so dangerous a neighbourhood, and anon returning with a swift rush to the surface, and furious dartings to and fro, as though meditating an attempt at the rescue of its companion.

And now, for the first time, the hunters were able to obtain a thoroughly clear and satisfactory view, at close quarters, of the gruesome-looking brutes, and a truly hideous and nightmare-inspiring sight it was; a sight which, as Escombe gazed at the ponderous, powerful, thick-skinned bodies, the enormous, protruding, balefully glaring eyes, and the long, cavernous, gaping jaws, armed with great serrated teeth—those of the upper jaw fitting in between those of the lower—caused him to feel, more strongly than ever, the conviction that in destroying the creatures he was a public benefactor.

The captured brute now hung so nearly motionless, with the point of the great barbed hook protruding through its upper jaw, that it was evident its strength must be practically exhausted; and Escombe, standing by to open fire with his magazine rifle in case of an emergency, gave the word to his companions to deal the death stroke, advising some to endeavour to reach the creature's brain by means of a spear-thrust through the eye, while others were to attempt to pierce the heart. But, with the arrival of the crucial moment, the nerves of the natives seemed to suddenly fail them; they became flurried and frightened in the very act of raising their weapons to strike, and every man of them missed his mark, inflicting many serious and doubtless painful wounds, but not one that seemed in the least degree likely to prove mortal. The result was the immediate resumption of a struggle so violent that for a breathless minute or two it really seemed as though the cutter, stout little craft as she was, would be dragged under water and sunk. And in the very height of the confusion one of the hunters must needs fall overboard into the midst of the boiling flurry of bloodstained foam raised by the struggles of the frantic brute, and was only dragged aboard again by Harry in the very nick of time to save him from the terrific rush of the second plesiosaurus. Then the young leader of the party, seeing that his companions were too completely unnerved to be of any use, and that the violent struggles of the wounded brute threatened to seriously injure, if they did not actually destroy, the cutter, stepped forward, and, raising his rifle, seized the opportunity afforded by a pause of a fraction of a second in the violent movements of the creature, and sent a bullet crashing through its right eye into its brain. That settled the matter. The struggles ceased for a moment or two with startling suddenness; a convulsive, writhing movement followed; then came a terrible shudder, and with a final gasping groan the monster yielded up its life and hung motionless, its body supported, still in an upright position, by the great hook through its jaw. With the crack of Escombe's rifle the second monster had suddenly vanished.

The question now was, what was to be done with the carcass of the dead plesiosaurus. As Harry stood there, contemplatively regarding it, it was perfectly obvious to him that if the great fish hook were cut out of the creature's jaw with an axe, the body would at once sink to the bottom of the lake, and there would be an end of it, so far as he was concerned, and the party would at once be free to resume their fishing, although he had his doubts as to whether, after what had already happened, another of the monsters could be tempted to take the baited hook. But it suddenly occurred to him that, the plesiosaurus being to all intents and purposes an extinct and antediluvian animal, the only remains of it in existence must necessarily consist of such fossilised fragments as had been accidentally discovered in the course of excavation, and that the complete skeleton of such a gigantic specimen as that before him would be regarded as a priceless acquisition by the curator of the Natural History Museum at South Kensington; so he at once resolved to take the necessary steps for its preservation. He gave orders for the line to which the hook was bent to be led aft, for convenience of towage, and then commanded his crew to set the cutter's sails, his purpose being to tow the carcass to a lonely part of the shore, and there have the body hauled up out of water, the flesh carefully removed from the bones, and the skeleton as carefully disarticulated, prior to packing it for dispatch to England.

But the cutter was scarcely under way, and heading for the spot that had been selected as suitable for the above operations, when a disturbance of the water near at hand indicated the presence of some bulky moving body, most probably the companion of the dead creature, which had been terrified into temporary flight by the report of Harry's rifle. The animal, however, or whatever it might be, remained invisible, the little swirling eddies and ripples on the surface of the water alone betraying its whereabouts. But while Harry and his friends were discussing this appearance, and wondering what it might portend, one of them happened to glance around him in another direction, and his startled exclamation caused the rest of the party to look in the direction toward which he pointed. And there, somewhat to their consternation, the party saw, not half a dozen yards away, on the cutter's weather beam, the indications that two more of the monsters were present, keeping way with the cutter, and, as was presently pretty evident, edging in toward her; indeed, so close were they to her that an occasional momentary flicker of the black back of the nearer of the two could already be caught through the gleaming water. Two or three of the nobles who had by this time succeeded in pulling themselves together and getting a grip upon their courage, proposed an instant attack upon the monsters; but Escombe felt that, for the moment, he had as much upon his hands as he could manage. For with that huge dead bulk in tow the cutter was scarcely under command, and he had no desire to scare the creatures away by commencing an attack upon them which he could not follow up.

The choice, however, was not left to him for long; for within five minutes of the discovery of the last arrivals all three of the plesiosauri, as with one consent and at a signal, closed in upon the carcass of their comrade, and, flinging themselves upon it with the utmost fury, gave themselves up to the task of tearing it to pieces, the work being accomplished in the midst of a foaming, splashing turmoil of water that was absolutely terrifying to witness, which caused the little cutter to pitch and roll to such an extent that it was almost impossible to retain a footing upon her heaving deck. Whether the creatures made any attempt to devour the great lumps of flesh that they tore from the violently swaying carcass it was quite impossible to determine, but in any case the process of disintegration was a speedy one, for in less than ten minutes from the moment of attack all that was left attached to the hook was the head of the defunct saurian.

Justly vexed at this malicious interference with his plans, and determined to save at least this last relic as a trophy of his prowess, the young Inca gave orders for the head to be hauled inboard; but upon the first attempt to do this, one of the monsters made a savage rush and seized the head in its great jaws, worrying it as a dog worries a rat, giving utterance as it did so to a succession of horrid grunting kind of growls that caused most of the hearers to break into a cold perspiration. So tenaciously did the brute retain its grip that for a few minutes the onlookers were almost persuaded that it was hooked; but ultimately it released the mangled fragment—which its powerful jaws had by this time crushed and splintered almost out of recognition—and, retreating some thirty yards, suddenly wheeled and came foaming back to the yacht, at which it made a furious dash, with the apparent determination to climb on board and sweep her deck clear of its human freight. So resolute, indeed, was it in driving home its attack that it actually succeeded in getting its two fore flippers in on the boat's deck, scattering its occupants right and left, and almost driving two or three over the side, while so heavily was the boat listed by the weight of the monster, that Harry, sliding upon the steeply inclined deck, had the narrowest possible escape of being precipitated headlong into the creature's gaping jaws, and indeed only saved himself by stretching out his hand and thrusting the snout violently aside, the violence of the thrust luckily enabling him to recover his equilibrium. Then Umu—who appeared to be the only native of the party blessed with any real courage or presence of mind—seeing his beloved master in imminent danger, as he believed, of being seized and devoured before their eyes, raised his bow, and hastily fitting an arrow to the string, drew the shaft to its very head and let it fly into the reptile's throat, where it stuck fast, inflicting so much pain that the beast at once flung itself back into the water, roaring and choking, coughing up blood, and throwing itself into the most indescribable contortions.

Then a very extraordinary thing happened. No sooner did the wounded plesiosaurus begin to vomit blood than the other two, which had meanwhile been swimming excitedly to and fro, hurled themselves upon it in what seemed to be a perfect frenzy of fury, and a most ferocious and sanguinary battle ensued, the swirling, flying, foam-flecked water being almost instantly deeply dyed with blood, while the air fairly vibrated with the terrifying sounds emitted by the combatants. The cutter, meanwhile, relieved of the heavy drag upon her of the carcass of the dead plesiosaurus, began to slide rapidly away from the vicinity of the fighting monsters, and would soon have left them far behind. But this did not at all suit Harry, who, having undertaken to destroy the ferocious reptiles, was by no means inclined to leave his task less than half done. He therefore put the cutter about and, to the mingled astonishment and dismay of his companions, headed her back toward the scene of the combat, steering in such a manner as to pass just to leeward of the spot where the violent commotion in the water showed that the battle was still raging with unabated fury. Then, as the boat ranged up alongside, with her foresheet hauled to windward, the great bodies of the monsters could be seen rushing and plunging and leaping hither and thither, whereupon the whole party of sportsmen opened a vigorous and well-directed fire of arrows and javelins upon them, Harry chiming in with his deadly rifle whenever a good chance for a shot offered itself. The result of this determined attack was that the young leader was lucky enough to get in a splendid shot close behind the left shoulder of one of the struggling brutes, which must have reached its heart, for upon receiving the bullet the great reptile flung itself more than half out of the water, uttering a dreadful cry as it did so, and then, falling back, turned slowly over, and with one last writhing, convulsive shudder, sank slowly to the bottom of the lake. Meanwhile the remaining two, both severely wounded, flung themselves upon each other with such a maniacal intensity of fury as was truly awful to see. Finally, one of the monsters succeeded in getting a firm grip upon the throat of the other, and hung on, despite the frantic struggles of the other to get clear. For perhaps two full minutes the commotion in the water was positively terrific; then it rapidly decreased until, probably quite exhausted by the intensity of their prolonged efforts, they lay practically still upon the surface of the water, their only signs of life being an occasional slight twist of the body on the part of one or the other of them. Such an opportunity was much too good to be missed, and, raising his rifle, Escombe was lucky enough to shoot both the monsters dead by a couple of rapid, well-directed shots through the head. The two carcasses immediately began to sink; but before they vanished completely out of sight, one of the cutter's crew, by means of a lucky cast, succeeded in hooking one of the defunct saurians with the great fish hook; and by this means the monster was eventually landed, with some difficulty, at the spot originally chosen for the purpose. Thus terminated the great plesiosaurus hunt, after nearly three hours of the most exciting work that Escombe had ever enjoyed.

Chapter Seventeen
Huanacocha the Plotter

About a fortnight after Escombe's destruction of the plesiosauri, it pleased Huanacocha, the late chief of the Council of Seven, to entertain a small but select party of his especial friends at a banquet, which he gave in his house, situate on the borders of the lake, the grounds of which adjoined those of the Virgins of the Sun, which, in turn, were contiguous to those of the royal palace.

Huanacocha was probably the most wealthy man in the City of the Sun, next to the Inca himself; for he had held the position of chief of the Council of Seven for nearly a quarter of a century, and previous to the appearance of Escombe upon the scene the portion of the national revenue that would otherwise have gone into the coffers of the sovereign had always been awarded to the Council of Seven; while, Huanacocha being not only an astute but also an utterly unscrupulous man, of exceptionally strong and overbearing character, the larger portion of this award had regularly found its way, by various devious channels, into his own private treasure chest. He was consequently well able to offer his guests an entertainment of almost regal magnificence. It is not to be wondered at, therefore, that when the Lord Huanacocha issued invitations to a banquet—which was not very often—the full number of the invited generally made a point of accepting, and being present at the function.

Upon the occasion in question the guests consisted of our old friends Tiahuana, the Villac Vmu, and Motahuana, together with the Lords Licuchima and Chalihuama, late of the Council of Seven, and the Lords Chinchacocheta and Lehuava—six in all.

It is not necessary to describe the banquet in detail; let it suffice to say that, for reasons of his own, the host had given special instructions that neither trouble nor expense was to be spared to make the function a complete success; and that therefore, so well had his instructions been carried out, the entertainment as a whole fell not very far short of that which had marked the occasion of Escombe's accession to the throne of the Incas.

There is no need to record in detail the conversation that followed upon the dismissal of the servants. It is sufficient to say that Huanacocha had arranged this banquet with the express object of eliciting the views of his guests upon a certain project that had been gradually taking shape in his mind, which he believed was now ripe for execution. But, to his astonishment and consternation, he now discovered that he had to a very important extent entirely misapprehended the situation; and after a long and somewhat heated discussion the meeting had broken up without result, save that the guests had departed from his house in a mutually distrustful and uneasy frame of mind.

When Huanacocha at length retired to rest that night not only did he feel somewhat uneasy, but he was also distinctly angry with himself; for although he had achieved the purpose with which the banquet had been given—which was to elicit a frank expression of opinion from certain individuals relative to the Inca and his schemes of reformation—he felt that he had blundered badly. He had used neither tact nor discretion in his manner of conducting the conversation; he had been reckless even to the point of suggesting opposition to the decrees of the sovereign; and when it was too late, when he had fatally committed himself, he had seen, to his discomfiture, that two of his companions—and those two the most powerful persons in the community, next to the Inca himself, namely the Villac Vmu and his deputy, Motahuana—were distinctly out of sympathy with him. True, the Villac Vmu had expressed himself as puzzled, disturbed, anxious at the attitude of the Inca towards the religious question; but it was perfectly clear that the frame of mind of the High Priest was not nearly acute enough to induce him to regard with favour, or even with patience, any suggestion at all savouring of sedition. And he, Huanacocha, in his heat and impatience, had been foolish enough to throw out such a suggestion. The question that now disturbed him was: what would be Tiahuana's attitude toward him henceforward in view of what he had said; nay more, what would be the attitude of the High Priest toward his friends in view of what they had said? Would the Villac Vmu and his deputy accept a suggestion which he had thrown out, that this momentous and imprudent conversation should be regarded as private and confidential, and treat it as such, or would they consider it their duty to report the affair to the Inca? If they did, then Huanacocha knew that he and his friends would have good cause to regret their imprudence; for, despite all his cavilling, the late Chief of the Council of Seven had already seen enough of Escombe's methods to feel certain that the young monarch would stand no nonsense, particularly of the seditious kind, and that, at the first hint of anything of that sort, if the culprits did not lose their heads, they would at least find themselves bestowed where their seditious views could work no mischief.

As these reflections passed through the mind of Huanacocha, that somewhat impulsive and overbearing individual grew increasingly uneasy, and he now began to fear that he had been altogether too outspoken.

For, be it known, this man Huanacocha had conceived nothing less than the audacious idea of overthrowing the Inca, and securing his own election in his stead. In his capacity of Chief of the Council of Seven he had for a long term of years enjoyed a measure of power scarcely less than that invested in the Inca himself; for, being by nature of an unusually arrogant and domineering disposition, while the other members of the Council had been exceedingly pliant and easy-going, he had never experienced any difficulty in browbeating them into tolerably quick compliance with his wishes, however extravagant they might happen to have been. As for the people, they had rendered the same implicit, unquestioning obedience to the Council that they would have rendered to the Inca, had there been one on the throne. Having enjoyed this power, together with all the privileges and emoluments attaching thereto, for so long a time, Huanacocha had found it particularly hard and unpleasant to be called upon to resign them all, practically at a moment's notice, when young Escombe made his appearance upon the scene. Possibly, had Harry chanced to conform to this man's preconceived opinion of what the Inca would be like whenever it should please him to revisit the earth, he might have accepted the situation with a reasonably good grace; but to be ousted by "a mere boy"—for as such he always thought of the young Inca—was altogether too much to be submitted to tamely.

At the first his mental revolt had been vague, indefinite, and formless; perhaps he had thought that in course of time it would pass away and he would grow reconciled to the new order of things, particularly if the young Inca should show himself properly willing to submit to the guiding hand of the Council of Seven, as represented by its late chief. But Escombe lost no time in making it perfectly clear to everybody that he had his own ideas upon the subject of government, and meant to act upon them. Upon more than one occasion—upon several, in fact—the young Inca had turned a deaf ear to the counsels of Huanacocha, and had carried out his own ideas because he had honestly believed them to be better and more advantageous to the community. He had put his foot down heavily upon many abuses of power on the part of certain of the highest nobles, and in this way Huanacocha had suffered perhaps more severely than anyone else. For this reason his condition of mental revolt, instead of passing away, gathered new force and gradually began to assume a definite form which ultimately resolved itself into the determination to cause Harry's "removal" by some means—he did not particularly care what they were—and procure his own election to the vacant throne, if that might be; or, if not that, at least the re-instatement of the Council of Seven, with himself, of course, as its chief.

With this object in view he had commenced operations by proceeding to manufacture sedulously a number of imaginary grievances from which he asserted that the people were suffering, and these he industriously spread abroad among his own friends, hoping that in course of time they would filter through to the people themselves, and be eagerly adopted by them; which delectable plan certainly met with some measure of success.

But as he lay tossing sleeplessly upon his bed he realised that he had that evening been both foolish and precipitate: he had seriously mistaken the nature of the views held by the two priests, and had betrayed himself and his friends in their presence. How would the Villac Vmu and his deputy act, or would they act at all, was the question which he now repeatedly asked himself? Could he by any means ascertain their intentions? He must, by fair means or foul: it would never do for him to remain in ignorance upon such a vital point after the reckless manner in which he and his friends had spoken. Ay, and more than that, he must make quite sure that they maintained silence upon the subject of that most imprudent conversation, otherwise—!

He flung himself over restlessly upon his bed: the longer he thought upon the matter the more glaring did his folly appear. He must guard himself and his friends from the consequences of that folly at all costs. But how? Who was there to advise him? Suddenly he bethought himself of Xaxaguana, the priest who ranked next below Motahuana. Of course, he was the very man of all others; for, first of all, he was Huanacocha's very particular friend, and a man, moreover, who was deeply indebted to him for many past favours of a somewhat exceptional kind; also he was young, comparatively speaking, very ambitious, and not over scrupulous. Yes, Xaxaguana was undoubtedly the man for his purpose, and Huanacocha told himself, with a smile of relief, that he had been a fool for not thinking of the priest before.

But although Huanacocha believed that he saw in Xaxaguana the "friend in need" for whom he had been so anxiously casting about, he was still much too uneasy to sleep, and he was up and about with the appearance of the first faint suggestion of dawn, too anxious to remain inactive any longer, yet fully conscious of the fact that the hour was altogether too early for him to seek his friend without running a very grave risk of attracting unwelcome attention by so unusual a proceeding. He therefore decided to take a long walk, and think the whole affair over again while his brain and his pulses were being steadied by the cool, fresh air of the morning.

Was it fate or was it mere chance that caused him to select a route which led him past that part of the temple which constituted the quarters of the priests? Huanacocha told himself that it was his lucky star that was in the ascendant; for as he was passing the building the door gently opened and the very man that he was so anxious to see stepped into the roadway and quietly closed the door behind him. Then he looked round and beheld Huanacocha, and a little ejaculation of astonishment escaped him.

"This is a fortunate meeting indeed," he exclaimed as he stepped forward to greet his friend; "most fortunate; for perhaps you will be astonished to hear that I am thus early astir with the express object of seeking you."

"Ah!" thought Huanacocha; "unless I am greatly mistaken that means that I must prepare for the worst." But, having by this time shaken off his panic to a considerable extent, and once more pulled himself together, he decided to allow his friend to speak first, as by so doing he would probably be better able to judge what he should himself say. He therefore responded to Xaxaguana's greeting by remarking:

"Then it is lucky that I chose this direction for my morning ramble, otherwise we should have missed each other. You look somewhat astonished at seeing me astir so early; but the fact is, my friend, that I was sleepless; I have therefore left my bed early, to take a walk in the early morning air. But I understood you to say that you wished to see me. Which way shall we go?"

"Let us go up the road toward the hills," answered Xaxaguana. "There will be the less chance of our being seen; and it may be well for me to mention, at the outset, that there may be several good reasons why you and I should not be seen together at this juncture, my Lord Huanacocha."

"Ah! and wherefore so, my good friend?" demanded Huanacocha.

"Because," answered Xaxaguana, "last night you betrayed yourself into the committal of a serious imprudence, namely that of presuming to criticise unfavourably certain acts of our Lord the Inca, which, as you are surely aware, is a crime punishable with death. Do you ask how I happen to know this? I will tell you. It chanced that I was kept late from my bed last night by certain business connected with the approaching Feast of Raymi, and I was therefore astir when the Villac Vmu and Motahuana returned from your banquet. You may possibly be aware that it is a rule among us that nothing which transpires within the precincts of the temple is ever to be referred to, or even so much as hinted at, outside the temple walls. It is therefore our habit, when within those walls, to speak before each other with the most perfect freedom; and, friend Huanacocha, I am breaking one of our most stringent vows in telling you even this much. I hope, therefore, that should the time ever arrive when you can do me a service, you will remember this fact, and allow it to weigh in my favour."

"Rest assured that I will do so, my good friend," answered Huanacocha; "although methinks that there are one or two services rendered to you for which I have as yet received no adequate return. But let that pass; I am interrupting you; pray proceed with your story."

"I will," returned Xaxaguana. "As I have already mentioned, I was astir when Tiahuana and Motahuana returned from your house last night. They entered the common room, in which I was at work—possibly because it was the only room in which any lights were burning—and, flinging themselves upon a couch quite near to me, began to talk. It was easy to see that they were much agitated and excited; but, being busy, I paid little heed to their conversation at the outset, and only pricked up my ears when I heard your name mentioned. Then I confess that I listened, and soon heard sufficient to convince me that you, Huanacocha, and your friends Lehuava, Chinchacocheta, Licuchima, and Chilihuama were, last night, guilty of such imprudence as may well cost you all your lives, unless you have the wit and readiness of action to prevent it!"

"But," ejaculated Huanacocha, all his former alarms returning to him with tenfold force, "how mean you, friend? Surely, neither the Villac Vmu nor Motahuana will dream of reporting what was said within the privacy of my house, will they?"

"What was said in the privacy of your house, last night, amounted to blasphemy," remarked Xaxaguana dryly; "and it is the bounden duty of every loyal subject of the Inca to report blasphemy, wherever it may be spoken. From what was said last night I gathered the impression that neither of the persons mentioned are likely to shrink from the performance of their duty, however unpleasant it may be; so for this reason I set out to warn you this morning. And it was for reasons connected with this that I ventured to indicate the exceeding undesirability of our being seen together just now."

"But—but—" stammered Huanacocha, completely thrown off his balance by what he had just learned—"if I understand you aright, my good Xaxaguana, all this means that the lives of my friends and myself have been put into the utmost jeopardy by my crass folly of last night, I knew—yes, I knew, when it was too late, that I had been a fool," he concluded bitterly.

"To be absolutely candid with you, friend Huanacocha, I think you were," rejoined Xaxaguana somewhat cynically. "Why did you do it?"

Huanacocha stopped short in the middle of the road and looked his friend square in the eye.

"Xaxaguana," said he, "when I was Chief of the Council of Seven it was in my power to do you several good turns—and I did them. Under certain conceivable circumstances it might be in my power to do you several others; and if you can indicate to me a way by which I can extricate myself from my present peril, rest assured that I will not prove ungrateful. I believe you are my friend; and I believe also that you are astute enough to recognise that I can serve you better living than dead. I will therefore be perfectly frank with you and will tell you all that has been in my mind of late. But see, there is the sun, and the good folk of the town will soon be astir, and we may be seen together; let us go over yonder and sit in the shadow of that pile of rocks; we can talk freely there without risk of being seen, or interrupted."

Without another word Xaxaguana turned and led the way across the upland meadow to a somewhat remarkable pile of rocks that cropped out of the soil about a hundred yards from the road, and, passing round to the shady side, which was also the side hidden from the road, seated himself on a bed of soft moss, signing to his companion to do the same. For nearly an hour the pair conversed most earnestly together; then Xaxaguana rose to his feet and, reconnoitring the road carefully to see that there was no likelihood of his being observed, stepped forth from his place of concealment. Then he hurried across the intervening stretch of grass, and on reaching the road, once more glanced keenly about him, and briskly turned his steps homeward. Half an hour later Huanacocha did pretty much the same thing; and it was noticeable—or would have been, had there been anyone there to see—that his countenance had lost much of the expression of anxiety that it had worn when he set out for his walk early that morning. He had scarcely bathed and finished his morning meal after his unwonted exertions when his favourite servant rushed into his presence and in agitated accents informed him that one of the underlings of the temple, on his passage into the town, had given forth the startling intelligence that the Villac Vmu and Motahuana, both of whom had been his lord's honoured guests at the banquet of the previous night, had just been found dead upon their beds!

Chapter Eighteen
Trapped!

The emotion of Huanacocha at this surprising piece of news was almost painful to see. As he listened to the hurriedly told story, poured forth by his man, his features took on a sickly yellow tinge, his eyes seemed to be on the point of starting out of his head, and his breath came in labouring gasps from his wide-open mouth; finally, when at length he seemed to have fully grasped the purport of the story, he hid his face in his hands, rested his elbows upon his knees, and sat there quivering like an aspen leaf. In the course of a few minutes, however, he regained his self-control, and with a sigh of such depth that anyone unaware of its melancholy cause might have almost mistaken it for one of relief, he rose to his feet and, muttering to himself something about the difficulty of believing so incredible a story, and the necessity for personally ascertaining the truth, he gave orders for his litter to be brought to the door, and presently sallied forth on his way to the temple, with this intention.

The distance to be covered was not great, and by the time that Huanacocha reached the temple he had almost completely recovered his composure. Alighting from his litter, and bidding his bearers to wait, he climbed the long flight of steps leading up to the building and, accosting the first person he met, demanded, in an authoritative tone of voice to see Xaxaguana. It was perfectly evident, even to one less experienced than Huanacocha in matters pertaining to the temple routine and its discipline, that some very unusual occurrence had happened, for everybody about the place seemed excited, agitated, distraught; but Huanacocha was, of course, well known to every inhabitant of the City of the Sun, and presently someone was found possessing enough authority to deal with the great man's request, or command, rather, and in the course of a few minutes he was conducted along a passage and shown into an empty room, there to await the arrival of the man he sought.

Apparently Xaxaguana was busy at the moment, for it was nearly a quarter of an hour ere he appeared, and when he did so his countenance was heavy with concern.

"Pardon me for having kept you so long waiting, my Lord," he said in a loud voice, "but this terrible occurrence, of which I presume you have heard, has thrown us all into a shocking state of confusion, and when your message reached me I was, in my capacity of senior priest, with the physicians whom we summoned, and who have been endeavouring to discover the cause of the death of our lamented friends the Villac Vmu and Motahuana." And, as he spoke, he closed the door carefully behind him.

"And have they succeeded?" demanded Huanacocha.

"Oh yes!" answered Xaxaguana. "They are in complete agreement that the cause of death in each case was senile decay. They were both very old men, you know."

"Senile decay!" exclaimed Huanacocha, in astonishment. "Surely you are not serious, Xaxaguana. Why, they were at my house last night, as you know, and nobody who then saw them will ever believe that they died of old age. They were almost as active and vigorous as the youngest of us, and neither of them exhibited the slightest symptoms of senile decay."

"Possibly not," assented Xaxaguana; "nevertheless that is the verdict of the physicians. And, after all, you know, these exceedingly old men often pass away with the suddenness of a burnt-out lamp; a single flicker and they are gone. I must confess that, personally, I am not altogether surprised; for when they returned from your house last night it occurred to me that they seemed to have suddenly grown very old and feeble; indeed I said as much when the news of their death was brought to me."

"You did, did you?" retorted Huanacocha. "By our Lord the Sun, you are a wonder, Xaxaguana; nothing less! How did you manage it, man, and so promptly too? Why it must all have happened within half an hour of your return home this morning."

"It did," said Xaxaguana. "I was still in my bath—for you must know that, being somewhat fatigued with my protracted labours of yesterday, I overslept myself this morning—when the intelligence was brought to me that our two friends had been discovered lying dead in their beds. And they could only have died very recently, for they were neither stiff nor cold."

"And—I suppose there were no signs—no marks of violence on the bodies; nothing to suggest the possibility of—of—foul play?" stammered Huanacocha.

"No," answered Xaxaguana; "the physicians found nothing whatever of that kind. How should they? It is certain that both men died in their beds, within the precincts of the temple. And who is there within these precincts who would dare to commit an act of sacrilege, to say nothing of the fact that, so far as is known, there is no one who would be in the slightest degree benefited by their death, or could possibly desire it."

Huanacocha looked at his friend admiringly.

"As I said just now, you are a wonder, Xaxaguana," he remarked. "But you have not yet told me how you managed it, and I am anxious to know. So set aside all further pretence, my friend; be frank with me, and satisfy my curiosity."

"No," said Xaxaguana firmly. "The man who has a secret and fails to keep it to himself is a fool, friend Huanacocha, and I am not a fool; therefore if I happen to have a secret I prefer to retain it within my own breast. But the matter stands thus. You told me certain things this morning, and among them was this. You said that if perchance anything were to happen to Tiahuana and Motahuana, that they died before it was possible for them to take certain action which you had reason to fear, you would use your powerful influence with our Lord the Inca to see that I obtained promotion to the position of Villac Vmu, as is, indeed, my right, together with certain other advantages. Is not that so? Very well. Singularly enough, that which you desired has happened—most fortunately for you; and now it seems to me that all that remains is for you to fulfil your promise. Do not you agree with me?"

"Yes," answered Huanacocha frankly, "I do; and I will proceed hence to the palace and officially inform the Inca of the sudden and lamented death of the Villac Vmu and his deputy, and will urge the immediate appointment of yourself to the vacant post of High Priest. There is no doubt that you will get the appointment, for in the first place you are entitled to it as senior priest; in the next, you will get the full advantage of my recommendation; and, in the third, the Inca has no personal friend to whom he would wish to give the appointment in preference to yourself. That matter may therefore be regarded as settled.

"But there is another, and an equally important, matter which I now wish to discuss with you, Xaxaguana, and in which I desire your advice and help. Tiahuana and Motahuana being dead, there is nobody, so far as I know, who has any particular interest in retaining the present Inca upon the throne. To that remark you may of course object that he is the re-incarnated Manco whose coming, as the regenerator of the ancient Peruvian nation, was prophesied by Titucocha, and that, in the event of anything happening to him, the regenerating process would be deferred indefinitely. But, I ask you, my dear friend, what if it were? In what way should we suffer? It is true that we have accustomed ourselves to look forward to our regeneration as the one thing to be desired above and before all others; but is it? We are perfectly happy here in this valley as we are. Do we in very truth desire to exchange our present happy and peaceful existence for an indefinite and doubtless long period of toil, and warfare, and suffering? And in what respects should we be the better at the end, even if we should be successful— of which, permit me to say, I have my doubts? And do we really desire that change in the character of our religion, and the so-called amendment of our morals upon which this young man insists? I doubt it, my friend, not only as regards you and myself, but also as regards the people generally. Now, I have spoken to you quite frankly; be equally frank with me, and give your view of the matter."

"I will, my friend, and in a very few words," answered Xaxaguana. "My view of the matter is identical with your own. And it is possibly identical also with that of many others. But how is that going to help us? Also, with all your frankness you have not yet given utterance to the idea that I see you have in your mind. You are far too cautious, friend Huanacocha, ever to become a successful conspirator."

"One must needs be cautious in broaching such a conspiracy as I have in my mind," answered Huanacocha. "Nevertheless," he continued, "boldness and caution are sometimes the same thing, therefore will I be bold with you, Xaxaguana, since I think it will not be difficult for me to prove to you that not only our views, but also our interests, are identical. In a word, then, I believe that it would be advantageous to you and to me—and possibly also to the rest of the inhabitants of this valley—if the present Inca were deposed, and I were made Inca in his place. The question is, how is the matter to be accomplished? If he were to die now, even as the Villac—"

"It would be the most unfortunate thing that could possibly happen," cut in Xaxaguana. "The Villac Vmu and Motahuana were both old men, and therefore that they should die is not at all remarkable. But that they should both die at the same moment is, to say the least of it, somewhat singular, and, despite all our precautions, is not unlikely to arouse more or less suspicion in many minds. Now, if the Inca also were to die, that suspicion would undoubtedly be converted into certainty and an investigation would assuredly be set on foot which could not fail to end disastrously for those found responsible for the three deaths, and especially for that of the Inca; for, as of course you are fully aware, practically the whole of the inhabitants of the valley are still old-fashioned enough to cling to the superstition that to murder the Inca is the blackest of black sacrilege.

"But on the day when the Inca was presented to us in the temple, you spoke certain words which, if they were now repeated, might find an echo in the mind of many an inhabitant of this city. You boldly expressed your doubts as to the identity of the youth with him whose appearance was foretold by the prophet Titucocha, and whom we of the ancient Peruvian nation have been expecting for the last three hundred years and more. Now, we know that many of the Inca's ordinances are regarded with disfavour by the people generally; and I believe that, as a consequence of this, it would not be very difficult to implant in the minds of the discontented a suggestion that the late Villac Vmu made a very serious mistake—if, indeed, he did not commit an unpardonable crime—in introducing this young man to us as the re-incarnated Manco Capac. That suspicion once instilled into them, it should be a comparatively easy matter to incite them to demand that the Inca shall establish his identity by submitting to the ordeal by fire, after which your election to the vacant throne should be a foregone conclusion; for, of course, neither you nor I believe for a moment that the young Englishman can possibly survive the fire ordeal."

Huanacocha gazed at his companion for several moments in silent admiration; then he exclaimed enthusiastically:

"I have already told you twice this morning that you are a wonder, and I now say it for the third time—you are a wonder, Xaxaguana, the possessor of the most astute and clever brain in the valley; and I foresee that, working together, you and I may achieve such dazzling results as we have scarcely yet dared to dream of. But how do you propose to bring about the result of which you have just spoken? It will be a slow and tedious process at best, and while it is being achieved many things may happen."

"Nay," answered Xaxaguana, "it will not be nearly so lengthy a process as you seem to think. This is my plan."

And, placing his mouth to his companion's ear, Xaxaguana proceeded to whisper a few sentences which appeared to fill Huanacocha with wonder and admiration.

"Do you think it will succeed?" Xaxaguana demanded, as he concluded his communication.

"It cannot possibly fail, if carried out with promptitude and discretion," answered Huanacocha in tones of conviction. "And its perfect simplicity is its greatest recommendation. When do you propose to commence operations?"

"At once," answered Xaxaguana, "now, this very day. Nothing will be talked of during the next few days save the sudden death of the Villac Vmu and Motahuana, and such a topic of conversation will afford me the precise opportunity which I require. And now, friend Huanacocha, you and I have been together quite as long as is either prudent or desirable. Go, therefore, hence to the palace, acquaint the Inca with the sad news of which you are the official bearer; inform him, if you will, that in the zealous discharge of your duty you have visited me for the purpose of obtaining the fullest information relative to the deplored event, and direct his attention to the extreme desirability of creating me Villac Vmu at once."

"Fear not, friend," answered Huanacocha, as he rose to take his leave, "you shall receive the notification of your appointment in the course of the day." And, followed by Xaxaguana, who accompanied him as far as the outer door, he left the apartment and proceeded on his way to the palace.

Huanacocha was as good as his word; for he not only secured from Harry the appointment of Xaxaguana to the dignity of Villac Vmu, but actually took the trouble to hurry back from the palace to the temple with the information of his success, and the royal warrant duly signed.

As Xaxaguana had anticipated, almost the sole topic of conversation during the ensuing fortnight was the death of the late Villac Vmu, and that of his deputy, at practically the same instant of time, as was determined by the physicians. For the first few days this circumstance was spoken of simply as a somewhat remarkable coincidence, but not very long after the obsequies—which were celebrated with unprecedented pomp in the temple—were over, it began to be noticed that, when the subject happened to be referred to, people were acquiring a trick of putting their heads together and whispering mysteriously to each other. The trick rapidly developed into something nearly approaching a habit; and as it did so, the whispers as rapidly changed into plain, open speech, and the words which were interchanged lost their original air of confidential mysteriousness, until, finally, people told each other without very much circumlocution that there was, in their opinion, more in the strange deaths of Tiahuana and Motahuana than met the eye. And if they were asked to express themselves more plainly they reminded each other that the two priests, who had died under such really remarkable circumstances, were the men who were responsible for the finding of the white Inca, and the introduction of him into the community, and this reminder was quite frequently followed by a somewhat pointed question as to whether, after all, they—the priests— could by any chance have made a mistake in their method of identifying the Inca, some people even going to the length of expressing the opinion that it was no question of mistake, but rather a case of deliberate deception of the people, with some mysterious purpose which would probably now be never brought to light, inasmuch as that our Lord the Sun, angry at the change in the form of the national religion, has cut off the offenders in the midst of their sins, as a sign of His displeasure. The transition from such talk as this to openly expressed doubts concerning the genuineness of the Inca's claim to be the re-incarnation of the divine Manco Capac was an easy one, made all the more easy by the unpopular character of many—one might indeed almost say all—of Escombe's decrees. Yet so consummate was the cunning and subtlety with which the campaign was conducted that scarcely a whisper of it was allowed to reach the ears of those who were suspected of being favourably inclined toward the Inca, and not the faintest inkling of it ever penetrated to Escombe himself. Such extreme care indeed was exercised by those who were pulling the strings that no sign whatever of the Inca's fast-waning popularity was for a moment permitted to manifest itself. The process of corrupting the palace officials and staff generally was found to be exceptionally tedious and difficult, for Escombe's genial disposition and straightforward character enabled him to endear himself without effort to everybody with whom he was brought into intimate contact. But it was accomplished at length by the exercise of almost superhuman ingenuity, with a solitary exception in the case of Arima, who, it was at once recognised, was so faithfully and devotedly attached to his royal master that it would be worse than folly to attempt to corrupt him; he was therefore left severely alone; the most stringent precautions being taken to keep the whole thing secret from him.

Matters had reached the stage above indicated when Escombe, having grappled with an exceptionally arduous day's work, retired to rest close upon midnight, and soon afterward sank into a heavy sleep, only to be, as it seemed, almost instantly awakened by the light of torches flashing upon his closed eyelids, and the scuffle of sandalled feet about his couch. Springing up into a sitting posture in his bed, he opened his eyes, still heavy with sleep, to find his chamber full of men—many of whom were armed—conspicuous among whom were Huanacocha and Xaxaguana, the new Villac Vmu.

"PASS THE WORD FOR ARIMA"
Page 264

"Why, my Lord Huanacocha," he exclaimed, rubbing his eyes to assure himself that he was awake, "what does this mean? How did you get in here? And what is the matter?"

"The matter, Lord," answered Huanacocha, "is one of the utmost gravity and importance, as the Villac Vmu, here, will inform you. It is nothing less than a revolt among the priests generally, most of whom have declared against the modifications in the form of the worship and service in the temple, instituted by my Lord, and have risen against the Villac Vmu and those others who have pronounced themselves in favour of my Lord's modifications. Some of those who were in favour of the modifications have been slain; but the larger number, amounting to between twenty and thirty, are even now being subjected to the fire ordeal, as would have been the Villac Vmu, had he not happily escaped and made his way to my house for shelter and help. That, in brief, is how the matter stands; is it not, Villac Vmu?"

"'Tis even so, Lord," answered Xaxaguana. "And when I had stated the facts to my Lord Huanacocha, he regarded them as of import serious enough to justify us even to the extent of disturbing the rest of my Lord the Inca, and—"

"By Jove, yes, I should think so," exclaimed Harry, interrupting the High Priest unceremoniously, and springing from his couch to the floor. "Where is Arima? Pass the word for Arima, somebody, please—or, stay, hand me my clothes; I'll get into them myself without waiting for Arima. How many of these revolting priests are there, do you say?"

"They number about a thousand, Lord," answered Xaxaguana. "We have already taken it upon ourselves to send to Umu, asking him to come to our assistance; but it will be some time ere our messenger can reach him, and he in turn can reach and order out the guard. We therefore thought it well to come to my Lord and ask him to hasten with us to the temple, there to use his authority to save the lives of those who must otherwise undergo the fire ordeal."

"Of course," assented Harry, as he scrambled into his clothes. "But what will happen if those mutinous beggars refuse to obey me, eh?"

"Refuse to obey you, Lord?" repeated the Villac Vmu in shocked tones. "Nay, they will certainly not do that. They have revolted now merely because they cannot be brought to believe that the innovations against which they rebel are in accordance with the orders of our Lord the Inca. You have but to personally assure them that such is the case, and they will instantly return to their allegiance."

"Very well," answered Harry, as he threw a heavy cloak over his shoulders to protect himself from the keen night air. "Now I am ready. Lead the way, somebody, and let us be going."

Emerging from the palace, and hurrying along the almost pitch—dark garden paths, the party swept through the palace gates into the main road, and made a dash for the temple by the nearest possible route, which happened to be through several dark, narrow, deserted side streets, in which not a soul was stirring; the little crowd of hurrying figures consequently passed on its way and soon reached the temple without having been observed by so much as a single person.

Somewhat to Escombe's surprise the temple proved to be in absolute darkness, when the party arrived before the walls; but Xaxaguana explained this by informing the young monarch that the revolted priests were all assembled in the opposite wing of the building, and that he had deemed it a wise precaution not to attempt to enter on that side, lest they should meet with resistance before the Inca could find an opportunity to make his presence known. As they drew in under the temple walls Xaxaguana called a halt, expressing some anxiety as to the possibility of the door being closed by means of which he proposed to effect an entrance, and he sent forward a scout to reconnoitre. His anxiety, however, proved to be unfounded, for the scout presently returned with the information that the door was unfastened and everything quiet on that side of the building. The party therefore moved forward once more, and presently Escombe found himself being conducted along a corridor, unlighted save by the smoky flare of the torches carried by his escort. Contrary to the young ruler's expectations, the building, even now that he was inside it, remained dark and silent as the grave; but this was explained by the statement of Xaxaguana that the revolting priests were all gathered together in the rock-hewn basement of the building, where they were at that moment engaged in putting their more faithful brethren to the dreadful "ordeal by fire". Accordingly, when Xaxaguana unlocked a massive bronze gate let into a wall, and invited Harry to descend with him to the chamber where the horrid rite was in progress, the young man followed unhesitatingly, as he also did through a door which the priest unlocked when they had reached the foot of the flight of stone steps and traversed some yards of corridor apparently hewn out of the living rock. The room was comfortably enough furnished, and looked almost as though it might have been prepared for his reception, for it was lighted by a handsome lamp suspended from the roof.

"If my Lord will condescend to wait here a moment and rest, I, his servant, will go and see exactly what is happening, and return to report," remarked Xaxaguana as he stood aside to allow Harry to pass him.

"But why wait?" demanded Harry, facing round to the High Priest. "Surely we have not a moment of time to waste. Would it not be—"

But, even as he was speaking, the Villac Vmu slid rapidly back into the passage, closing the door behind him with a slam, through the thunderous reverberation of which in the hollow vault Harry thought he caught the sound of a sharp click. With a muttered ejaculation, expressive of annoyance, he sprang to the door and endeavoured to open it; but it was fast, and, as he listened, he heard the sounds of hastily retreating footsteps in the passage outside. And in that same moment the truth flashed upon him that, for some inscrutable reason, he was trapped and a prisoner!

Chapter Nineteen
Umu takes a Hand in the Game

The first rays of the next morning's sun had scarcely flashed over the ridge of the sierra which hemmed in the eastern side of the valley, when Arima, awaking with a most atrocious headache, and the feeling generally of a man who has just passed through an unusually prolonged bout of dissipation—or, alternatively, has been drugged—arose from his bed and, staggering across the room, plunged his throbbing and buzzing head into a large basin of cold water, preparatory to dressing. Once, twice, thrice did he plunge head, neck, and hands into the cooling liquid, with but little satisfactory result, for the relief which he sought, and confidently expected to derive, from the process, refused to come; and he groaned as he sank upon a seat and tightly gripped his throbbing temples in his hands. Never before in his life had he felt so ill, so utterly cheap and used-up, as he did at that moment. In addition to the violent headache from which he was suffering, his blood felt like fire in his veins, his skin was dry and rough; he was so giddy that he could scarcely stand. The truth was that he had been drugged with such brutal severity on the preceding night, by Xaxaguana's emissaries, to make sure of his being out of the way at the moment of his master's seizure, that it had been due more to chance than anything else that he had ever again awakened. After a few minutes' rest he felt so much better that he was able to dress, and afterwards make his way to his master's room. For, ever since the slaying of the monsters in the lake, it had been Escombe's habit to rise early in the morning, and, making his way to the bottom of the garden, embark on a balsa, from which, after Arima had paddled it a few hundred yards from the shore, master and man had been wont to bathe together. And now, according to custom, the faithful Indian hurried away to awaken his master, as usual, for indulgence in the regular morning dip.

But upon entering the sleeping chamber he of course found it untenanted, and for a moment the thought occurred to him that possibly he was late, and that his master, having awakened at his usual hour, had risen and gone down into the garden alone. A single glance out of the window, however, at the length of the shadows cast by the various objects lighted by the sun outside, sufficed to satisfy him that habit had triumphed over even the influence of the narcotic which had been administered to him, and that he was certainly not more than a few minutes late. Then, with the instinct of the semi-savage, he flung his glances quickly about the room, and instantly detected signs that it had been invaded during the night by a number of people, and that his master had arisen and dressed in haste. Quick to take the alarm where Escombe was concerned, he at once hurried out, and, without waiting to find any of the palace officials to whom to report his discovery, proceeded forthwith to question as many of the servants as he met. But here again he only found matter for further alarm and apprehension; for not only did the whole service of the building appear to be in a state of complete disorganisation, but it at once became evident to him that every man he met was confused, agitated, and more or less anxious of manner; and, although each and all professed themselves unable to throw any light upon the mystery of the Inca's inexplicable disappearance, he felt instinctively that they were all lying to him.

Realising at length that no information was to be obtained from these people, Arima passed from the palace into the grounds, making his way, in the first instance, down to the shore of the lake, for the purpose of satisfying himself beyond all possibility of question whether or not there was any foundation for his first surmise, that Escombe had risen early and left the palace without waiting for him. But no; there was no sign of his young master in that direction; moreover, the balsa was lying moored in its proper place; also the cutter was at her usual moorings. There was therefore no possibility that the Inca had taken it into his head to go for a solitary early morning sail. Satisfied upon this point, the Indian next made his way round to the front of the palace, and here at once the evidences of a visit of a large party of people to the palace, some time during the preceding night, once more presented themselves, the latest—that is to say the topmost—set of footprints showing that quite a crowd of people had hurried from the main entrance of the building down the broad path leading to the entrance gates of the garden and thence into the main road. Moreover, the "spoor" remained undisturbed in the road for a distance sufficient to indicate the general direction in which the party had gone, although it was lost in the ordinary signs of traffic within a few yards of the gates. Having ascertained thus much, Arima returned to the spot where the footprints first showed outside the palace doors, and, going down upon his hands and knees, patiently set himself to the task of endeavouring to discover his young master's among them. But before he had had time to achieve any result in this direction one of the palace officials appeared and, angrily demanding to know what he was doing there, ordered him back into the palace to attend to his duty; explaining, by way of reply to Arima's agitated representations, that the Inca had left the palace during the early hours of the morning, with a party of companions, to hunt the vicuña. The Indian at once knew this to be a falsehood, for the hunting grounds lay many miles down the valley, and hunting parties never dreamed of proceeding thither otherwise than on horseback, and Arima was prepared to swear that none of the party had been mounted. Moreover he was convinced that his master would never have dreamed of leaving his favourite servant behind had he been bound upon a hunting expedition. The official, however, was curt and peremptory in his manner, and Arima soon understood that he must obey his orders or suffer arrest. He therefore returned to the Inca's rooms and proceeded to put them in order, as was his duty. But the very curtness and peremptoriness of the official's manner to him, as well as the improbable story which he had told, only had the effect of strengthening and confirming the suspicions in the faithful fellow's mind; for the attachment of the young Inca to this man was well known, and even the highest officials of the palace had thus far not disdained to be extremely civil to him.

But the question in Arima's mind now was: what precisely was it that had happened to his young master, and whither and why had he gone? For even thus far no glimmering of the hideous truth had reached the Indian's mind. His suspicions and apprehensions were all as yet chaotic and formless, and he was very far from fearing that Escombe's life was in danger. But as he proceeded with his business, seeking from time to time to get some relief from his splitting headache and the other extremely disagreeable symptoms from which he was still suffering acutely, it gradually began to dawn upon him, as his mental faculties slowly shook off their stupor, that every one of those symptoms were synonymous with those following upon the administration of an overdose of a decoction made from a certain poisonous plant growing here and there in the valley, and which was sometimes used as an anaesthetic by the local physicians. He was fully aware of the tremendous potency of the extracted juices of this plant, as also of its tastelessness, and the consequent ease with which it could be administered, and he recognised clearly that if anyone had wished to administer such a draught to him on the previous night it could easily have been done. The question which next arose in his mind naturally was: why should anyone desire to administer such a draught to him? But his mental powers had by this time sufficiently recovered from the effects of the drug to enable him quickly to trace a connection—however obscure as yet—between this act and the extraordinary fact of his master being missing. When once the faithful fellow had reached the length of connecting the two circumstances together he was not long in realising the terrible possibilities that lurked in such a sinister combination of circumstances. And with this realisation he suddenly took fright, for at the same moment the significance of certain apparently trivial remarks and occurrences that had lately come to his knowledge suddenly dawned upon him. Could it be that these matters, scarcely noticed at the moment, really bore the significance which he now attached to them, or was it all the result of some bodily disorder reacting upon his mental processes and causing him to take a distorted and unnatural view of things that were actually of no moment whatever? He could not tell; his brain was still in too muddled a condition for him to feel that he could trust it. But there was one sensible thing that he could do, he told himself. He could go to Umu and lay the whole matter before him. Umu was a shrewd sensible man, who would soon say whether or not there was anything in those mad fantasies that were now beginning to chase each other through his bewildered brain. Besides, Umu was the Inca's most devoted friend—next to himself, perhaps. So, slipping out of the palace by the garden entrance—lest perchance he should be seen and stopped if he attempted to pass out by way of the other—he plunged at once into the most unfrequented paths, and so betook himself, by a circuitous route, to the lake shore, where he at once got aboard the balsa, and, paddling the primitive craft some half a mile beyond the royal demesne, beached her in a secluded spot, and thence made the best of his way to Umu's house.

The morning was by this time so well advanced that the hour for the first meal of the day was past, and it became a moot point with Arima whether to seek Umu at his house or at the barracks of the Inca's bodyguard. He decided, however, upon trying the house first, and it was well that he did; for, although Umu was not at home, neither, it seemed, was he at the barracks. But Maia, his daughter, had an impression that she knew where he might be found, and Arima had not poured into the girl's ear half a dozen sentences of his somewhat disjointed tale before she cut him short by explaining that she was about to seek her father, and that he (Arima) must on no account whatever attempt to stir from the house until her return, unless, of course, her father should make his appearance in the interim. Having bestowed that injunction, Maia, wild-eyed and white-lipped, rushed into the street and hurried on her way; for she, too, had heard words said, to which at the moment she had given scant heed, but which in the light of what was hinted at by Arima now bore to the quick-witted girl an awful significance.

As it happened, she had not to go very far, for she had not left the house more than five minutes at the utmost when she caught sight of her father, mounted, on his way to the barracks, a good mile distant. Fortunately for her he reined up to exchange a few passing words with an acquaintance, and that afforded her the opportunity to overtake and stop him. She did not dare, however, to mention the errand which had brought her out in search of her father until the two friends had parted, when she briefly explained that Arima was seeking him, and urged him to hasten back to the house without delay, at the same time telling him sufficient of what had passed between herself and the Inca's henchman to cause Umu to realise something of the gravity of the situation; for he dug his heels into his charger's ribs and dashed off at a gallop.

When Maia arrived back at the house, she found Arima in the midst of the relation of his story to her father, and, quite as a matter of course, sat down to listen. The Indian had, in the interim between her departure and Umu's arrival, found time to pull himself together and properly arrange his thoughts, and he related his narrative with due regard to sequence of events, beginning with such apparently casual words and trivial occurrences as had come under his notice, and had only assumed a significance in the light of more recent happenings. Then going on to describe his sensations upon awaking that morning, he completed his story by relating in detail everything he had done, and the thoughts and suspicions that had occurred to him subsequent to his discovery of his master's absence.

"Yes," agreed Umu, when Arima had brought his story to a conclusion, "the whole thing seems reasonably clear, up to a certain point. I have not a shadow of doubt that certain disaffected persons have adopted the extreme, and altogether unprecedented, step of seizing the person of our Lord the Inca; and they caused you, my friend, to be drugged in order that you might not interfere with their plans. The question which we now have to decide is: who are those persons, and what is their object in seizing the Inca? They must be individuals of very great power and influence, otherwise they would never dare—"

At this point Maia, who had been betraying rapidly increasing signs of anxiety and impatience, cut in with:

"My father, to me it seems of the utmost importance that not a moment should be lost in discovering what has become of the Inca, whose life may at this moment be in the utmost jeopardy; for those who were desperate enough to carry him off would probably not hesitate to kill him, if need were: indeed that may be their purpose. Your task, therefore, must be to rescue him without an instant's unnecessary delay, which you should be easily able to do with the aid of your troops. Probably if the officials of the palace were carefully questioned they could be persuaded to tell you what has become of the Inca, for doubtless they know, since he could not have been carried off without their knowledge and acquiescence."

"Yes, you are right, Maia. I see exactly what you mean, and I have no doubt that I can devise a method of making the palace people tell what they know," answered Umu. "I will ride to the barracks at once, and order the guard to turn out in readiness to proceed wherever required; after which I will proceed to the palace with a squadron, and it will be strange if I do not find means to make somebody tell me what I require to know. You, Arima, had better go to the barracks and await my return there from the palace, when you can ride with us. And now I will go; for, as Maia has said, even moments may now be of importance."

Some twenty minutes later a troop of the Inca's mounted bodyguard, led by Umu, dashed at a gallop in through the gates of the palace gardens, and, at a word from their commander, surrounded the building, a party of a dozen of them following their leader into the palace, to the consternation of all who encountered them. This dozen constituted a search party, which, with drawn swords, systematically swept the building from basement to roof-tree, gathering together every official and individual of the palace staff that could be found, until the whole, with the exception of some dozen or so underlings, had been captured. Then all were marched out into the vast palace garden and surrounded by the now dismounted troopers, who meanwhile had made prisoners of four of the chief officials as they were endeavouring to slink out of the palace and make good their escape.

Marching the whole of the captives off to a secluded part of the gardens, where nothing which might happen could be seen save by those immediately concerned, Umu ordered the chamberlain and his three immediate subordinates to be brought to him, and said to them:

"Now, sirs, my business here is to ascertain from you what has become of our Lord the Inca. I have not the slightest doubt that you can tell me; but whether you will tell me the truth or not is quite another matter. I intend to arrive at the truth, however, either by persuasion or force, and I will try the former first: let me very earnestly advise you not to compel me to resort to the latter. And to make as certain as I can that the information with which you are about to furnish me is true, you will each withdraw from your comrades to a distance at which it will be impossible for you to communicate with each other, and where you will each inform the officer—who, with a file of men, will accompany you—of everything that you know concerning the mysterious disappearance of the Inca—where he has been taken, by whom, and for what purpose. If your stories, when compared with each other, are found to agree at all points, I shall consider that I am justified in believing them to be true; if they do not—" He turned to the other captives and said: "Go to work at once, collect timber, and build a large fire in this open space." Then, turning to the officers who had been deputed to examine the four prisoners, Umu concluded: "Take them away; hear their story; and then bring them back to me, that each man's tale may be compared with those of the others."

Umu knew his fellow countrymen well. He was fully aware that while the South American Indian, like his brother of the northern continent, will endure the most frightfully excruciating tortures with stoical fortitude if the occasion happens to demand it, he will not willingly subject himself to even a very minor degree of suffering for the sake of shielding those whom he has no particular object in serving. He felt pretty well convinced that these craven wretches who had allowed themselves to be corrupted into betraying their monarch would have very little hesitation in also betraying their corrupters, especially as they might feel assured that, Umu having taken the matter in hand, those corrupters would henceforth have scant power or opportunity either to reward or to punish. The hint conveyed by the building of a large fire therefore proved quite sufficiently persuasive. In little more than ten minutes the commander of the bodyguard found himself in possession of all the information which the palace officials had it in their power to communicate. This information, in brief, was to the effect that they had, one and all, from the highest to the lowest, been heavily bribed by the emissaries of Huanacocha and Xaxaguana to allow those two powerful nobles, with a strong party of followers, to enter the palace in the dead of night and abduct the person of the Inca, and to hold their peace upon the matter until either Huanacocha or Xaxaguana should personally give them leave to speak and tell them what to say. As the stories of all four of the officials happened to agree, even down to the smallest detail, Umu decided that he might venture to accept them as true; whereupon the whole of the prisoners were hustled back into the palace by way of the back entrance, driven down into one of the basement chambers, and there securely locked up, with a corporal's guard in the passage outside. The palace then being locked up, the troop mounted and departed at a gallop for the house of Huanacocha.

This house, or palace as it might be more appropriately termed, was, like most of the residences of the great Peruvian lords, a large and sumptuous edifice, standing in its own spacious grounds. Umu's tactics upon approaching it were similar to those which he had employed upon approaching the palace; that is to say, upon entering the grounds he caused his men to dismount and surround the building, which he then entered, accompanied by a sergeant in charge of a squad of troopers. As he unceremoniously made his way into the great entrance hall he found himself confronted by the chief steward of the establishment, who, followed by the entire staff of terrified servants, was hurrying to the garden, anxious to ascertain the meaning of this unwonted invasion of his master's privacy.

"Where is your lord, sirrah?" thundered Umu, as a file of soldiers promptly arrested the quaking functionary.

"I know not, Lord Umu," answered the unfortunate man, as well as his chattering teeth would allow; "indeed I was about to send out the servants to seek news of him, for I am beginning to fear that evil has befallen him. He left the house alone last night, less than an hour before midnight, saying that he knew not when he should return; and he has not since been seen."

"Then, if he told you that he knew not when he would return, why do you fear that evil has befallen him?" demanded Umu.

"Because, Lord—nay, I know not, except that—that—well, it is a most unusual—for my Lord Huanacocha to absent himself for so many hours without saying whither he intended to go," stammered the steward.

"Say you so?" sneered Umu. "That seems to me strange indeed; for it is not the usual custom of a noble to acquaint his steward with his business. Nay, friend, I cannot believe your story: you must have some better reason than the one which you have given me for your anxiety as to your lord's safety, and it will be to your great advantage to acquaint me with it forthwith."

"Lord, I have told you the truth; indeed I have," protested the unfortunate man, making as though he would throw himself upon his knees before Umu.

"So much the worse for you," growled Umu savagely, for the delay was beginning to tell upon his patience. "Is there any man here," he continued, "who can tell me where my Lord Huanacocha is to be found?"

He glared round upon the assembled servants, the whole of whom had by this time been quietly herded together by the soldiers. There was no answer.

"Very well," continued Umu, addressing his men. "Take these people down to the cellars below; lock them in securely; and then set fire to the house and burn it over their heads! I can waste no more time here."

As the troopers, in obedience to this order, closed round the prisoners, and with coarse jests began to hustle them unceremoniously toward the head of the flight of steps leading down to the basement of the building, the steward, suddenly realising the desperate nature of his own and his fellow servants' predicament, turned to Umu and cried:

"Stay, Lord, I pray you, and visit not upon us the misdeeds of our lord. When I said just now that I knew not the whereabouts of my Lord Huanacocha, I spoke only the truth, for indeed I cannot tell for certain where he is—nay, Lord, have patience, and hear what I have to say ere you condemn me to a frightful death for a fault which is not mine. It is indeed true that I know not where my Lord Huanacocha is to be found, for he did not deign to tell me his business when he went out last night; but I believe I can form a very good guess as to where he now is."

"You can?" ejaculated Umu. "Then say on, and that right quickly. For within the next five minutes this house will be ablaze, and you within it, if you have not by then told me what I want to know." Then, turning to a sergeant, he said: "Take with you a dozen men; bring everything in the house that will burn, pile it in this hall, and pour on it all the oil you can find. Now, sirrah, proceed with your tale."

"Then, Lord, in brief, it is this," answered the wretched steward, speaking as well as his chattering teeth would allow. "From words which I have overheard from time to time of late passing between my Lord Huanacocha and others, especially the new Villac Vmu, I believe that when my master left this house last night he did so with the purpose of accompanying the High Priest and an armed party to the palace in order to seize the person of our Lord the Inca and convey him to the temple, that he might be subjected to the fire ordeal, to prove whether or no—"

"The fire ordeal, say you?" roared Umu in a paroxysm of fury, as the full horror of the situation at last dawned upon him.

"Even so, Lord," answered the quaking steward. "I heard my—"

"You had reason to believe that your master had conspired with the Villac Vmu to seize the Inca and subject him to the fire ordeal, yet you never took the trouble to come and report the matter to me?" roared Umu.

"I—I—Lord, I knew not that—it was no part of my duty to—" stammered the wretched steward, as too late he began to realise the terrible nature of the predicament in which he had placed himself by his too great fidelity to his master.

"It is enough," interrupted Umu. "Bind him hand and foot; lay him upon that pile yonder; and set fire to it. Sergeant Huarima, you will remain here with six men to ensure the utter destruction of this house, after which you will follow the rest of the corps to the temple. As for you," he continued, turning to the staff of servants, who were huddling together, paralysed with terror at the tragic turn which affairs were taking, "you would only be receiving your just deserts if I were to order you to be consumed, with your chief, upon that pile. I am merciful, however; you are therefore at liberty to go. But let the fate of the steward be a lesson to you all henceforth, that fidelity to the Inca comes before fidelity to your master. And now, men, pass out and mount. Our next place of call is the temple."

Chapter Twenty
In the Nick of Time!

"Well," soliloquised Harry, as he glanced about him upon realising that he was indeed a prisoner, "what does this mean? Is it mutiny, or treason, or what is it? And as to there being a revolt of the priests, I don't believe a word of it. Had there been any such thing it would not have been possible for me to have entered this building without encountering some sign— either sight or sound—of it. No; that was just a yarn, a ruse to get me to come here willingly. Now, I wonder what the dickens they want with me, and what they intend to do with me now that they have me. Nothing very serious, I expect; for I am the Inca, and they would never dare to lay violent hands upon the Inca; that amounts to sacrilege of the very worst kind. Yes; no doubt. And yet I am by no means certain that that fact would exercise any very powerful restraining influence upon our friends Huanacocha and Xaxaguana. They are both ambitious men, and I am very much inclined to question whether the religious convictions of either man are powerful enough to hold him back from sacrilege, if his ambition urged him in that direction. Ah, well! time will show, I have no doubt; meanwhile I have not had half my night's rest, so I will do what I can to recover arrears." And, thus thinking, he quietly stretched himself upon a couch which stood against one wall of the room, and composed himself to sleep.

With the light-hearted carelessness of extreme youth he actually did sleep—slept so soundly that he was not even disturbed when, some hours later, the door was quietly opened and two attendants entered bearing food and drink, which, seeing that the prisoner still slumbered, they placed upon the table and departed, securing the door again as they passed out. It was past ten o'clock in the forenoon when the young man, having completely rested, opened his eyes and looked about him in wonderment at finding himself in strange quarters. The next moment, however, memory returned to him: he recalled the proceedings of the past night, and once more began to speculate upon the purpose which could have been powerful enough to induce Huanacocha and Xaxaguana to resort to so extreme a measure as that of his abduction from the palace. And now, with the more sober reflections following upon a sound night's rest, he began to take a somewhat more serious view of the situation. He began to realise that what these two powerful nobles had done was no hasty, ill-considered act, undertaken upon the spur of the moment, without thought of the probable consequences, but was doubtless the result of long and anxious premeditation; and, if so, they would surely have taken every possible precaution to guard themselves against evil consequences. And—a slight shudder thrilled through him as the thought obtruded itself upon his mind—for aught that he could tell to the contrary one of those precautions might take the form of providing that he should never return to the light of day, and that no one should ever know what had become of him! But here again the optimism of youth came to support him, and he dismissed the grim reflection with a smile; the matter, of course, could not be anything like so serious as that, he told himself, and without doubt in an hour or two hence he would be back in the palace, heartily laughing at the whole adventure.

He drew forth his watch and looked at it. To his astonishment he found that it was a quarter after ten o'clock—for, his place of confinement being below the ground level, and hewn out of the heart of the rock, there were no windows to it, and the only source of light was the lamp suspended from the roof, which still burned brightly. For an instant he was under the impression that his watch had stopped overnight at the hour indicated, but upon putting it to his ear he found that it was still running. Then his eye felt upon the viands on the table, and he suddenly discovered that he was hungry. Without further ado, therefore, he seated himself at the table, and, dismissing for the moment all further considerations of the future, fell to and made a most excellent breakfast.

Escombe had finished his meal a full hour and more, and had found time once more to become distinctly apprehensive as to the intentions of Huanacocha and Xaxaguana toward him, when the sound of footsteps approaching along the passage outside his door warned him that the crisis was at hand, and the next moment the door was flung open and a priest entered.

"My Lord," he said, "it is the command of the Villac Vmu that you accompany me into his presence."

"The command, did you say?" retorted Harry. "Surely the Villac Vmu strangely forgets himself and his position when he presumes to send commands to the Inca. However," seeing that the passage outside was full of armed men who were evidently quite prepared to enforce obedience to the orders of the High Priest, he continued, "I will not stand upon ceremony, or carp at a mere form of words, but will obey the summons of the Villac Vmu. Yet, let him and all who hear me remember that I am the Inca, and that my power to reward obedience is as great as it is to punish presumption. Now, lead on."

The priest led the way into the passage, Harry following, and the moment that the latter emerged from the room in which he had been confined an armed guard of a dozen men closed in around him, rendering escape on his part impossible. In this order the procession passed along the passage, up the steps which Harry had descended upon his arrival, and thence along a corridor into a room crowded with priests and civilians, where, raised upon a dais, sat the Villac Vmu enthroned. Still surrounded by the guard, Harry was halted in front of this dais, and directed to seat himself in a handsome chair that had been placed there for his reception. This done, the proceedings at once commenced, and Harry immediately perceived that he was about to be subjected to some sort of a trial, for no sooner was he seated than the Villac Vmu cried:

"Let my Lord Huanacocha stand forth."

There was a moment's bustle and confusion, and then from the midst of the assembled crowd Huanacocha shouldered his way through, and placed himself near Harry, but outside the encircling guards.

"My Lord Huanacocha," said the Villac Vmu, "at your instigation, and because of certain representations made by you, I have taken the unprecedented course of causing our Lord the Inca to be brought hither, that he may answer, before those here assembled, to the charges which I understand you desire to bring against him. State, therefore, those charges; but before doing so ye shall swear by the Light of our Lord the Sun that your motive in instigating these proceedings is free from all bias or personal ill will; that you are animated therein solely by anxiety for the public welfare, and that you will say no word save what you, personally, know to be the truth."

"All this I swear!" answered Huanacocha, raising his right hand aloft.

"It is well," commented the High Priest. "Proceed now with your charges."

"My Lord," answered Huanacocha, "my first and most serious charge against the young man who sits there, and whom we have for these many months past honoured and served as the re-incarnated Manco Capac, the father and founder of our nation, is that he is an impostor, with no right or title whatsoever to the service and reverence which we have given him.

"My second charge," continued Huanacocha, "which, however, should be preferred by you rather than by me, O Villac Vmu, is that this youth has blasphemously forbidden us any longer to worship our Lord the Sun, our Father and Benefactor, and the Giver of all good gifts, and has commanded that we shall worship instead Pachacamac, whom he calls God, of whom we know little or nothing, and whom we have never until now been bidden to worship. I am strongly opposed to this change of religion—for it amounts to nothing less—as is everybody else with whom I have spoken on the subject. We all fear that such change will certainly bring disaster and ruin upon the nation. There are other charges which could be preferred against the prisoner," concluded Huanacocha; "but I am content that the case against him shall rest upon those which I have already enumerated."

"It is well," commented Xaxaguana. "My Lord Huanacocha, the gratitude of the community is due to you for the public spirit which has prompted you to come forward and perform what we all recognise to be an exceedingly disagreeable task, and doubtless the public generally will be careful to see that your disinterestedness is suitably rewarded. Is there anyone present who desires to support the charges preferred against the prisoner by my lord?"

There was. The ball of high treason once set rolling, everybody seemed anxious to add to its momentum, and man after man came forward, either to support the charges made by Huanacocha, or to ventilate some petty grievance, real or imaginary, of his own, until at length so much time had been consumed that Xaxaguana, growing impatient, refused to listen to any further evidence. He then turned to Escombe and said:

"Prisoner, you have heard the charges that have been brought against you. What answer have you to them?"

"I might well answer," said Escombe, "that I am the Inca, and that no one has the right to question my actions, and no one—not even the Villac Vmu—has the right to bring me to trial, as you have dared to do; for I am supreme and infinitely above and beyond you all. But I have no desire to take refuge behind my dignity. If anyone considers that he has a grievance against me, as appears to be the case, I prefer to answer it.

"And first as to the charge which Huanacocha brings against me of being an impostor. Let me remind you who were present of what took place in the temple upon the memorable occasion when I was first brought here by Tiahuana and Motahuana. Tiahuana was the man responsible for my presence in this valley, and my elevation to the position of Inca. It was he who, having heard certain particulars concerning me, sought me out, satisfied himself and his colleague that I fulfilled in my person all the conditions referred to in a certain prophecy, and brought me hither without even going through the preliminary formality of asking my consent. It was he who, when he presented me before you all here in the temple, convinced you all, with two or three exceptions, of whom Huanacocha was one, that I was the re-incarnated Manco Capac, the Inca destined to restore the ancient Peruvian nation to its former power and grandeur; and it was you who, convinced by his arguments, placed me on the throne. I had nothing whatever to do with that; I made no claims or pretensions of any kind; I was simply passive throughout. But when, convinced by Tiahuana's arguments and proofs, you had placed me on the throne, and I learned what was expected of me, I devoted all my energies to the performance of the task which I felt had been laid upon me; and you know how far I have succeeded. You know that those of pure Peruvian blood are being daily gathered into this valley from every part of the kingdom; you know that they are being trained to play their part as fighting men; and you know also—at least Huanacocha does—that I am even now engaged in making plans and arrangements for the secret introduction into the country of an adequate supply of the most modern weapons, in order that, when the proper moment comes, you may be able to fight upon equal terms with your enemies.

"As to my having decreed an alteration in your religion, I did so because when I came among you I found you to be idolaters, worshippers of the Sun, which is but one of the many beneficent gifts which Pachacamac—whom I call God—has given to His children. The sun can only give you his light and heat according to God's will and pleasure; and therefore it is God, and not the sun, whom you should worship. And I tell you that until you transfer your adoration from the sun to Him who made it, you will never be a prosperous and happy people; nor will I consent to rule over you, or help to restore you as a nation to your ancient power and glory. Choose, therefore, now, whether you will worship God, or continue in idolatry; whether you will achieve the great destiny which Titucocha, your prophet, foretold for you, or whether you will remain the mere remnant of a once powerful and splendid nation, lurking here in obscurity in this valley from which you dare not venture forth lest those who now hold the land that once was yours fall upon and destroy you. If you choose the latter fate, as you seem inclined to do, then must I go forth from this valley, and leave you to your own devices; for, as I have said, I will not rule a nation of idolaters. But if you choose to obey me, and submit unquestioningly to such ordinances as I shall promulgate from time to time for your advantage, then will I undertake to make you all that Titucocha foretold you should become."

It was evident that Harry's address had produced an exceedingly powerful impression upon the bulk of his audience, for the moment that he ceased to speak there arose a great hubbub among those who composed it, the assembly almost instantly breaking up into little knots and groups, the members of which at once proceeded to discuss eagerly the several points of the speech. It was a result as unwelcome as unlooked for by the prime movers of the conspiracy, and the glance which Huanacocha shot at the Villac Vmu was full of dismay and apprehension. The latter, however, who had noted something of the effect which Harry was producing, saw also how to avail himself of that effect and at the same time achieve his own and his friend's purpose. He therefore allowed the commotion to continue unchecked for full ten minutes, before he rose and held up his hand for silence. Then, when the disturbance had subsided sufficiently to allow his voice to be heard, he said:

"My friends, I perceive that, like myself, you are in a difficulty, and know not what to believe. You feel, as I do, that if this youth is in very truth the re-incarnated Manco whose return to earth was promised by the prophet Titucocha, it would not only be rankest folly but absolute sacrilege to reject him. But how are we to know; how is this most important, this vital point to be determined? There is but one way—a way which I have already provided for: we must subject him to the ordeal by fire! If he survives that ordeal, well and good; we shall then know for certain who he is, and we will serve and obey him in all things. But, if not—"

He got no further; for at the mention of the ordeal by fire Harry saw at once, as in a lightning flash, the villainous trap into which he had been betrayed, and the hideous fate to which it was intended to consign him. Leaping to his feet, he snatched the drawn sword from the hand of one of the astonished guards who surrounded him and, before any of them could interpose to prevent him, had leapt upon the dais and seized the terrified Xaxaguana by the throat with one hand, while with the sword which he held in the other he threatened to run the quaking wretch through the heart.

"Oh no, you don't," he cried, as he tightened his grip upon the struggling priest's throat; "no fire ordeal for me, thank you! Sit still and give over struggling, you villain, or I'll pin you to the back of the chair you sit in. Do you hear me? Ah, that's better; put your hands down by your sides and keep them there. And you other fellows stand still where you are, and don't attempt to lift so much as a hand against me, unless you wish to see me slay this man before your eyes! Now, Villac Vmu, grasp the seat of your chair with both hands—just to keep them out of mischief, you know—and do as I tell you. First order those men of yours to lay down their arms and march out of the building—see, I release your throat that you may draw breath to give the order—ah! would you, you treacherous scoundrel? Then take that!"

For as Harry released his grip upon the priest's throat the latter sprang to his feet and endeavoured to clasp the young Englishman round the arms and body, at the same time shouting to the others to come to his help. But Harry was too quick for his would-be captor; he sprang back a single pace, thus just eluding the grip of the priest, and at the same time lunged at him with the copper sword which he held, driving it straight through the man's scheming, treacherous heart. Then, as a great roar of dismay and execration arose from the assemblage, he quickly withdrew his reeking weapon from the quivering body and, hastily wrapping his cloak about his left arm, leaped to the wall, placed his back to it, and prepared to sell his life as dearly as might be.

He gave himself about half a minute more to live; for what could he single-handed do against the swordsmen, to say nothing of the rest of that howling, bloodthirsty crowd who now came surging toward him. They could overwhelm him in a moment, by sheer force of numbers! But as the swordsmen sprang upon the dais, with gleaming eyes and threatening points, the voice of Huanacocha rang through the chamber as he shouted:

"Take the young fool alive, and harm him not, as you value your lives! He has slain the Villac Vmu; and for that reason, if for no other, he must pass through the fire. Hem him in, take his weapon from him, and then bind him hand and foot!"

It was, however, very much easier to give that order than to obey it; for Escombe had always been passionately fond of sword-play—to such an extent, indeed, that he had placed himself in the hands of a certain well-known *maître d'armes* in Westminster, and had been pronounced by that gentleman to be his most promising pupil—so now, with a tolerably good weapon in his hand, and his back to a solid, substantial wall, he felt quite in the mood and form to put up an excellent fight.

The swordsmen closed in round him and, as by tacit consent, flung themselves upon him in a huddled mob, with the evident intention of bearing him to the ground by sheer preponderance of numbers. But the next instant three of them recoiled, shrieking, with their faces slashed open, as Harry met their charge with a sweeping circular cut from left to right. Then a fourth man staggered and fell with a ghastly wound in his throat, while the rest drew back in dismay and wonder at a feat of swordsmanship that to their comparatively untrained minds seemed to savour strongly of either magic or the supernatural. As to Escombe, he took a long breath, and told himself that perhaps, with luck, he might be able to hold out for as much as five minutes; for that first encounter, brief though it was, showed him that these men had not the remotest idea of how to handle a sword, while as for himself, he had no sooner gripped the hilt of his weapon than he felt all the keen delight of the practised fencer thrill through him at the prospect of an encounter. Oh yes! he would put up a good fight, such a fight as these people should remember to their dying day; though of course one of them would get him, sooner or later, when his weapon happened to be plunged in the body of an enemy.

These thoughts flashed through the young Englishman's mind in the drawing of a breath. Then he braced himself afresh against the wall to meet a second and much more wary attack—his enemies had learned caution already, for instead of flinging themselves upon him pell-mell, as at the first rush, they attacked him three at a time, one in front, and one on either hand, thus allowing plenty of room for the play of their blades. Also they strove, by every stratagem they could think of, to entice him away from the wall, so that they might be able to slip round and take him in the rear; but to keep one's back to the wall was one of the fundamental rules of self defence that had been dinned into him until it had become impossible to forget it, and Harry was not to be tempted. Close to the wall he kept, allowing himself only just sufficient room for the free play of his blade; and when at length the attacking trio, losing patience, attempted to rush in upon him, his point seemed to threaten all three at once, and the next moment two of the three were *hors de combat,* one with his sword hand half severed at the wrist, and the other with his right arm laid open from wrist to elbow.

The ineffectiveness of the attack proved too much for Huanacocha, who had thus far been looking on at the fray with a sardonic grin upon his countenance. Now, as he saw the swordsmen hanging back, obviously afraid to approach that charmed semicircle, the whole of which Escombe's blade seemed to cover at the same moment, he lost patience, and, with an angry roar, dashed forward, snatched a weapon from one of the disabled fighters, and called upon all present to help him to capture the audacious young foreigner who seemed determined to make fools of them all. Then, as the others sprang at his call, an idea suddenly seized him. Tearing the cloak off his shoulders, he flung the heavy garment straight at Harry, whose blade became entangled in the folds for just the fraction of a second. But it was enough; the others, seeing in an instant what had happened, tossed away their weapons and, flinging themselves upon Escombe before he could clear his sword, tore his weapon from his grasp and bore him, still fighting savagely with his fists, to the ground. In another minute it was all over; with men grasping each of his limbs, and two or three more piled upon his prostrate body, poor Harry was soon overcome and reduced to a condition of comparative quiescence, after which it was not a very difficult matter to enwrap his body with so many turns of a thin, tough, raw-hide rope that further movement became an impossibility.

Immediately the whole place rang with howls and shouts of fiendish rejoicing at the brilliance of the feat which had culminated in the capture of this pestilent young foreigner, whose gallant resistance, so far from exciting admiration in the breasts of his captors, seemed to have filled them with the ferocity of wild beasts. As he was raised to his feet preparatory to bearing him away to the place where a fiery death even now awaited him, first one and then another fought and struggled through the yelling crowd to glare into his face with ferocious glee, and to hiss into his ear bloodcurdling hints of the doom prepared for him.

The uproar was at its height when Escombe's preternaturally sharpened ear detected a new note in it, a note of astonishment, consternation, and terror that quickly overbore and drowned the tones of savage exultation. The next instant the air was vibrant with shrieks and cries for mercy as the crowd, scattering right and left, made way before the levelled spears and whirling blades of the Inca's bodyguard; while the voice of Umu, harsh and tense with concentrated fury, was heard high above the din, exhorting his followers to let not one of those present escape. Within a moment Umu himself, whirling a heavy battle mace about him with savage freedom, had forced his way to Harry's side, and had either beaten down or driven off those who had constituted themselves his custodians.

"Are you hurt, Lord; have these sacrilegious beasts dared to harm a hair of your head?" he panted, as he flung a supporting arm about Escombe's bound and helpless body.

"No," answered Harry, smiling rather wanly upon him; "I am as sound as ever I was, thank God! But you have only arrived in the very nick of time, Umu. In another five minutes you would have been too late, my good and trusty friend. How did you know where I was, and what was happening?"

"The tale is too long to tell just now, Lord," answered Umu, as he busied himself in freeing Harry from his bonds; "it shall be told later, when I have disposed of these vile wretches. It was Arima who brought me the first hint of what was afoot. Pachacamac be praised that I was able to get here in time! What were they about to do with you, Lord?"

"They talked of putting me to the fire ordeal," answered Harry; "but I had a word to say against that, as you may see. Xaxaguana, one of the chief conspirators, has already paid the penalty of his perfidy, and lies there dead."

"Truly, Lord, you fought well," exclaimed Umu admiringly, as he glanced about him at the dead and wounded. "And Huanacocha—is he among this rabble?"

"He is—unless he has escaped," answered Harry.

"If he has, every tenth man of your bodyguard shall lose his hands and feet," snarled Umu savagely. And then his brow cleared as, glancing at the mob of prisoners which the troopers were now forming up, he detected Huanacocha alive, and apparently unhurt, among them. "Ah, no! he is there, I see," he continued. "Very well; this plot was of his hatching. He shall undergo the fire ordeal himself."

"Nay, not that, good Umu; not that," protested Harry. "Such a fate is too horrible to be thought of. Punish him by all means, if you will, for indeed he deserves punishment; but not in that way."

"Very well, Lord," answered Umu; "it shall be as you wish. Meanwhile, I pray you to return to the palace, escorted by your bodyguard; while I, with a few men, attend to the safe disposal of these fellows."

Five minutes later, Escombe found himself, he scarcely knew how, mounted on a trooper's horse, wending his way back to the palace, surrounded by his devoted bodyguard, while the populace, quick to detect how matters were going, rent the air with their acclamations.

An hour later Umu bowed himself into Escombe's presence to report progress.

"The prisoners, Lord," he said, "are, with the exception of Huanacocha, safely confined, and now await such punishment as you may be pleased to inflict upon them. In the presence of a great multitude I have caused the head of Huanacocha to be struck from his body in the grounds of his own palace, and have thrown head and body together upon the smoking ruins of the place. I have likewise posted a notice upon the entrance gates forbidding anyone to interfere with the body or give it burial. It is to be left where it lies, for the dogs of the city to devour, as a warning and example to others of the fate of those who conspire sacrilegiously against the authority or person of the sovereign. And I have left two armed troopers to mount sentry at the gates, to ensure that my orders are obeyed."

"Two only," ejaculated Harry in horrified tones. "My dear Umu, if I may judge of the temper of the people at large by those with whom I had to deal in the temple to-day, those two unfortunate men have been torn to pieces before now. You must send supports at once to them. I want no more bloodshed over this unfortunate business."

"There will be no more, Lord," answered Umu grimly. "The sentries are as safe as if they were in barracks. The people know me. They know that at the first sign of disorder I would sack the city from end to end, and put every one of its inhabitants to the sword; and there will be no more crime of any sort for many a day to come, after what has befallen Huanacocha, who was the most powerful noble in all the land."

"I am sure I hope not," answered Harry. "And if you should prove to be right in your estimate of the salutary influence exercised by the example which you have made of that turbulent fellow, his death will not have been in vain. And now, Umu, what about the palace servants? I see that an entirely new staff has been installed here, by your orders, Arima tells me; and he also tells me that the others are safely lodged in prison. Surely they had nothing to do with the conspiracy?"

Whereupon Umu, by way of reply, proceeded to recount to his royal master the whole history of the affair, so far as he had learned it. And that included pretty nearly everything that was worth repeating; for in the course of his investigations during that eventful morning the soldier had come upon thread after thread, until, taking into account what he then learned, and adding to it such stray hints as had previously reached him, and to which he had, up to that morning, attached no significance, there was very little left to be learned relative to the conspiracy. The result of it all was that, after thinking the matter over very carefully, Escombe was driven to the conclusion that this curious people, into whose midst he had been so strangely brought, were not ripe for those reforms which he, as their ruler, would have felt it his duty to introduce; that they did not want them, and would never willingly accept them; and that, consequently, he must either govern them as they desired to be governed, at the expense of his own conscience, or else abandon the idea of ruling them at all:

Having come to this conclusion, he summoned all the nobles to a conference, at which he put the case frankly before them, inviting them as frankly to express their opinion upon it, with the result that he was fully confirmed in the opinion which he had formed. The day after the close of the conference he definitely announced to Umu his intention to abdicate and quit the valley; at the same time asking that officer's advice as to the best and most desirable mode of procedure in so exceedingly delicate a business.

"The affair can be arranged quite easily, Lord," answered Umu. "There is not the slightest need for you to abandon us. After what has happened to the Villac Vmu and Huanacocha, who were the two chief conspirators, and the example which I shall make of all those who were foolish enough to listen to them, you will be troubled by no more conspiracies; and I will see that whatever laws you may choose to make are obeyed, whether they happen to be to the taste of the people or not. There are a few, who, like myself, are able to recognise that such laws as you have thus far made are for our advantage, and you will always be able to reckon upon their support; while, for the others, who have not sense enough to understand what is good for them, they must be compelled to bow to the decrees of those who are wiser than themselves.

"But if, as you have intimated, you are quite resolved not to enforce your wishes upon the people against their will, I will issue a proclamation declaring that, since the inhabitants of the valley have rejected the enormous benefits and advantages which you had desired to bestow upon them, you have decided to leave the valley and abandon them to their fate, and that I have assumed the reins of government and will henceforth rule them in your stead. It is for you, Lord, to say which of these two alternatives shall be adopted."

"Very well, Umu," said Escombe, "I have already quite made up my mind. I will not remain here to force upon the people laws and ordinances which are unacceptable to them; therefore issue your proclamation as soon as you please, and I will make arrangements to leave forthwith. I presume I may depend upon you to furnish me with guides and an escort as far as Santa Rosa, from which I will take the train to Islay. Also, as I shall require money to defray my expenses back to England, I shall take the liberty of withdrawing one bar of gold from the palace treasure chamber for that purpose."

"Assuredly, Lord," answered Umu. "You shall be furnished with a reliable guide—you can have none better than Arima—and also such an escort as will enable you to perform your journey in perfect safety and comfort. As to the gold, it must of course be for you to determine how much you will need to defray your expenses back to your own country; but what of the remainder of the treasure? You will scarcely be able to take the whole of it with you; for to transport it across the mountains would need the services of every man in the valley, and so large a following as that would be apt to attract undue and unwelcome attention."

"Ay, that it would," laughed Harry. "But I have no intention of robbing you of all your treasure, Umu; very far from it. A single bar of gold will suffice for all my needs, thanks!"

"But the whole of the treasure is yours, Lord, to do what you will with it," answered Umu. "It was given to you on the day when you were proclaimed Inca; and—"

"Oh, yes, I know!" interrupted Harry; "it was given me for a certain purpose, to wit, the reconquest of the country and its restoration to its former owners. But since the people are too indolent and too self-indulgent to allow me to do this for them, of course I have no claim upon the treasure, and could not possibly dream of appropriating it to my own uses."

"So let it be then, Lord," answered Umu. "Take what you require; and, for the rest, I will deal with the matter."

A week later witnessed Escombe's departure from the Valley of the Sun, with Arima as his guide, and a troop of the Inca's bodyguard as his escort. As Umu had promised, every possible arrangement had been made for his safety and comfort on the journey; and that portion of it which lay between the valley and Santa Rosa was accomplished far more agreeably than was that which lay between Santa Rosa and the sea. The bodyguard escorted him to within twenty miles of Santa Rosa, which was as close to the city as it was prudent for them to approach, and then left him to complete the journey in the company of Arima and the porters who bore his baggage for him. There was not very much of the latter now remaining; nevertheless his following amounted to some twenty-five men; for in addition to Escombe's personal belongings, tent, etcetera, there were three stout wooden cases measuring about eighteen inches each way, containing, as Umu, at parting, informed Harry, the smallest possible share of the treasure which he could be permitted to leave with. When these were ultimately opened, they proved to contain gems—diamonds, rubies, and emeralds—of such enormous value as to constitute their owner a multi-millionaire. It is not to be supposed that Escombe succeeded in conveying all this treasure down to the coast and getting it safely embarked upon the mail boat for England without tremendous difficulty and trouble. But by the exercise of immense ingenuity and tact, and the expenditure of a very considerable amount of time, he ultimately managed it.

Harry is now safe at home, and settled down very comfortably, with his mother and sister, in the most lovely part of Devonshire, where he divides his time pretty evenly between enjoying himself, converting his store of gems into coin of the realm, and seeking opportunities to employ his enormous wealth for the benefit and advantage of his less-fortunate fellow men.

Let it not be thought, however, that Harry's adventures in the City of the Sun had banished from his mind the fact that he still owed a very important duty to Sir Philip Swinburne. On the contrary, it was the subject which became the most important one in his thoughts after he had finally completed his arrangements for the safe transport of his treasure to England. Indeed it claimed his attention immediately upon his arrival at the coast, and one of his first acts was to write to Sir Philip, acquainting that gentleman with the fact of his escape from the Indians—for so he put it—and his impending departure for England, adding that he would afford himself the pleasure of calling at the office in Westminster at the earliest possible moment after his arrival home. He had already ascertained that the survey party had completed its operations, and that Bannister had left for England some two months prior to the date of his own arrival upon the coast. He knew that there were many points in connection with that portion of the survey which had been executed prior to Bannister's arrival upon the scene which nobody but himself could make clear, and accordingly he had no sooner started upon the long homeward voyage than he betook himself to the task of preparing voluminous explanatory notes on those points, so far as his memory served him, in order that he might have all his information cut and dried for submission upon his arrival home.

In conformity with his promise, he duly presented himself in Westminster within twenty-four hours of his return to English soil, receiving an enthusiastic welcome from his former confrères, and especially from Bannister, whom he found busily engaged in plotting the result of the soundings taken at Lake Titicaca. He was also effusively welcomed by Mr Richards, who had already wrought himself into a state of distraction in his futile endeavours to clear up those very obscurities which formed the subject of Harry's notes. But with the return of Escombe to the office the troubles of the chief draughtsman on that account ceased, and he found himself once more able to sleep at night; for Harry promptly made it clear that he held himself absolutely at Sir Philip's disposal until the whole of the plans relating to the survey should be completed. He presented himself at the office punctually at ten o'clock every morning, and worked diligently throughout the day for the succeeding two months until the entire work had been brought to a satisfactory conclusion, and Sir Philip had written his report and dispatched it with his proposals to the Chairman of the Peruvian Corporation.

Whether those proposals will be carried into effect the future only can tell, for they involve the expenditure of a formidable number of millions. But it is safe to say that, if they are, Harry will take no part in the work, his view being that, since he has no need to earn his living, it would be wrong of him to accept a post and thus shut out someone who has that need.

Still, he has the satisfaction of knowing that, although his future is independent of the goodwill of any man, he so conducted himself during the trying time of his service under Butler, and afterwards, while working singlehanded, as to win the warmest approval and esteem of Sir Philip Swinburne and the worthy Richards, the latter of whom is now wont to quote Harry Escombe as the pattern and model of all engineering pupils.

It is also due to Harry to mention that he made an early opportunity to call upon Butler's widow for the purpose of personally acquainting her with the details of the surveyor's unhappy end. But in doing this he contrived so to modify the particulars of the story that, by judicious omissions here and there, without any sacrifice of truth, he succeeded in conveying an impression that was very comforting and consoling to the unfortunate lady in the midst of her grief. As he found that the poor soul had been left in very straitened circumstances, he made it his business promptly to arrange with his lawyers that she should be paid anonymously a sufficient sum quarterly to place her beyond the reach of want.